THE HAUNTING OF MISSISSIPPI

THE HAUNTING
OF MISSISSIPPI

BARBARA SILLERY

PELICAN PUBLISHING COMPANY

Gretna 2011

*The word "Pelican" and the depiction of a pelican are trademarks
of Pelican Publishing Company, Inc., and are registered in the
U.S. Patent and Trademark Office.*

Library of Congress Cataloging-in-Publication Data

Sillery, Barbara.
  The haunting of Mississippi / Barbara Sillery.
    p. cm.
  ISBN 978-1-58980-799-0 (pbk. : alk. paper) 1. Haunted places—
Mississippi. 2. Ghosts—Mississippi. I. Title.
  BF1472.U6S535 2011.
  133.109762—dc22
                                        2010053125

All photographs by Barbara Sillery

Printed in the United States of America
Published by Pelican Publishing Company, Inc.
1000 Burmaster Street, Gretna, Louisiana 70053

To my newest muses:
Michael Timothy Moore
Leila Sillery Moore

Contents

Prologue

The Magnolia State is rich in history and haunted lore. Many of its place names—Biloxi, Natchez, Pascagoula—have their origins with the first people of the land, the Native American tribes who fished the rivers, hunted the game, established clans and communities, and were the original storytellers. Myths, legends, and fear of the unknown have fueled imaginations. Oral history, the passing on of knowledge gleaned from elders—parents, grandparents, and great-grandparents—enrich our lives. Everyday trials and victories, large and small, enable people to endure, to thrive, and celebrate a shared heritage.

Ghost stories are the crossover genre. They venture into the fields of archeology, architecture, anthropology, biography, geography, philosophy, psychology, religion, sociology, and history: her-story, his-story, our-story. From Edgar Allan Poe's dark-as-night-talking raven to nursery rhymes, phantoms lurk behind every portal.

Someone came knocking
At my wee, small door;
Someone came knocking
I'm sure-sure-sure;
I listened. I opened,
I looked to the left and right;

But naught there was a-stirring
In the still dark night.
—Walter de la Mare

I am grateful to so many flesh-and-bone Mississippians for opening their doors and sharing family histories, legends, and personal encounters with their favorite spirits. Many, many, thanks to: Marsha Colson, Mattie Jo Ratcliffe, Gay Guerico, Lynn Bradford, Carolyn Guido, Margaret Guido, Jeanette Feltus, Cheryl Morace, Elizabeth Boggess, Katherine Blankenstein, Patricia Taylor, Kay McNeil, Judy Grimsley, Thomas Miller, Eric Williams, Chris Brinkley, Tom Pharr, Phyllis Small, John Kellogg, Joe Connor, Kathy Hall, Leonard Fuller, Bob Mazelle, Leyland French, Nancy Carpenter, Dixie Butler, Grayce Hicks, Leigh Imes, Melanie Snow, James Denning, Donna White, Richard Forte, Al Allen, David Gautier, Aimée Gautier Dugger, Mark Wallace, Wesley Smith, Lisa Winters, John Puddin' Moore, Dominick Cross, Warren Harper, Mike Jones, Woody Wilkins, Clay Williams, Ruth Cole, Lucy Allen, William Griffith, Drew Chiles, Dick Guyton, Sybil Presley Clark, Lisa Hall, Tracie Maxey-Conwill, and Tom Booth.

For their on-going support and encouragement, thanks to my lifelong friends Grayhawk and Glinda and Tom Schafer. To my teammates at Aurora, especially partner Lisa Fox, and the members of the Aurora Book Club, thank you. Thanks to Oak Lea, my picture wizard, and to all the staff at Pelican Publishing, especially the editor in chief, Nina Kooij, and associate editor, Heather Green, you've been terrific to work with.

To my daughters Heather Bell Genter and Rebecca Genter, who bring me joy and urge me on, I wouldn't make it through anything without you. An extra special thank you to my eldest daughter Danielle Genter Moore, who patiently poured over the chapters and tried to keep me on track. Her on-target corrections and notes always elicited a smile, a few groans, and occasional chuckles.

To the lively and intriguing spirits of Mississippi, it's been a pleasure. Hang in there.

THE HAUNTING OF MISSISSIPPI

McRaven House hidden in a forest of trees near Vicksburg.

1

McRaven House

Ah, distinctly I remember it was in bleak December,
And each separate dying ember wrought its ghost upon the floor.
—Edgar Allan Poe, "The Raven"

McRaven House may well be the most haunted in Mississippi. With each tenuous step from chamber door to chamber door, there is a stirring up of that which has lain dormant, a sense of disquiet that those within prefer their solitude.

The house is well-hidden. A rusting, wrought-iron gate, its white paint chipped and peeling, its decorative grape clusters ripped off by vandals, offers a meager clue that there may be something more beyond this dead-end street. A heavy padlock and chain discourage visitors. McRaven House is for sale. Eighty-two-year-old caretaker Leonard Fuller is saddened by its current condition. He withdraws a key from the pocket of his blue work pants and inserts it into the ponderous padlock. A squeal of protest and the gate creaks open. A forest of mature trees, overgrown shrubs, fallen limbs, and a carpet of decaying leaves obscure the winding brick path. A hundred feet ahead, a pale, moon-yellow corner of the house pokes through the green-brown vegetation. Another S-curve to the right and the galleried-Italianate front façade beckons. Mounted in the middle of the otherwise unadorned hunter-green front door is a ghostly white doorknocker shaped like a female hand.

A chill pervades the front hall. Leonard's hands are shaking. His green jacket and blue-plaid, flannel shirt do not insulate him from the dampness of the interior. Short spikes of grayish-white hair frame an angular face dotted with brown age spots. As he turns on the light, a gravely, weathered voice delivers a preemptive warning. "We've had so much activity here I couldn't even begin to tell you all the things that happened."

The straight-backed chair to his right triggers an early memory. "My mother was still living. She had been sick and I was sitting up with her at night and working as a guide during the day. We always used to have two guides here when the house was open for tours. One takes the tour group around and the other hangs by the door." An arthritic finger points at the offending chair. "I was sitting right there. I was kinda tired and I had put my hands over my face, and I reckon I was kind of nodding off a little bit. All of a sudden, I got hit so hard that I was knocked out of the chair and I hit the floor." A whoosh of air escapes from Leonard's mouth. His chest deflates. "I thought maybe it was the other guide, she was a young lady, and sometimes she did a bit of foolishness." Leonard's first instinct was to catch his fellow guide in the act of escaping. He juts his chin to the right. "I popped up and run back into the parlor there." He describes his puzzlement at finding the parlor empty and, at the same time, hearing the other guide's voice giving the tour upstairs. "She couldn't have gotten up there that quick, and even if she had been able to done it, she wouldn't have been able to talk 'cause she would have been out of breath from running up the back staircase." Dejected, Leonard drops his arms to his sides. "So there I was all by myself when that *force* knocked me out of my chair." When pressed to identify his tormentor, the caretaker doesn't hesitate. "I think it was one of the old ladies. She thought I was sitting there and not paying attention, so she gave me a little whack to wake me up. It was one of the two sisters that lived here. They're dead, you know."

Annie and Ella were the last of the Murray children to live in McRaven House. The elderly spinsters resisted modern conveniences and, except for their doctor, had no contact with the outside world. Although they inherited a huge mansion, the sisters' entire world consisted of one room—the dining room. Leonard explains the unusual set-up. "They moved their bed in here. They were old and they didn't want to go up and down the steps. The last two years of their lives, the sisters couldn't stand the cold so they cooked in the fireplace. To get to the old kitchen, you have to go outside. They chopped up antique furniture for firewood." Leonard's thin lips compress into a straight line of disapproval.

Ella Murray died in the house at the age of eighty-one. In 1960, Annie, the surviving sibling, sold McRaven and moved into a nursing home. Leonard remains convinced that the spirits of the peculiar pair have never left.

In the front parlor, on the wall nearest the piano, matching four-by-six, sepia-toned photographs capture Annie and Ella as happy, pampered little girls, with long brown curls caught up in large bows, wearing white eyelet dresses. As lonely adults, the sisters turned to hoarding. Leonard saw the evidence first hand. "As the ladies got older, a good bit of their diet was sardines. They saved every single sardine can they ever used; there were sardine cans everywhere." However, there was an up side to their hoarding. "Most of the furniture and artifacts that are here are original to the house. Ninety percent," boasts Leonard. "We were very fortunate; we had two ladies live here their entire lives. They are still the guardians of McRaven House."

McRaven House is a time capsule crammed with the priceless heirlooms and mementos of every family who ever crossed its threshold. From

From the side, McRaven House appears as a series of steps.

front to back, the house descends like stepping-stones: 1882 Italianate, 1849 Greek Revival, 1836 Empire, 1797 frontier cabin. Time travel is possible here; follow in the footsteps of each of the prior inhabitants. If you get lost, they will find you.

In 1985, Leyland French acquired McRaven. He is believed to be the first person to live in it since Annie and Ella Murray. When Leyland moved in, he was startled to discover that he was not alone. Many of the former residents still check in and out.

In 1882, William Murray purchased McRaven. Over the course of the next seven decades, five immediate Murray family members died in the house: William (1911), his wife Ellen (1921), daughter Ida (1946), one of three sons (1950), and daughter Ella (1960). Three of the Murrays have been known to return. Annie, Ella, and their father, William, seem to have a proclivity for whacking current occupants.

Long before the caretaker was shoved unceremoniously out of his chair, Leyland French also received some rough treatment. French reopened the historic home for tours following an exhaustive restoration. While this greatly pleased the general public, it did not sit well with the spirit of William Murray. Leonard shuffles over to a corner in the dining room opposite the brick fireplace. "One day Mr. French was on his hand and knees just about here. Someone had spilled something and it left a stain on the wood floor. He was trying to get the dark spot out, when a force pushed him down to the ground and held him there, like it was a heavy man's foot on his back." Leonard stares at the wide-planked floor. "You never know what's going to happen at McRaven."

McRaven's haunted reputation attracted the media. "We've had all the major networks," says Leonard. "Ghostbusters from California came here about three years ago. They were going to spend *two days* in Vicksburg." Leonard chuckles. "They ended up spending *two weeks* just at McRaven." In August of 1999, CBS News correspondent Susan Spencer produced a piece for *48 Hours,* a primetime television series. In the interview, Leyland French revealed that one ghostly encounter was not pleasant. "He slammed the desk drawer on my thumbs!" Shaken by the resemblance of the ghost to the portrait of William Murray in the parlor, the new owner called on an Episcopal priest to bless the house. The exorcism did not banish all the ghosts.

During the heyday of the tour years, one mother had a hard time keeping her young child in check. Leonard remembers the incident well. "The little boy wouldn't stay put. He kept running through the house and his mother was embarrassed. She finally grabbed hold of his hand and told him to behave. He was about four years old. He looked up at his mother and tried to explain: 'Mother, all I want to do is go over there and play with that little red-headed boy.'" Admiration tinges Leonard's voice. "There were twenty people on that tour and this child was the only one who could see that little red-headed boy. The Murray boy who died in the house had red hair, and there's no way this little boy could have known that. People may say he made it all up, but *nobody* knew that one of the Murray boys had red hair."

The tale of a playful little boy ghost in the twenty-first century pales in comparison to the horrendous deed that occurred on the grounds. On May 14, 1864, former owner John H. Bobb was cut down in a fuselage of bullets. It was the start of the Siege of Vicksburg. John H. Bobb noticed six drunken Union soldiers destroying his gardens. He ordered them to leave. The soldiers cursed him and refused to move on. The enraged homeowner picked up a brick and threw it in their direction. John H. Bobb reported the disorderly intruders to Gen. Henry W. Slocum, Federal commander of Vicksburg. On his way back to McRaven, John H. Bobb was assailed by a mob of twenty-five disgruntled Union soldiers. "They were all drunk," says Leonard. "They got their guns and shot him twenty times in the back." John H. Bobb's murder was the first recorded act of violence by Union occupation troops during the Siege of Vicksburg. John's widow, Selina, sold the house and moved to another family plantation in Louisiana. Selina may have left, but John's outraged spirit remains behind.

After John H. Bobb purchased the house in 1849, he added on to the front and transformed the home into the then popular Greek Revival style. Over 150 years later, he refuses to leave. "He has a habit of walking the front galleries," explains Leonard. "A lot of times we can hear heavy footsteps up there. When I go to check, there's nobody there. Nobody that you can see anyways. But I know it's him 'cause I smell the pipe tobacco. Mr. Bobb liked his pipe, and Mrs. Bobb did not allow smoking in the house." The tragic figure of John's wounded spirit also prowls the gardens keeping a vigilant watch for unruly visitors.

The balcony where the ghost of John H. Bobb paces and smokes his cigar.

Before John and Selina Bobb left their mark on McRaven, their predecessors, Sheriff Stephen Howard and his wife, Mary Elizabeth, called McRaven home. Mary Elizabeth is the good ghost at McRaven. Unlike the troubled spirit of John H. Bobb, Mary Elizabeth enjoys visitors. "In the spring, we used to always have tour groups of school kids. One group came with their coach. The coach brought all of them out to the front porch, taking their pictures four at a time." Leonard's grin reaches his blue eyes. "One of the pictures had five people in it. Mary Elizabeth's face just popped up. Guess she wanted to be included."

Touring McRaven is akin to navigating a maze. There is a temptation to leave a trail of breadcrumbs behind or, at the very least, have the benefit of the guiding hand of a friendly ghost. The spirit of Mary Elizabeth Howard likes to oblige, but Leonard feels that sometimes that doesn't work so well. "She diverts our tours. We send the tourists up the back staircase to go into the old section of the house and we tell them to turn left. When we get to the top of the stairs, they're in the bedroom on the right, Mary Elizabeth's room. We ask them why are they over there, and they always tells us, 'The lady that was standing here told us to come in.' We ask them, *What lady?* See, there's only supposed to be one guide up here at a time. Anyways, the people will say, 'The nice lady' or 'the one in the long dress with brown hair.' We know it's Mary Elizabeth getting them off track. She likes to torment us a little bit. She's bad about turning the lights on at night when the place is supposed to be closed." The twinkle in Leonard's eye contradicts his attempt at disapproval. "Now, I'm not sure why she is foolin' with the light switches. They didn't have electric lights back them, but I guess she's showing us she's learned all about 'em." Another deep chuckle. "Sometimes the police will call us and say every light in the house is on. And I'll come over, and sure enough the house is all lit up." The twinkle flashes again. "Mary Elizabeth is just having a little fling. It's just one of those things that happen to us here."

Mary Elizabeth's ghost is inordinately fond of having her picture taken in the bedroom. Leonard shows off a gauzy white shape in a small photo. "If you look right here, you see the lady's bust and the rest of her figure. That's Mary Elizabeth Howard. Here's another, and you can see her in the webbing of the bed." Many of Mary Elizabeth's personal items are scattered about the room: ivory-handled opera glasses, white gloves, make-up kit, and a silver brush rest on the top of a dresser. "That little ceramic bowl there," says Leonard, "ladies used to hold hair from their brush so later on they could make hair pieces, like those extensions girls put in their hair now. Back then they called them rats' tails. If a lady had thin hair, after she had gotten sick maybe, she put them in." Several dark, chestnut-colored "rat tails" poke out of a cubbyhole over the dresser. A quilt, a many-hued kaleidoscope of triangles in reds, blues, plaids, and tiny prints, spills over the foot of Mary Elizabeth's bed. It was a wedding gift from her grandmother.

Mary Elizabeth was a young bride, just twelve years old when she married Stephen Howard. The middle bedroom and the dining room below are additions completed in 1836 by Stephen in anticipation of a large family to come. In August of 1836, fifteen-year-old Mary Elizabeth Howard gave birth to her first child, Caren. In that same hot summer month, Mary Elizabeth died in the newly completed bedroom of complications due to childbirth.

The September 1, 1836, notice in the paper requested that *"friends and acquaintances of the late Mary E. Howard attend her funeral to-morrow at three o'clock, P.M. . . . at the old family burying ground . . . the procession to take place from S. Howard's plantation, three miles below Vicksburg."* The printed notice with its black border is propped up on a pillow at the head of the bed, an epitaph for one who died too young.

A devastated Stephen Howard left town immediately after the funeral. "When Mary Elizabeth died, he sold off everything he had accumulated in Vicksburg and moved to Yazoo County where baby Caren could be cared for by her grandparents." Leonard's eyes come to rest on a raised baby cradle swathed in mosquito netting. "People ask me all the time why I think Mary Elizabeth comes back so much. One is, she was only fifteen, and she might think her life is incomplete, and she wants to finish growing up." Leonard locks his hands behind his back and squares his shoulders. "The other thing is that as soon as that baby was born, they carried it off to Yazoo County and Mary Elizabeth may be looking for that child even today. When a lady has a child, it don't make no difference if she dies right away, she always remembers that child. Mary Elizabeth wants her baby."

Each item in the room leads to new tales. Next to a large spinning wheel is a spinner's weasel, an early measuring device for yarn. When the device is full, it makes a popping sound. According to Leonard, that's where we get the phrase "pop goes the weasel." But it is a small, hooded, canvas-covered trunk under the window that elicits the most amazing narrative. Leonard clears his throat and draws a deep, wheezing breath. "Back when they were trying to trace the history of this house, they wanted to find Caren Howard that would be Mary Elizabeth's daughter. By then, she would have been well advanced in age. They sent a researcher to Yazoo County where the baby was taken. He goes to the local library—too late. The librarian says she's sorry 'cause Caren passed away recently, but just when he's getting discouraged, she hands over an address and tells him to go talk to the lady who lives there. Now he's pretty sure it's a dead end, but he goes anyway. When he gets there, the old lady surprises him saying that she's been expecting him. He asks if the librarian had called ahead; she shakes her head no. She says Caren was her friend and told her that he would come looking for her and to show him a trunk. See, Caren wanted the trunk to be returned to McRaven House. Inside were all of Mary Elizabeth's personal items. Mary Elizabeth had labeled every single one. That's how we know," adds Leonard, "that the quilt on her bed was made by her grandmother in 1728. Mary Elizabeth put the date on it."

It is impossible to know if Mary Elizabeth had a premonition about her impending death and whether that was the reason behind her methodical labeling of all of her personal items. What is truly inexplicable is how Caren, who left McRaven House when she was just days old, would know that one day someone would come looking for her mother's trunk and return the items to their rightful positions in the restored bedroom. The unsolved riddle is part of the legend of McRaven House.

Mary Elizabeth Howard died giving birth to her baby in a bedroom created for her by her loving husband. Andrew Glass, the original owner of McRaven House, died trying to return to the safety of his home. His loving wife slit his throat. Leonard recaps the local legend. "The gentlemen who lived here in the house back in 1787, they were very vicious. The Glasses, the first ones, belonged to a gang who would raid people going up and down the Natchez Trace. The Trace being under the direction of France, and Vicksburg being under the direction of Spain, the Glasses knew that after they robbed the travelers on the Trace,

Mary Elizabeth Howard's trunk returned after a long absence.

the French wouldn't follow them all the way back to McRaven House in Vicksburg, so they would be safe. Well," says Leonard after a lengthy pause, "Mr. Glass got wounded in one of those raids, his wife had to kill him, cut his throat, rather then let him be taken prisoner. Andrew Glass wanted to die so the French wouldn't torture him. Now, Mrs. Glass could have shot him, but that would have alerted those Frenchmen to where they were hiding and then captured the whole group."

The 1797 section of the house, the Pioneer or Frontier portion, is gloomy; a two-room structure attached to the rear. A small bedroom sits directly over the original kitchen. The twisting back staircase is steep and narrow. The steps are worn; the middle of each step is cupped like a bowl from the tramping of so many feet. Leonard argues that the claustrophobic staircase is actually an improvement. "Originally, the Glasses had a rope ladder here. And they would throw that rope ladder from that landing up here to go down to the kitchen and then at night they would pull it up after them so no one could attack them while they were sleeping."

The original Glass family frontier bedroom.

"Some of our guides get the feeling that there is *something* moving around them in the room. They have seen things and heard things up here; they don't like it so much."

Ghostly manifestations are everywhere at McRaven—within and without. During the Civil War, the house was under attack. Confederate soldiers dug in. The phantom presence of these men is felt all around the wooded area, beyond the strolling gardens, where they set up camp.

T-shaped trenches, nearly six-feet deep are carved out close to a strategic bend in the railroad tracks. Leonard's voice rises and falls as the tale of the gory battle resumes. The singsong cadence of the birds, the soft rustle of the wind in the trees fade. "The men in the first trench line up and load their rifles. They know the Union troops have gotten bogged in at the north end of the county; they was having a hard time moving their heavy cannon and ammunition wagons. The railroad tracks that pass right by the front of the house have a good road bed underneath, so the Confederate guys knew the Union ones would be coming to Vicksburg right along them railroad tracks." Leonard cranes his neck to the right as if sighting the blue uniforms of the artillery coming into the turn. "They fire the cannon right at 'em. The troops in the trenches, up here in the T, fire into 'em. They slip back into the long arm of the T to reload, and the soldiers back there move up front— continuous firing." Leonard's head swivels right, left, right, following the pounding feet of the soldiers running through the trenches. *Load. Fire. Shoot. Retreat.* The wounded are lifted up on to a mound in the middle of the trenches, an island of blood staining the ground. During brief lulls, they are dragged into the makeshift hospital set up inside McRaven. When the skirmish is over, the number of dead reaches twenty-eight, a jumbled heap of blue-, gray-, and khaki-colored cloth united now by the deep red of their fatal wounds. Their shouts, their screams, their pain, their passion are embedded in these trenches, these deep cuts of a once divided nation.

A century and a half after the Siege of Vicksburg, one of the wounded posed for a contemporary paranormal photo. "We had a reenactment going on that day in the side yard. This young lady, one of the reenacters' daughters," explains Leonard, "she wanted to take some pictures. So I went back to the house with her and unlocked the door. She took pictures in the front parlor. After she got them developed, she sent me copies." An enlarged five-by-seven color photo clearly shows the reflection of a Confederate soldier in the gilt mirror over the marble mantle. "You know he was a wounded soldier because he even has a yellow arm band on his left arm. Like I say," says a self-satisfied Leonard, "you never know what you are going to wind up with at this house." As a child growing up near McRaven, Leonard Fuller admits that sightings of phantom shapes in uniform, stalking the grounds were not unusual.

Fortunately, the acres of grounds surrounding McRaven are commodious enough to accommodate a host of phantoms, including the homeless souls forced to march along the Trail of Tears. In 1830, with the signing of the Indian Removal Act, Andrew Jackson became the first United States president to order Native Americans to leave their ancestral lands. The removal began with the Choctaws, November 1, 1831. The Okla Hannali and southern Okla Falaya bands of Choctaws were to be gathered at Vicksburg. McRaven House and grounds were used as a way station. Over the course of three years, 1831 to 1833, 17,000

Choctaws were relocated. French historian and political thinker Alexis de Tocqueville, a witness to the Choctaw removal, wrote, *"There was an air of ruin and destruction . . . one couldn't watch without feeling one's heart wrung . . . the expulsion . . . of one of the most celebrated and ancient American peoples."* In October of 1832, an epidemic of cholera swept through Vicksburg. The fleeing citizens of the town infected all they encountered including the Choctaws entering the city. Due to the highly contagious nature of the disease, the bodies of the dead, Choctaw and white, were heaped in piles, covered with brush, doused with kerosene, and burned.

In the dressing room next to the master bedroom once occupied by William Murray and his wife, Ellen Flynn, a peace pipe, or a calumet, rests on a blue-velvet armchair. This sacred Native American ritual artifact, its wood darkened by age and tobacco smoke, might have been used by a medicine man to heal sickness or ward off danger. Sadly for the Choctaws who passed through Vicksburg, the calumet did not bring good fortune. The number that died during their sojourn at McRaven is unknown.

What has come to be accepted as fact at McRaven is that a host of spirits moves freely, unhampered by the passing days and years. Leonard believes they are as anxious as he is for the right buyer to come along and reopen the home for tours. The ghosts at McRaven are not shy. They are adept at darting in and out among hordes of visitors and will even pause for a photo op if given the opportunity.

Postscript: When the carriage gates swing open once more, an extended visit is a must. Every room, every chamber is crammed with often weird and intriguing artifacts upstairs and down: an ear trumpet, Mrs. Bobb's silver *chatelaine* (key chain), a *Third Hand* (a silver bird whose beak opens to momentarily hold a sewing project in progress), sad irons, a folding surgeon's table, cutting instruments, bullet casings, shells, ram shots, and rifles.

Leonard delights in educating the uninitiated. A ram shot, a cylindrical object about two-feet high and eight inches in diameter sits under the dining room window. "The first shot out of the cannon would be that opening salvo with the idea that the ram shot would penetrate the wall of the building. The second round out of the cannon would have a charge in it and it would go in through that same hole and explode inside. This one weighs about sixty-five pounds and came through the kitchen wall. We're lucky those Union guys never got to fire that second round." Leonard strokes an old rifle hanging over the bedroom fireplace. "Sometimes the flintlock musket didn't go off. See this small pan here that holds the charge. Well, Mr. Glass could pull the trigger and the gunpowder would flare up, but the bullet wouldn't fire. They call that a 'flash in the pan.'"

On first view, an assortment of clay pipes over the mantle seems broken and in disrepair. Not so, states the knowledgeable caretaker. "These are pub pipes, available for anybody to use. You'd go into a tavern, pick up one, break off a piece of the stem, and you'd have a clean pipe stem to put your mouth on."

The unusual paint color slathered over the walls and ceiling of the 1797 bedroom leads to another story. "It's made from crushed blueberries and buttermilk. People might think that kind of odd that somebody would use buttermilk, but you know, the most economical grades of paint today are alkaloid base and the base of buttermilk is alkaloid. This room," Leonard says with pride, "has never been painted over. It's the original blue color."

The most recent mystery centers around a fire set by an arsonist three years earlier. Inside the old kitchen, Leonard raises his hand to the transom over the door. "See how the glass is buckled and pushed out? That's from the heat of the fire." The kitchen structure is unusual in that it is attached to the main house. "Fear of fire," confirms Leonard. "Most of your house fires started as grease fires because they used lard. Combustible. They had a law back then that if you had your kitchen attached, you had to have a cistern added so you could have water to fight the fire with." The raised stone cistern is just steps from the kitchen door, but it wouldn't have been enough to save the house from the determined arsonist. "He set fire to this house and nine more homes before that." Outrage pours from Leonard. "The day he set fire to McRaven, he had just gotten out of prison for other acts of arson." How did McRaven, a wooden structure, survive the conflagration? An odd chain of coincidences still baffles the senior caretaker. "A neighbor saw [the fire] and

Caretaker Leonard Fuller in the Glass bedroom.

called it in, but since we're pretty far from the nearest fire station they never would have gotten here in time. Now, there's a Baptist church in that neighborhood right behind us. Somebody turned in a false alarm and so the fire trucks were just three blocks away when the arsonist set the fire. If they hadn't been so close by, we would have lost McRaven. It would have been gone. Nothing left. Just ashes." Perfect timing or a little assist from the paranormal protecting what was theirs?

No matter its savior, McRaven House in Vicksburg stands tall— shrouded in mystery, filled to the rafters with haunted tales, and waiting for the right buyer to embrace it, ghosts and all.

2

Anchuca

Anchuca Mansion in old town Vicksburg is an elegant bed-and-breakfast establishment where the ghosts really do go bump in the night. These spectral guests are very particular about their accommodations. One attention-seeking couple even set off an indoor waterfall while another expressed disfavor with the décor.

Dressed casually in a green T-shirt and Anchuca baseball cap, co-owner and chef Chris Brinkley expertly wields a large knife. The cheerful chef is prepping fresh pineapples for a fruit salad. Wonderful aromas permeate the small kitchen. "We bought the house March 1, 2001. My first experience with a ghost occurred pretty much right away. Initially, I lived in the servants' quarters, which are upstairs in the rear wing. I had hung three little masks from South America on a wall in the living area. Brian, a friend of mine, was in there and I was in the kitchen making dinner. All of a sudden, Brian ran out of the living room, yelling that one of the masks came out from the wall and hovered in midair for a second and then fell to the ground." Chris pauses mid-chop. Cubes of pineapple slide off the wide blade of the knife into a bowl brimming with fruit. "I had no idea how this could have happened, but I went in and picked up the mask from the floor. I had never thought too much about ghosts or anything like that. So, I said out loud to *whoever* or *whatever,* 'I don't know who you are, and I don't know what's going on, but these masks I've had for several years and they are important to me, so I would like for you to leave them alone.'" A jovial Chris concludes, "I hung the mask back on the wall, but after that, my friend Brian did not want to come back up to the apartment."

Anchuca, a charming bed and breakfast in Vicksburg.

To Chris's consternation, this mysterious incident was followed shortly by another. "In the fall, I was by myself; we had no guests here at all at that time. I had come down the back staircase from my apartment to get some ice cream from the kitchen. I'll show you where." Chris puts the knife down on the chopping block, wipes his hands on his black-and-white striped apron, and steps out of the kitchen into the formal dining room.

Anchuca was built on a hill; the front bedrooms are a level above the main floor. Chris re-creates his path through the house. His left arm arcs upwards; he points to the multi-tiered landing. "We have this X-shaped staircase, so I was headed back up this way. The door up there in the middle of the landing leads to a balcony. I was on this landing, and I felt like someone was watching me. All the lights were off, and the hair is standing up on the back of my neck. About that time, I saw a real bright light up against the inside of that front door. I watched kinda dumbfounded as this shape, just like a woman in a long, period dress, came through from this side and flew around. She was all white, and I really couldn't see facial features or anything. She hovered there in front of that solid door for a minute, and then she went straight through the door to the bedroom on the right. Then I kinda snapped out of it. And I always thought that if I saw a ghost in this house I would stop and question it. Well, instead, I turned around and I said, 'That is not even funny.' I went out the back door. I locked it real quick, went in my room, and put the chain on the door." An embarrassed smile slips out. "As if it would make any difference after I just watched the thing go through two closed doors. For quite a while after that, when I came through the house, turning out lights or whatever, I would just say, '*Goodnight, everybody!*' And would wish them well. I never had any problems after that; *she* didn't come see me out in the servants' quarters."

But Chris's elusive visitor did pop in on someone else. "It was about three years after we moved in. I was in Atlanta and Tom [Tom Pharr, co-owner of Anchuca] had a funeral to go to in Memphis. We still had Snickers, a golden retriever, in the house because we didn't have any

The ghost landing inside the front hall of Anchuca.

fenced area that we could leave a dog in, so Georgia, a good friend of ours, who was working at the D.A.'s office, volunteered to come and let Snickers out. It was around Christmas time. Georgia came over. She didn't have a lot of time because they had the grand jury in session. She let Snickers out to do his business and then brought him back inside." Chris explains the dog's health issues. "Snickers was prone to having seizures and was afraid of storms and lightning and would actually try to dig to get inside."

Chris takes a stand near the bottom step of the main landing. "Snickers was sitting here, looking up at the same place that I had [the front door] and he started to shake all over. Poor Georgia thought that he was having a seizure because Snickers wouldn't respond at all. She said, 'Are you okay, honey?' When she reached over to touch him, he kind of snapped out at her. Then she looks up and realizes she's got another problem because she sees drapes blowing in the breeze. She mutters to herself: 'Oh, great, now I've got to go and shut that window.' And then it dawns on her, wait a minute, that's a door, not a window. Those are not drapes floating out. She screams and runs out the back door by the kitchen here. She's outside thinking, *I don't know what to do because I've got to get back to work. The dog has followed me out here scared to death. I don't want to go back in there.*'"

Chris vouches for his friend. "If you knew Georgia Lynn, she is now the director of the Humane Society. She is a complete animal lover. She's got as many animals as I do. But in this case, after she thinks she's seen a ghost, she's shaken up. She ends up telling Snickers, 'Honey, I am sorry, but I've got to leave this house.' She pushes him back inside, locks the door, and goes back to her office. Tom said when he got home that night there was a message on the answering machine from Georgia Lynn." Again, Chris comes to his friend's defense. "Georgia is very clearheaded. . . . She was a victims' assistance coordinator for the D.A.'s office, dealt with some horrible things." Chris then quotes verbatim from Georgia Lynn's answering machine message: "*I don't know what you all have going on over there, but house-sitting is out of the question. I love the dog. I love you, but don't ask me to go in the house by myself again.*"

Chris takes a stab at giving the female entity a name. "We knew there was a lady, Jane Collins, who owned the house in 1835. In that era, Mississippi was kind of unique in that it allowed women to own property. There is a deed in her name, and I believe she died of yellow fever in the house while she was engaged to be married. So we've always surmised that she might still be here. Tom used to sleep in the Jefferson Davis suite and he would see her periodically in the middle of the night. When we compared notes, he had more details because he saw her more clearly. But, he usually brushed it off saying it was just a dream."

Chris's issue with the female apparition is where she hangs out. "That is the newer section of the house, built in 1840 by the Wilsons, after Jane died." With a bemused shrug of his shoulder, Chris speculates, "Maybe she's trying to figure it all out."

Tom Pharr joins his partner, Chris, in the kitchen. Tom, dressed in red shirt and casual slacks, is a tall man, powerfully built. The pair works in tandem with varying styles: Chris, gregarious; Tom, a bit more laid back. Both are excellent hosts. Each agrees that a few guests have had difficulty coming to terms with the realm of the paranormal.

Chris: "We had some guys staying here for about three months who were working on the outage down at the Grand Gulf nuclear power plant at Fort Gibson. One claimed that someone would pound his pillow at night, and the other was scared to sleep in his room because he would see *her* [the ghost of Anchuca], and these," says an incredulous Chris, "were nuclear physicists."

Tom: "He didn't want to actually say he saw something. Our housekeeper who was in charge of keeping the rooms fresh came to me, and we had this strange conversation:

'Do you want me to keep changing the linens? You know he's not using that bed; he just stays in the back room and watches TV.'

'Yes, he watches TV in the back, but he sleeps in the front room.'

'No, nobody is sleeping in that bed.'"

Chris chimes in: "You know they work hard, come back here, have a beer, watch TV, and fall asleep on the couch."

But Tom was bothered by the erratic behavior. "I thought maybe the bed was uncomfortable, so I went to him and asked if the bed was okay, and that's when he admitted the whole story to us. He was an engineer with a very factual outlook, but he couldn't get over what was happening to him."

Chris: "But he did share it with his wife and invited her to come down and visit, and she said, 'Oh, now you want me to come. You won't sleep in a bed with a ghost, and now you want me to come and sleep with you. This is hilarious.'"

Tom: "You just never know how some guests are going to react."

Chris: "And it was really funny because there were some women who were working on the same project and they stayed here too. One of them—she was absolutely beautiful, athletic, and she went in some of the most dangerous parts of that nuclear power plant, and she just rode those guys because they were afraid their rooms were haunted."

Anchuca caters to numerous luncheons, dinners, and parties. Chris recalls one lady from Alcorn State: ". . . very prim, proper and sophisticated. She sat next to Tom having a glass of wine. She just announced, 'I feel them. Don't you feel them? The *ghosties* are here.'" Chris gently pokes fun at the woman's choice of words. "I am trying to not laugh, and I look over at Tom and he's got this flat smile plastered on his face."

Tom gives a shot at the more diplomatic route. "Maybe there are people more in tune than others. We had one guest who checked in and then came directly back and said she couldn't stay here."

Chris fills in. "She had a room in the Carriage House."

"She came to dinner that night," adds Tom.

"She was a poet who was doing a reading. She said she couldn't stay here because . . ."

Tom finishes for Chris. "Because it was *too emotional* for her."

Chris rolls his eyes.

Tom, well versed in the history of Vicksburg and the tenure of the various owners of Anchuca, speaks up. "Well, Joe Davis, the president's brother, did die in this house in 1870."

The president Tom refers to is Jefferson Davis, the beleaguered leader of the Confederacy. In 1869, Jefferson Davis reunited with his elder brother Joseph Emory Davis, who owned Hurricane Plantation as well as Anchuca, which he used as a townhouse while in Vicksburg. According to oral history accounts, Jefferson Davis spoke to friends and neighbors from the front balcony of Anchuca, making one of his last public addresses to the people of Vicksburg.

Chris adds a few more sad notes to the history of the house. "We had a lot of people die here. They used Anchuca as a hospital during the Siege of Vicksburg in 1863. And then that baby died here. Eliza. She was only three years old. They buried her here."

"The Wilsons only buried her here temporarily," Tom argues. "Then they took her to Cedar Hill Cemetery. The city was under martial law. Mr. Wilson died here too, but it was a natural death."

The tally goes up. Chris reminds Tom of their diaphanous female apparition who slips through closed doors. "Then there is Jane Collins."

After a few run-ins with the spirits who roam Anchuca, some of the employees who work for Chris and Tom have made a clear line between what they will and won't put up with.

"We did have a housekeeper, Zella," says Tom. "She was upstairs ironing. The laundry room is on the upper floor of the rear wing, the old servants' quarters. I was in the courtyard below. It was summertime, warm. She ran out on the balcony screaming." Tom imitates Zella; his voice takes on a high-pitched quiver: *The cold wind blew right through me! The cold wind blew right through me!* Tom is regretful. "Zella will not come back to work here at all."

Zella's sister, Annie, is a little less stringent about her working environment, but she too has her limits. She wants Tom and Chris to give the laundry room a good cleansing. And Annie's not talking dirt. Tom groans softly. "She tells me somebody locks her out of the laundry room. I say, 'Annie, it's an old lock. Sometimes it sticks.' She comes right back with, 'No, sometimes you can't get in, and then other times, it opens right up.' Annie believes there's a ghost or something blocking the way."

The shower in Tom's room has also become a haunted site for Annie. "She's in my room, she hears the shower running. She starts talking to me through the door." Tom rubs his forehead. "The problem is I'm downstairs. When I didn't respond to her questions, Annie comes downstairs, sees me, and wants to know if somebody is using the shower in my room. I tell her, no. She insists the water is running. I go upstairs; the shower stall is not even wet. Annie is upset. She insists the shower was running and she heard voices."

Tom throws up his hands in resignation. "Annie has been here for eight years. She will work during the day but not at night, not after dark. Zella won't do it at all."

Unlike Annie, who now has an aversion to running water, one

forgotten couple felt justified in using the "wet method" to be reinstated in their former residence.

Anchuca's formal dining room is glorious. A French bronze gasolier casts a golden glow over the baronial dining table. A magnificent 1850 silver, Sheffield epergne serves as the centerpiece. English porcelain coronation cups grace the shelf over the rosewood sideboard. It is perfection, but all Tom Pharr sees are two pinprick holes and the small rectangular patch in the ceiling above the head of the table. The handiwork of a phantom couple. They wanted out, and if it took a little damage to set them free, then so be it.

"The plumber actually found them when he was trying to find out where the water was coming from." Tom is in the front hall. Two oval portraits hang over the entry sideboard. The handsome couple face each other; he stares to his right, she to her left. Encased in separate bubbles of convex glass, the man with a full mustache and beard above a starched, white collar is stern-faced. The woman, also in formal dress, has a fixation with crosses; a pair dangles from her ears, and a larger one drapes across her ample bust. "From the style of dress, we believe they are the Hennessys. Mr. and Mrs. Hennessy purchased the house in 1875, that's right after Joe Davis died here at Anchuca."

Tom walks into the dining room. He takes a position near the head of the table and directly under the "escape hatch" in the ceiling. "It was about eleven o'clock one night. It was late. I came back here to turn off the light, and I heard this splat, the sound water makes when it hits a soft surface like this carpet. It was wet enough here that it was starting to make a noise. I looked around, and I couldn't figure out where it was coming from. And then I realized it was dripping from the ceiling, and I thought, *'Oh, no, there must be a pipe leaking up here.'* I go upstairs into the bathroom where the shower is and there is a cased-frame doorway leading to the hall, and water is coming from the ceiling, hitting the casing, and down to the floor, and that is what is directly above this." Tom realizes the problem must be extensive; the water is coming from above the bathroom in the attic, where the hot water heater and air condition condenser are located. He has no choice.

"I call, Donny—he's the plumber—at eleven o'clock on a Saturday night, and it hits me that there is going to be a triple charge for an emergency, late-night, weekend fix." The only good news in this home repair equation is that the plumber on call has serviced the air conditioners before and is familiar with the house. However, the working conditions are less than ideal. "In the 1980s renovation, they blew in extra insulation, so it's just like picking through cotton up there in the attic." A slight shudder courses up Tom's back and down his arms. One hand flicks off invisible fibers from the other as he relives the midnight foray into the attic with the plumber. "Donny turns his flashlight on the drip pans underneath the condensers that are there to keep any overflow from leaking through." The mystery deepens. "The pans are all just as dry as a bone. The same with the pans under the water heaters; dry as well. No sign of any recent water in the pans, and it was summer."

Determined to find the source of the water leak, the plumber dives in. "He just started taking his bare hands and just squishing in that insulation trying to find some dampness." The task is tricky. A partial wood floor supports the equipment, but the rest is open between the joists; one false step and his foot will go through the ceiling. "He's feeling for dampness, a sign maybe of a broken pipe, although there is no plumbing over that part of the house." And then, just like in the nursery rhyme where little Jack Horner "sticks in his thumb and pulls out a plumb," Donny sticks in his hand and pulls out a man, a portrait buried underneath the insulation. "He hands it to me, and I'm so distracted by this portrait, I stop watching what Donny is doing until he sticks his hand back in and hands me another one."

Tom carefully carries the framed portraits down to the bedroom level of the house. "I go into the bathroom and I'm wiping them off. I got so engrossed cleaning them up, paying attention to the couple, that I stop focusing on the drip. Donny's still in the attic looking for the source of the leak. He can't find anything that is wet up there at all, anywhere. He goes down each floor to retrace the trail of the drip from the attic to two floors below. It wasn't until Donny said, 'Well, I don't know where it could be from, but it is not dripping anymore.' And I go, 'It's not?'" To Tom's stunned amazement and the plumber's professional dilemma, the mysterious leak is no more. The waterfall in the dining room has ceased, stopped dripping. "It's not happening anymore. And we didn't know what to think."

Tom recaps: "A water flow sufficient enough to soak the carpet dripped from the dining room ceiling. The water wasn't from a leak in the shower on the floor above because the water started in the ceiling above the shower; the pipes for the shower come from below. The drip pans of the water heater and the air condenser in the attic were desert dry. The insulation in the attic is dry."

If a plumb line were dropped from the spot in the attic where the portraits were hidden, it would lead to the very spot in the dining room ceiling that filled the carpet with water. Can spirits inhabit portraits? And, if so, are they powerful enough to set a waterfall in motion? And when they've attracted sufficient attention, can they exert an opposite force to turn the spectral spigot off? Tom Pharr has no answers. Donny the plumber's parting advice? "Call me if it starts leaking again."

"Luckily," says a relieved Tom, "We've never had to."

Still, there was a wet carpet to dry out and wet plaster to be replaced, but the two drill holes would remain. "We put in those holes to let any pooled water out, but it wasn't filling up anymore. We've left the holes there just in case."

Whether it's a case of squatters' rights or the he-who-screams-loudest-gets-the-most-attention principle, Tom is happy to have the portraits. "The chain reaction caused this couple to come to the surface. The result is we found both of those portraits in the attic, and they are now hanging in a prominent place in the house."

Tom pursued the identity of the mysterious couple. Anchuca was built in 1830 by local politician J. W. Mauldin. In 1847, Victor Wilson, a coal and ice merchant, enhanced the structure with a Greek Revival front and a two-story dependency in back. "I talked to people who knew the history of the house. In 1875, this house was purchased as a wedding gift for a new young family, the Hennessys. They lived here until 1921. For over forty years, they raised their children. I even talked to John Hennessy, one of the descendants, who wrote our insurance for the house. Unfortunately, he doesn't know what his ancestors looked like; he has no old photos of them."

Tom researched further. "The style of clothing of the couple in the portrait and the frame is 1870 to 1880." The jewelry was also a clue. "It has to be the Hennessys. They were very Catholic, and in the portrait, the woman has crucifixes in her ears and around her neck."

Believed to be Mrs. Hennessy, one of two oval portraits discovered in the attic.

The discovery was four years ago. Tom says that since the pictures have been on display, "everything is cool—and dry." Yet, a ghostly phenomenon leaves this otherwise practical man baffled. "This started out as a household emergency. I wasn't seeing any shiny light, no orbs, none of the usual paranormal trivia. Two pictures pulled me upstairs." Tom laughs at the weird circumstances. "I never would have been able to make up a ghost tale like this." He reaches over to adjust Mr. Hennessy's framed portrait on the wall, making sure it is in alignment with Mrs. Hennessy. "I guess they just wanted to be back out. They haven't seen daylight in a long, long time. And I am just so happy to find them. I just think they are really great."

Postscript: Anchuca is a Choctaw word meaning "happy home." Chris Brinkley and Tom Pharr have created an inviting retreat where guests are welcomed like family. This impressive landmark is on the National Register of Historic Places, but it retains a refined simplicity enjoyed by visitors and appreciated by a small cadre of sophisticated spirits.

3

Cedar Grove Inn & Restaurant

This historic inn is all about options. Antique beds, armoires, gilded mirrors, and a cornucopia of lavish rooms await the arriving guests. Ghosts—the haunted spirits of Cedar Grove—slip in and out of the ballroom, the dining room, the library, the gentlemen's parlor, and the bar. The younger spirits—the children—are seen and heard in the Bonnie Blue room, the nursery, and the entry hall. They all enjoy the freedom of five acres of gardens where they've been spotted near the gazebo, the front hedges, and the back staircase. "They come and go in spits and starts," explains co-owner Phyllis Small. "Cedar Grove Inn is just a very pleasant haunted house."

Cedar Grove Inn and Restaurant sits on a bluff with panoramic views of the Yazoo and Mississippi rivers, about a mile from the historic downtown district of Vicksburg. Phyllis Small, her husband, and daughter Colleen purchased the property in November of 2003. The spirits came out to greet them.

"Colleen had issues one morning when she arrived to open up. She was on the property across the street for awhile [Cedar Grove's Country Cottages], and when she came over here to the inn, she smelled cigar smoke." Phyllis is a true Southern woman—warm, gracious, accommodating. Reddish hair is pulled back from an amiable face. A matching black jacket and dress form the day's ensemble. She readily shares details of that first encounter. "No one is allowed to smoke inside the house. No cigars, pipes, cigarettes, or anything like that. So Colleen starts to investigate. She comes in the back door, where the guest registration is, and follows the smell to the front of the house. She's in

Cedar Grove Inn & Restaurant overlooks the Yazoo and Mississippi rivers.

the main entryway, when a voice says, '*Hello.*' She turns around. No one is there. She checks upstairs. The house is empty."

Phyllis explains that she is working on site because her daughter is expecting her second child and is back at her home in Natchez. Besides overseeing the management of a thirty-three room inn, bar, and restaurant, Phyllis is getting up to speed on the idiosyncrasies of the resident ghosts. "Mr. Klein, the original owner, he's the one who won't give up smoking his cigars."

Joe the bartender concurs. "I was in the hallway between the house and the restaurant. I smell a *pungy* odor," Joe wrinkles his nose, "like sweet tobacco. We were closing up around 11:30 at night. The cook came out and said, 'Wait, it smells like someone just lit a cigar.' I said, 'Yeah, I smell it too.' I'm thinking it must be Mr. Klein; he's the one who built Cedar Grove."

Executive chef John Kellogg didn't just smell the cigar; he saw the flare of its flame. "Marlene, the events manager, and I were walking and talking in the hall. We're near the dining room. You always have a tendency to look in as you pass." Eight Chippendale chairs surround a long, walnut, banquet table. The room is reserved for private parties. On this day, there are no reservations. "Marlene and I look in, and over the head chair, there's a wisp of smoke curling up as if someone has just taken a puff on his cigar. Marlene and I do a double take. I look back at her and jokingly say, 'I didn't see it either.'" For the executive chef, it's no contest. "It had to be John Klein. That's where he would have sat—at the head of the table."

Front desk manager and morning tour guide Kathy Hall is a contradiction. She runs the desk like a drill sergeant, but her phone voice is all sweet Southern drawl. Her snow-white hair rises in spikes of stiff white bangs in front; in back it falls in waves of soft curls to below her shoulders. She handles the guests and the ghosts of Cedar Grove with equal measures of good cheer, dry wit, and forbearance of all their foibles. She understands that John Klein's smoking addiction is a habit he can't kick even in the afterlife. "There's always the smell of cigar smoke in the gentlemen's parlor; that's where he entertained his business acquaintances." Kathy also concedes, "I've seen an outline, not very clear, but it was a man standing in the center of that room."

The steady drone of a vacuum cleaner is jarring in the stunning double parlors framed by deep-blue drapes, gilded cornices, and Italian marble fireplaces. Phyllis navigates around the small army of cleaning crew. "Some of our housekeeping staff has told us they feel a presence in here. When they face the pier mirror between the windows, they see a reflection of a man that we all believe is Mr. Klein behind them." Phyllis interrupts Mike, a man consumed with nervous energy. He is dressed in black slacks and a red shirt with the Cedar Gove logo over the breast pocket. "Have you seen anything today?" Mike's response is hesitant, unsure of the correct answer. "No, ma'am." He sneaks a look past Phyllis's shoulder in my direction. "We hope that won't deter you from coming." He makes a quick exit and rejoins the work in progress.

John Alexander Klein built Cedar Grove in 1840 as a wedding present for his wife. Klein family history claims that it was love at first sight when John spotted fourteen-year-old Elizabeth Bartley Day. John

Klein moved from Waterford, Virginia, to Vicksburg in 1836 at the age of twenty-four. By twenty-eight, he shrewdly diversified his wealth in the fields of banking, lumber, and cotton. While John waited for Elizabeth to mature, he began work on the Greek Revival-style mansion. John and Elizabeth married in 1842. The groom was thirty, his teen bride sixteen. The couple left for a yearlong European honeymoon and shopping expedition, where they purchased many of the furnishings in the house today.

When the honeymooners returned from Europe, they moved into a small cottage behind the main house, awaiting the finishing touches and installation of their recent acquisitions for Cedar Grove. Today, this cottage has been converted into two guest rooms: the Pool Court and Garden Court suites. Occasionally, there is a *spirited* objection to the use of modern conveniences. "We've had people complain that their TVs don't work. We'll go in and check and they work just fine. The lights go on and off." Phyllis does not believe it's a flaw in the electrical system. She feels it is more of a personality clash. "It doesn't happen all the time. I think our ghosts have issues with certain visitors, and they pick on them a little."

While some are irritated by John Klein's cigar smoke, other aromas are a welcome change. Executive chef John Kellogg arrived at Cedar Gove to breathe new life into the restaurant. A graduate of Ecole de Cuisine La Varenne in Paris and with thirty years of culinary expertise, he has infused the menu with succulent flavors: fried green tomatoes with roasted aioli, grilled shrimp with andouille sausage, and baked Mississippi farm-raised catfish topped with crawfish bisque. The aromas are hypnotic. John's wife's senses are equally acute. "When I first arrived, my family lived on the property until we found a house. My wife asked the front desk manager where the lavender bushes were because that was the scent she smelled. The manager told her there were no lavender bushes on the property. My wife insisted, 'I keep smelling lavender all over the house and grounds.' The manager smiled and said, 'Well, yes, Elizabeth Klein wore lavender perfume. She always grew a bunch of lavender. She liked the scent and the color purple.'"

Joe Connor is a fixture in the lounge. His medium-length, salt-and-pepper gray hair is brushed straight back off a high, wrinkle-free, brown forehead. He wears a khaki Cedar Grove polo shirt and dark slacks. Joe says there was a reason Elizabeth Klein used heavy doses of lavender

A family portrait of John Klein who haunts Cedar Grove.

Elizabeth Klein's spirit likes to visit with the guests.

perfume. "She was trying to mask the smell of the cigar smoke." Joe believes Elizabeth is still at it. "Every now and then something of that nature pops up, and a guest will come to me and say, 'Do you smell that?' And I'll say, 'Smell what?' And they'll insist that it smells like a lady's perfume. I just say, 'Maybe so,' because I don't want to alarm nobody."

Elizabeth Klein also refuses to relinquish her role as hostess; she frequently checks up on the guests. In the 1980s, Ted Mackey purchased Cedar Grove and turned the Kleins' home into a bed-and-breakfast establishment. Enamored with Margaret Mitchell's epic novel *Gone with the Wind,* Mackey named many of the rooms and suites after the book's characters: Scarlett, Rhett, Bonnie Blue, Aunt Pittypat, Mr. O'Hara, Prissie, and Ashley Wilkes.

In a deep voice that rumbles like distant thunder, Joe speaks amiably about Elizabeth's midnight visits to room number 8, the Ashley Wilkes suite. "There was a lady who stayed in that room, and she came into the bar and told me she had an *experience* the previous evening. Before she got into telling me what happened, I told her that I already knew: she woke up and someone was sitting beside her on the bed. The lady guest wanted to know how I could know that, and I told her it wasn't the first time. The only difference was that the other lady who booked the Ashley Wilkes suite had to call her fiancé in the middle of the night to come get her because she said she couldn't sleep with a ghost in the room."

From her central post at the desk, Kathy hears it all. "When the kids and teens come and tell me that they've seen a ghost, I don't pay too much attention. The other day I had one young girl on a school group wanting to know if we had ghosts. I said that sometimes we have a little *activity* but nothing bad. She comes back after going around the house and she's got an attitude." Kathy does a good impersonation; hands on hips, she tosses her hair back with a flip of her head. "This kid walks up to the desk and announces, 'I've got a statement to make. You said you had good ghosts here?' I look her square on. 'That's correct. They are not harmful.' The girl waves her camera in the air and claims that she was upstairs taking a picture when 'all of a sudden, there's a face in the picture and it's yelling at me.'" Kathy takes such accusations in stride. "Our ghosts may be sad, they may be troubled, but they don't yell."

They do have other traits, sometimes helpful, sometimes not. Elizabeth is a very energy-efficient ghost. She does not believe in waste. "Number 22, the General Pemberton room, is downstairs; we had a couple check in there, a husband and wife," says Kathy. "The next day the couple approaches the desk and tells me a story. The wife, a very nice lady, says she went to bed, and left the light on in the bathroom so if she had to get up in a strange room during the night, she could find her way. She's barely asleep when she realizes the room is dark; the light in the bathroom is off. She's not happy. She gets out of bed, feels her way to the bathroom, and turns the light back on. She goes back to sleep. A few hours later something wakes her up again, and the bathroom light is off. Same routine, gets up, turns it back on. The couple wake up in the morning, and the bathroom light is off." Kathy chuckles. "At least the husband had a sense of humor. He turns to his wife and says, 'I guess the ghost can't sleep with the lights on.'"

The spirits of Elizabeth and John Klein do not limit their visitations to inside the house; they have both put in personal appearances around the grounds.

"Our chef saw a person sitting by the gazebo on the left side of the house." Phyllis Small spreads her hands open, palms up. "And then the ghost-person disappeared."

Chef Kellogg has just completed dinner service. His double-breasted chef's smock is unbuttoned at the neck. He glances out through the window and begins. "Very, very early in the morning, typically that's when you see him—a gentleman on the bench under the cedar trees. When you turn off of Klein Street into this top entrance, it's a *lit-tle* precarious." The chef refers to the side entrance that leads to the visitor parking area. "When you turn in you've got to focus on the driveway because of the sharp curve. At the next curve, you're looking at him because he is right in your direct line of vision; you see the guy sitting there, and then, immediately, you have to look back at the road. In a matter of a second or two, he's gone. I had heard Joe talk about him so I knew it was Mr. Klein."

Joe wipes at an invisible spot on the bar's immaculate surface. He flips the cloth over his left shoulder and leans on the back bar. "I am not the only person that saw this, but what happened was, one night

I was leaving. I saw a figure sitting on the bench out there under the cedar tree—a real short person, dark clothing. I started walking closer, but when I got to the bench, he was gone." Joe takes the cloth off his shoulder, folds it neatly, and squares it next to the sink. He lifts his head and makes eye contact. "It was the same figure John, our chef, has seen. We both agree that it is Mr. Klein."

The nocturnal wanderings of Mr. Klein's better half, the lovely Elizabeth, have caught a few guests off guard. Joe is an expert on the layout of Cedar Grove. The lounge area occupies a former open porch. A bank of windows runs parallel to the long and narrow bar. There is a view of the Country Cottages on the opposite side of Washington Street. These pale-yellow bungalows are leased for extended stays, from a few weeks to a few months. "There are some people who used to stay in number 26 across the street over there. The lady, she likes to come over here for a drink in the evening. The first time she told me about seeing Miss Elizabeth, she hadn't had anything to drink that night. She says, 'I was closing the winders, the shades on the winders, and I could have sworn that I saw a female in a white gown walk through the hedges.' She said she called Miss Kathy and told her about this, and Miss Kathy goes . . .'" Joe gives an exaggerated version of Kathy Hall's slow drawl: "'Weeelll, you are not the first somebody to see Miss Elizabeth.'" Joe tacks on his own footnote. "Miss Kathy told me three or four years before that a couple was just driving by and saw somebody on a balcony up there in a white dress, and Miss Kathy said there ain't nobody supposed to be there. The door to that balcony is locked at night."

Elizabeth Klein gave birth to ten children at Cedar Gove, six boys and four girls. Three died in infancy. The death of the fourth would undo Elizabeth. During Halloween, Cedar Grove offers a special haunted tour of the mansion led by a costumed guide portraying the grieving mother. "Elizabeth" explains that she was six months pregnant during the Siege of Vicksburg. She moved to a plantation north of the city where she gave birth to a son, William Tecumseh Sherman Klein. The baby was named after Elizabeth's uncle by marriage, the famous Union general, who spared Cedar Grove from burning when Elizabeth agreed to its use as a field hospital. When Elizabeth returned to Vicksburg, "my neighbors were hostile toward me and my son. . . . They told me he would be cursed. I was proud to prove them wrong as he grew into a young man who was intelligent, bright, and handsome."

Elizabeth's malicious neighbors believed the curse on young William came true. The actress in the role of Elizabeth has her audience's rapt attention. She takes her place in the rear garden next to the filigreed, black iron staircase leading to the second-floor gallery.

"One morning Willie went hunting with a neighborhood friend and returned to sit under the magnolia tree that was once planted there. His friend awoke with his gun in hand and began to get up when he accidently engaged the gun and it went off, hitting our young Willie in the chest. Willie managed to make it half way up this iron staircase and then stumbled to his death at the base of the stairs. My husband never overcame his grief, and I draped myself in black the rest of my days."

Willie's wounded ghost has been seen many times. Phyllis selects a key from the ring and inserts it into the keyhole of the door leading to the upper back gallery. "We have to keep this door locked because sometimes it seems to open by itself." Phyllis pushes open the door to the second-floor back gallery off the children's rooms. As if on cue, the theme from *Gone with the Wind* booms forth from a loud speaker in the garden below. "Isn't that ironic that *that* music just started?" Phyllis's gold hoop earrings twirl about her lobes as she shakes her head in wonderment. If there is a choice to be had, staff and some alarmed guests would prefer hearing Tara's theme full blast, rather than the dreadful *thud, thud, thud,* like a body tumbling down the stairs, a sinister reminder of a young boy's fatal plunge that sometimes invades the quiet reverie of the gardens.

Often arriving early and leaving late, the executive chef has had to deal with the inn's paranormal peculiarities. "It was Christmas time and the whole banister out there in the hallway was covered with garland and ribbons. I came in that morning, and they said, 'You left the front door open last night.' And I said, 'No, I didn't.' They said, 'Yeah, you did.' I repeated, 'No, I didn't. I am very good about locking up. I double-check doors.'" John was upset. He took the maintenance man with him to review the tapes from the surveillance monitor. "There is a security camera above each door. Motion activated. We rewind the tape. About

The rear staircase where Willie was accidentally shot to death.

one o'clock in the morning, the front door opens, closes, opens, comes about halfway shut, opens the rest of the way, closes. The maintenance guy states, 'Oh, a gust of wind blew it open.' I said, 'Look at the garland, it doesn't move.' The other thing is the motion sensor camera at the other end of the hall should have come on too if it was the wind." John shakes his head. "It didn't. Only the camera above the door came on." Whoever was playing with the front door had the last laugh. "There are a lot of nights, especially in the slow winter season when we have no overnight guests in the house, you'll hear doors shut upstairs and footsteps in the hallways, especially room 6, the children's room, above the front desk."

John's own son has experienced the haunting vibes of Cedar Grove. "He was visiting me at work. We closed up one night. Everything was locked; he was standing at the registration desk, and he heard the door handle rattle. He looked at me because I didn't make a move to go over to it and asked, 'Do you want me to let them in?' I said, 'You can if there is anybody there.' Of course, he goes, 'What do you mean?' So I told him to go ahead and see if anybody is there. He opens the door. No *body*." John puts the emphasis on a flesh-and-blood figure. "He closes the door and I tell him, 'It happens all the time.' He's excited. He's sixteen. Ghosts are cool stuff."

The Kleins' master bedroom is a guest favorite for disparate reasons. It's called Grant's Room in honor of Gen. Ulysses S. Grant's overnight visit on his travels through Vicksburg. The adjoining Bay Room is the original nursery. The Klein children still play in the house. "There have been three or four occasions, all different times when people will stay in the Grant Room, and somewhere between 2:30 and 3:30 in the morning, they'll hear children laughing in the hall, but they don't seem to mind," says Joe. "It's happy times," brags Phyllis.

Unlike the dreadful echo of Willie's falling body on the outside staircase, the soft thumps coming from the inside stairwell strike a cheerful note. "We hear children's voices upstairs and then the *bump, bump, bump* of a ball bouncing down the steps." Desk manager Kathy welcomes the childish games. The chef adds his endorsement. "They giggle. *Hee. Hee. Ha, Ha, Ha.* Good sounds."

The Bonnie Blue room on the second floor has a view of the east garden. A floral Laura Ashley print falls in graceful swags over the canopy bed. It is a room for a princess to conjure magical dreams. One mischievous tyke who inhabits the space wants people to know she's still around. The mantle over the black-and-white marble fireplace features a matching pair of golden candelabras. Just above the candelabra on the right, a child's handprint appears as if on a whim. Today, the smudged outline is visible. "It was not here yesterday," swears Phyllis. "And I can't figure out how a child could reach that high, unless she's standing on a chair."

Phyllis is just as frustrated with the condition of the single sleigh bed in the corner. She bends over and with outstretched hands smoothes out the wrinkles in the white coverlet. "This bed always looks like someone is sitting in it. The housekeeping staff goes crazy."

"Even though the maids go up there and clean up, you'll see pranks on the bed where somebody left the impression of their feets as if they was bouncing on that bed." Joe's head nods up and down. "Then when they gets to sitting on the edge, you know with their legs on the sides, you see

The haunted Bonnie Blue room where little ghosts play.

Owner Phyllis Small reaches up to touch the handprint.

The vanishing handprint over the mantle in the Bonnie Blue room.

that too." Joe often offers to help. "I was going upstairs to get a towel, and I looked in the Bonnie Blue room, and I saw that bed a mess. I came down and got Rhonda, another staff member. I told her to go upstairs and check the room out, but I didn't tell her what to look for. When she got back, I asked her what she saw. Rhonda says, 'Footprints on the bed.' I was glad because I just wanted to make sure she saw the same thing I did. I didn't want anyone to think I was just making something up."

However, he finds other childlike impressions around the house easier to explain. "I was in the ballroom once and there was a child's white handprint on the glass. Somebody on the staff got all excited thinking it was a ghost print." Joe grins. "Wasn't nothing like that. The afternoon before we had a birthday party and some people brought their kids. The air-conditioner was on all night. Room got cold and the winder got condensed. So this little kid's fingerprints looks all frosty white just like a ghost."

Back in the Bonnie Blue room, Phyllis wishes there was a good explanation for what she encountered. With a hint of trepidation, she demonstrates. "This is where the cold spot was. I came in here, saw the bed looked as if someone had been bouncing on it, I took a step in to straighten it, and the space around it was chilly cold, freezer cold." Her round, wire-framed glasses have slipped down her nose. She pushes them back up with her index finger. "There was nothing here to cause a draft." Phyllis rocks one step forward, one step back. "When I backed up, the temperature was normal. It was the most eerie feeling I have ever had. I said to myself, *They're here. I know they're here.*"

As the surviving Klein children grew, papa Klein built homes for them as wedding presents. Daughter Susan married Isaac Bonham. Their home, the Corners, was directly across the street from Cedar Gove. Susan gave birth to two children, but both died of childhood diseases. While trying to intervene in a duel, Isaac was killed by a stray bullet. The young widow moved back to Cedar Gove. After the death of her parents— John in 1884, Elizabeth in 1909—Susan sold Cedar Grove, with all its furnishings, to Dr. Antoine Tonnar. Dr. Tonnar sold it to the Podesta family, who were looking for a party house.

Cedar Grove's large ballroom served as the perfect setting for their many lavish soirees. But the Podestas were harboring a secret. Their daughter

Phyllis Small standing next to the cold spot in the Bonnie Blue room.

was not well, not of "sound mind." She spent most of her young life sequestered in state asylums. When her occasional visits home coincided with a party night, the troubled young woman was locked in her room to prevent any potential "embarrassment." Family lore does not reveal if this young girl ever threatened to kill herself if she was forced to return to the asylum, but on the evening before her departure, she did just that. She escaped from her room, marched straight into the ballroom, drew a pistol from her gown, and shot herself in the head. Phyllis confirms that this is the most haunted room in the house. "People tell us they hear the sound of a gun going off, screams, and music. They always talk about the music." Phyllis has never experienced any of this. She and her daughter Colleen have only had to deal with the drapes—and a ghostly decorator who has a decidedly upside-down point of view.

The ballroom décor is all frothy wedding-cake pink and white. Rose-colored damask drapes frame the tall windows. The swags at the top are held in place with matching bows. Phyllis adjusts her glasses. Pale-blue eyes lock on the window nearest the corner. "See that bow up there? I have come in here before and it is flipped backwards. There is no draft anywhere that can cause that. Colleen has had the housekeeping staff fix it over and over. They have to get a ladder to do it. It's an on-going problem." Phyllis admits that as comical and annoying as this poltergeist activity may be, it seems disconnected from the tragic suicide in the ballroom. "If someone is trying to get our attention, or wants us to do something, we wish we knew what it is all about."

Cedar Grove has an entire family of "old" ghosts and one new one. The novice ghost haunts the bar. "I don't think that ghost is a member of the Klein family," says Phyllis. "I really, truly feel that it is Andre, our former chef. He was very emotional, very flamboyant, you know, sometimes chefs have that over-the-top ego."

Expert mixologist Joe is in place behind the bar. "I'll give you a demonstration of what happened." Joe plucks four red wine goblets from a shelf and places them stems up on a drying rack behind the bar. They form a square, almost touching each other. "This was last summer. There were three people over there—a waitress and two guests." Joe indicates the short length of the L-shaped bar. "I had turned my back to get some more wine to refill a glass when the man shouts, 'Look at that glass, it's flying through the air.'" Joe's compressed lips disappear under his thick mustache. "Yup, it flew off the counter, flipped over, and landed bottom side up, right between these four." The glass with invisible wings is a hefty beer glass with a thick bottom. Joe sticks the beer glass in the center of the square of wine goblets. "Nothing got broken."

"I had no idea before I worked here they had ghostly stories about the place. When I got to Cedar Grove, the ghosts must of decided to test me out, see if I could figure out what was going on, see if I would freak out. Once they knew I wasn't going to panic and take off, they realized, we can't mess with this one."

For Joe, the second incident was less harrowing than the first. "There were house glasses stacked here." The bartender moves over to reveal a three-tiered shelving arrangement to the side of the mirrored bar. "The wine glasses were lined up on shelves on the back bar." Joe holds a house glass in his hand. "This glass came down, crosses over to the wine glasses, breaks them off at the stem, but the globe parts are not shattered." Joe shrugs. "Of course, there's this crashing sound, and Miss Kathy at the front desk is hollering, 'Mr. Joe, Mr. Joe, what are you doing?' I yell back, 'I ain't doing nothing.'"

Kathy's version of the events is similar. "I was sitting at the front desk that afternoon, and I heard a glass hit the floor. I wasn't paying too much attention until I heard a second one, a third one, and then I got up and started walking down the hallway towards the lounge. I'm hollering, 'Mr. Joe, are you okay?' I'm thinking maybe he fell or something. 'That's not me,' he yells back. 'These glasses are edging themselves up to the edge of the shelf and are falling off.'" The phone rings. Kathy reaches for it, but before she picks up, she says, "I don't know how that could happen. I don't know why it doesn't scare me, but it doesn't."

Chef John Kellogg has also been on the receiving end of the paranormal prankster. "I've seen the glasses fall in the bar. I've actually had a glass hit me in the bar." The chef rests his hands on the carved back of a chair in the formal dining room. Cedar Grove's lounge is on the other side of the hallway. "I went in there one day before the bar was even open. As I started around the corner, at the end of the bar, three glasses came off. Two went straight down, and one hit me in the head. It traveled laterally about this distance to get to me." John stretches his hands about four feet apart. "Everybody says they think it is Andre. There were a couple of cooks between me and him, but no other real chefs. They say Andre had a temper; maybe he doesn't like my style."

Another ghostly hand made it clear that he/she objected to Colleen's style as well. "Colleen ran the house before her mother, Phyllis. She had this painting hung. Only it wouldn't stay up." The massive, gilt frame nearly overpowers the image of a young mother cradling her baby. John has no easy answers. He runs his hand through a tangle of brown hair flecked with gray. "You'd come back in the room and it would be off the wall, resting on top of the buffet. The hook would be still in place, and the wire on the back of the painting would be fine. Colleen would have the staff rehang it, and as soon as they'd leave, it would be off again. Colleen gave up. That's why its sitting on the buffet the way it is." John likes to point out that the buffet with its white marble top is not a piece of furniture, but a skillfully disguised, three-thousand-pound, cast-iron safe. "Kick it," he urges. "It was made to look like wood and sounds like wood. They did a good job. It fooled the Union soldiers." This was a successful case of hiding in plain sight. Sherman and his men passed it every day while they occupied the house. They had no inkling that John Klein's stash of cash was safely stored inside. Secrets and mysteries reside in every room of this fine inn.

For those on the lookout for a haunting good time, is it possible to reserve a room *with ghosts* at Cedar Grove Inn? Are they on call? Do they take requests: *Come out, come out, wherever you are?*

Kathy says such questions are common. "Some guests who book a room will ask, 'Do y'all got ghosts?' We have to tell them there is no set room where things are guaranteed to happen. Sometimes they play around, sometimes they don't, but when they are here, they're mischievous, and they're having a *gooood* time."

Chef John goes along with Kathy. "We have a lot of people come here and say we want to see a ghost and we say, 'We do too, but they don't quite work for us.' People ask which room has ghosts in it. I can't say one room is more haunted than the next. I just know what I have seen and heard. If you pay attention you are going to hear things; you are going to see things."

During Halloween, the Cedar Grove lounge is humorously renamed "Lost Souls Tavern." Even then, Joe is the most discreet of bartenders. "Some peoples when they come here, they want to know, others when they find out will say, 'I can't stay here, I got to go somewhere else.' So I don't talk about ghosts and such unless someone asks."

Phyllis believes it's all about perceptions. "I am one of those kind of people that get feelings about it. When we purchased the property, it was three o'clock in the afternoon; the lights went off in the entire mansion. We couldn't get them back up. It was the first day." She holds her arms out in front and inspects them for goose bumps. "I am getting a chill, just thinking about it. I looked at my husband and said, 'That's Mr. Klein letting us know who's the boss. It's his way of saying, 'This is my house, and I will allow you to stay if you respect my house.'" The lights did eventually come back on. Phyllis says all is well; the spirits of the Kleins are part of the extended family, and they can continue to reside at Cedar Grove Inn for as long as they so desire.

Postscript: If you have an open mind, and are not the squeamish sort, then reserve the Library Suite in the main house or a suite on the first floor of the original Carriage House. All are exquisitely furnished, come with private parlors, and have a dark past.

The best view of the Southern-style, columned Carriage House is from the rooftop garden of the mansion. During the Klein era, the ground floor of the Carriage House served as the stables. On hot summer nights when the air weighs thick and heavy and fog rolls up off the river, the sharp crackle of flames and the high-pitched whinnies and pounding hoofs of spooked horses return. "There was a mother and her two daughters staying in one of the Carriage House suites," relays Kathy, "when she checked out she told me she was bothered by what she thought were horses stomping in a mass cluster of confusion. It hit me that what she was probably hearing were the groomsmen trying to get the horses out of the stable. There used to be two stables here, one of them burned to the ground."

Inside the main portion of the inn, room 21, the bilevel Library Suite, has a different problem. "Oh, you mean the dead smells?" Kathy is blunt. "Yeah, it is kind of eerie." The library is an Elizabeth Klein alteration to Cedar Grove. Elizabeth desired more space to entertain her female acquaintances. The quick fix? Appropriate the adjoining gentlemen's parlor to double the size of the ladies parlor. Elizabeth had an agenda: move John and his cigar-smoking friends to the outer regions of the mansion. The shrewd wife waited until her husband was out of town before hiring a contractor to do the deed. And how could John Klein object? He returned to a magnificent library, walls the color of deep claret, cabinets for his books, a private outside entrance, and a circular staircase that led to an immense wine cellar below.

During the Siege of Vicksburg, when General Sherman commandeered Cedar Grove for use as a field hospital, the wine cellar's cool depths were the perfect environment for a morgue. In an excerpt from Cedar Grove's haunted Halloween tour, the spirit of Elizabeth stands before the ground level entrance to John's wine cellar and reveals its history.

"This room was where the dead bodies of dearly departed souls would be placed for safe keeping during the Civil War. . . . It was dark and

View of the haunted Carriage House from the rooftop of Cedar Grove.

cool so the remains would be preserved until shipment home or burial. However, it was sometimes a long time between death and burial, and odors would come from this room. Many believe they can still smell the odor of decaying bodies."

Guests staying in the suite enjoy the full use of John's office and sitting room, and at night, they descend the spiral staircase to a spacious bedroom in muted shades of pink with an attached spa bathroom. For most, the privacy and luxury of the accommodations usually offset any lingering phantom odors.

Phyllis Small unlocks the French door of the bedroom. The suite's outdoor space has a private, bricked courtyard with a fountain where guests, says Phyllis, can "sit and smoke." Phyllis surveys the patio for any telltale signs of cigarette butts. "Colleen doesn't know. She hates smoke."

Before leaving the patio, Phyllis ticks off the uncanny similarities between her daughter Colleen and the Kleins:

John Klein was twenty-four when he acquired the property.

Colleen was twenty-four when she purchased Cedar Grove.

Elizabeth Klein went to great lengths to rid the house of the smell of cigars.

Colleen has an aversion to all smoking odors.

John Klein met Elizabeth, his bride, in Natchez, Mississippi.

Colleen's middle name is Elizabeth, and she is from Natchez.

The Kleins are of German lineage.

Colleen's ancestors are German.

Klein in German means small.

Colleen's maiden name is Small.

Alluring Madeline hangs over the fireplace in the dining room of King's Tavern.

4

King's Tavern

Madeline. Alluring Madeline.
Sweet sixteen and a dimple in her chin.
Love for the tavern keeper sealed her fate
when the coy barmaid chose the wrong mate.

For the tavern keeper had a wife,
who knew too well how to wield a knife.
Now, alluring Madeline, a pretty little ghost is she,
haunting King's Tavern for all eternity.
—B. Sillery, "Alluring Madeline"

In the 1700s, the Natchez Territory had a largely rough-and-tumble population. King's Tavern, known then as the Post House, sat strategically near the entrance to the Natchez Trace. The Trace was a trail road, a lawless highway infested by rogues, robbers, vagabonds, the destitute, and ne'er-do-wells. Wary travelers, traders, adventurers, and flat boatmen often banded together at the Post House before embarking on their journey overland up the 450-mile trace, extending between Natchez, Mississippi, and Nashville, Tennessee. For some, their trek began in New Orleans and stretched more than six months to their home in the northeast. The original trace was a footpath carved out by Native Americans as a trade route between the southern and central areas of the continent.

On May 31, 1789, Prosper King secured a Spanish land grant, deeding an entire square of grounds and its buildings. From 1789 to

1820, Prosper owned and operated what would later be rechristened as King's Tavern. The ground floor with brick walls served as stables. Two smaller dirt-floored rooms housed the slaves. The tavern occupied the main floor. Exposed beams, cypress-paneled walls, and a stone fireplace with a blazing hearth welcomed visitors. The second floor, reached by an exterior staircase, provided simple living quarters for Prosper and his wife. The third floor attic was often rented out to poor travelers desperate for a place to lay their weary heads.

To this establishment came the hapless Madeline, who went from barmaid to mistress of the owner Prosper King. Mrs. King had other ideas: she executed a swift and decisive end to the ill-fated affair. According to local lore, the offended Mrs. King either stabbed Madeline or hired killers to do the dastardly deed. And to ensure that Mr. King never saw his young lover again, Mrs. King had Madeline's body bricked inside the fireplace in the main dining room. All of this seemed like a fanciful tale until the 1930s.

Crumbling bricks revealed a gruesome grave. In 1823, the Postlethwaite family purchased the Post House and made it into a cozy home. The transformation was so successful that succeeding generations of Postlethwaites lived in the home for the next 150 years. Old structures require constant maintenance, and as the sun-dried, clay fireplace bricks began to disintegrate into dust, masons were hired to shore the fireplace back up. Carefully trying to salvage the remaining bricks, the workmen unearthed bone fragments among the bricks and mortar. The shaken workers recovered the skeletal remains of three people—two adult males and one teenage female. Buried with the skeletons was a jeweled dagger. Speculation abounds; the female had to be poor Madeline. The males? By one account, slaves murdered for some unknown transgression. By another, the male skeletons were the hired assassins, who in turn were murdered and entombed with Madeline. If the latter was the case, then Mrs. King certainly had one busy day and one very powerful arm.

And here's where the tale of Madeline lives on. By the 1970s, the remaining Postlethwaites had moved out. The two-hundred-plus-year-old structure, made of bargeboards and rough-hewn timber held together with wooden pegs, began to crumble. Members of the Natchez Garden Club were reluctant to let what might be the oldest dwelling in the Natchez Territory fall to the ravages of time and the elements. They banded together to restore the original structure with its large galleries. The successful restoration garnered a listing on the National Register of Historic Places. The ladies of the Natchez Garden Club were not interested in running a tavern or an inn. But Yvonne Scott was. She opened the Post House as a combination restaurant and tavern and renamed it King's Tavern after the early owner.

Yvonne was fascinated with Madeline's story. She wanted a portrait of Madeline to hang over the fireplace in the main dining room. She searched in vain; a poor serving girl would never have been able to afford such an extravagance.

Tom Miller, the current tavern keeper, picks up the story. "Yvonne went to a local thrift shop and was digging around. In the back of the shop, hidden deep in a pile of discarded furniture and picture frames, she spies a portrait of a young girl. The girl looks Spanish with dark alluring eyes and hair, and she is holding out an apple, kind of offering it up. Yvonne feels like this is what Madeline would have looked like. She goes to the sales clerk and says she wants to buy it. But the sales clerk doesn't know who it belongs to or where it came from, so she gets on the phone and calls the manager, calls everybody, and no one has any answers. Yvonne negotiates back and forth and finally purchases it for fifteen dollars. She hangs it over the fireplace, the very fireplace where Madeline's bones were discovered, and from that point on, the portrait became Madeline."

Miller says that poltergeist activity frequently occurs involving the portrait. "There have been times when that picture is on the wall and it starts swinging violently back and forth. From the time Yvonne hung it here, that is very common." Miller also states that Madeline's portrait was a condition of his purchasing the tavern from Yvonne. "Yvonne didn't want to let her go, but I told her that Madeline had to stay with King's Tavern. She belongs here."

Diners at the restaurant agree. Madeline's portrait is a big draw. After hearing her story, tourists love to take pictures of the portrait. One visitor added an intriguing new twist, which the tavern keeper found to be a remarkable coincidence. "I had a European tourist who came in, knew nothing about the ghost, about Madeline. He kept staring at the picture and called me over and said, 'Somebody must have gone to Europe.' He claimed that this was a copy of a very famous picture. I was dumbfounded. He said, 'Yes, the painting over the fireplace is called *The Alluring Madeline.'* And I mean, I just got goose bumps, and I said, 'You're pulling my leg. You know the story about our Madeline.' He said, 'Well, I don't know who she was, all I know is that this picture is titled *The Alluring Madeline.'* I said, 'Well, our ghost here, her name is Madeline and that's who we see in the picture.'"

The staff at King's Tavern attributes all types of pranks to Madeline. Again, Tom Miller acknowledges, "She's a prankster. At least we think it is her. There is a chain at the back of the restaurant that swings back and forth. One time, I had to move a couple from the table against the wall, because she was making the chain swing so hard that they felt the need to duck. She makes water pour from the ceiling where there are no pipes up above. Her hot spots are on the staircases." Miller refers to the wood-railed, steeply rising staircase that winds in a narrow trail from the main floor to the attic. "A lot of times she will tap people on the shoulder. And women, especially women, she will tug at their hair as they are coming down. They tell us they smell lavender, which we like to think was Madeline's favorite scent."

And if that is not enough manifestations for this lively ghost, the spirit of Madeline likes to pop into the bedroom on the third floor. "Madeline haunts that part of the house too. A lot of our waiters say that that is Madeline's bedroom, but that is probably not correct. This was a tavern and inn to make money, and the owners would not have let a servant sleep there, but we let people go up and see what the room might have looked like when it was an inn."

The bedroom is sparsely furnished with a plain armoire, night table, and wooden bed. The faded quilt coverlet is the source of on-going phenomena. "She leaves warm spots on the bed as if someone was laying there and they just got up. That happens almost every day, every day constantly, the spots move around. We tell our guests to go up and see if they feel the hot spots. Sometimes, the warm areas are near the head of the bed; other times it will be near the foot as if someone has shifted around under the covers."

As active as Madeline is, she has competition for haunting rights at

King's Tavern. And this next little spirit's departure from the world is more horrific than Madeline's demise.

Along the Natchez Trace, there were no highwaymen more feared, more brutal than the Harpe brothers. Big Harpe and Little Harpe were the worst of the worst. Their murderous rampages spared no one.

Tom Miller recounts the legend of one vile deed that happened when King's Tavern served as the post office for the Natchez Territory. "Big Harpe was in the tack room over here when a woman came in to get her mail. She held a crying baby to her chest. The baby's wails annoyed Big Harpe. He grabbed the baby by its legs and whacked the child's head on the wall and killed it."

The exact location of the infant's cruel death has become another ghostly "hot" spot. Tavern keeper Miller points to the staircase that runs along an interior brick wall that separates the restaurant into main dining room and party room. "There are tables on both sides of the brick wall, table number 11 and table number 12. If you sit right there at either of those two tables, you can hear the crying." For those who inquire if justice was ever meted out to the vicious highwayman, Miller is quick to respond. "Big Harpe got away that day, as he had in the past. He was known to have killed quite a few children. He even strangled one of his own babies for crying." However, says the tavern keeper with a satisfactory nod, "his last horrible deed finally got him. After he killed the baby here, he slipped away to Tennessee and murdered his friend's wife and child. They got a posse together and chased him all the way down to just north of Jackson. Killed him. Chopped his head off, put it on a tree, and put a sign up that said *This is what happens to highwaymen.*"

King's Tavern lays claim to a third ghost who hovers near the tavern but never crosses the threshold. Miller sits casually on a stool with his back to the bar and shares a bit of early Natchez history. "This was the frontier. This place at night was a safe place for people to sleep. They would close all the shutters up, like a little fortress. People were afraid of attacks by highwaymen, river pirates, and Indians." Miller's elbows are on the bar, arms crossed on his chest. He issues a disclaimer. "Now, I've never seen him, but some of my guests have. This ghost is dressed like an Indian with full headdress like a chief. He stands at the original front door which is no longer in use."

King's Tavern in Natchez.

To the right of the current canopied entrance to the restaurant is a six-foot panel of glass that replaced the former doorway. This modern touch is glaringly out of place with the weather-beaten timber exterior, but the expanse of glass provides necessary daylight to what would otherwise be a dark and gloomy interior. According to the legend, the phantom Indian chief probably lived on the land before the house was built. And says Miller, "He is curious as to what is going on; he peers in the window, checks it out, and then leaves. He knows he is not welcome, and Mr. King would never have allowed an Indian inside his place."

Grayhawk, a Native American elder of the Houma Nation speaks of his contemporary encounter with a belligerent ghost who tried to ban him from exploring King's Tavern. Grayhawk, whose father is Choctaw and mother is Houma, was in town to attend the annual March PowWow at the Grand Village of the Natchez. Grayhawk is drawn to old structures. After dinner at the tavern with friends, and listening to the ghostly saga of Madeline, he went up the stairs to see the bedroom and feel the "hot" spots on the bed. But as he made the turn on the first landing, it became quite clear that "someone" did not want him to go any farther. "I put my hand on the railing, and I felt this pressure like another hand had grabbed my wrist and was holding it down." Grayhawk said he felt as if he was engaged in an actual physical struggle, although there was no one in front of him. "I had to fight to free my hand from the rail."

For Grayhawk, a well-muscled man, sturdy of stature, the phantom confrontation did not surprise him. Until well into the twentieth century, Native Americans were not welcomed into white establishments, many unable to attend public schools until the passage of the Civil Rights Act of 1964.

Grayhawk has a pretty good idea as to the identity of his ghostly adversary. "It was probably Mr. King, the original owner. He was letting me know that he didn't want me upstairs." Grayhawk did finish his tour, but he walked away with a physical reminder of the encounter. "As I was leaving King's Tavern, I felt my wrist aching. I looked down and there were four raised, red welts on my wrist like the imprint of fingers grabbing hard and holding on tight."

A young woman entombed behind a brick wall, a baby with a crushed skull, a curious Indian, and an adversarial Mr. King: phantom spirits all—apparitions whose appearances provide endless ghostly fodder to the haunting of King's Tavern.

Postscript: The Natchez tribesmen were seen in the area as late as 1782. Natchez Indians did not wear the full feather headdress often associated with Plains Indians of the Southwest. In *The Historic Indian Tribes of Louisiana,* authors Fred B. Kniffen, Hiram F. Gregory, and George A. Stokes describe the mode of dress of Native Americans typical in the Southeast including the Natchez:

"Neither sex normally wore any distinctive form of headgear. . . . Prominent men, on occasion, wore silver headbands connected with nettings. . . . After 1740, silver headbands were wrought from European coins, some of them highly ornate and identifying a chief."

If guests at King's Tavern do see a vision of an Indian chief in full headdress peering in the window, he must have traveled very far indeed from his ancestral homelands.

Stanton Hall occupies an entire city block in historic downtown Natchez.

5

Stanton Hall

The ghostly alter ego of Frederick Stanton is an early riser; he startles sleeping guests with a hearty *GOOD MORNING!* This predawn, wake-up call has been a problem in the past. Now that Stanton Hall no longer hosts overnight guests, the disruption is confined to more civilized hours.

Mattie Jo Ratcliffe jokingly refers to herself as the *Godmother* of tour guides. As chairwoman emeritus of the Natchez Pilgrimage Garden Club, which owns and operates Stanton Hall as a historic house museum, she has trained them all during her fifty-plus-year tenure. Mattie Jo takes a seat in the lobby of the Carriage House Restaurant on the grounds of Stanton Hall. A parade of well-wishers, including the head chef, stop to greet her. The flow of acquaintances ebbs and Mattie Jo eagerly delves into the mysterious habits of the spirit world; she plunges into a recent paranormal incident between hostess Kathleen Butler and the ghost of the original owner of Stanton Hall. "Kathleen told me that Frederick spoke to her. It was right after she finished a tour, and he called her by name."

The tour of Stanton Hall is a looping down-up-down, back-to-front-to-back labyrinth. Visitors enter the house through the gift shop in the rear courtyard. They are guided through the first-floor living spaces from dining room to parlors, and then they ascend the main staircase to the second-floor bedrooms. The tour ends at the entrance to the servants' quarters where visitors descend a narrow exterior staircase to the courtyard below.

Mattie Jo explains that on that particular day Kathleen watched the last of her group clutch the wooden handrails as they treaded gingerly downward. She closed the door securely behind them. Kathleen then turned and headed to the inside staircase to return to the gift shop for the next tour. This was the "the proper procedure" for all hostesses. Kathleen was now alone at the top of the baronial main stairs.

The matriarch of the Pilgrimage Garden Club settles into the tale. "She heard this voice calling, 'Kathleen.' She thought maybe she was behind schedule and someone was calling her to hurry up. She looked over the banister and there was no one there." What really threw Kathleen off, according to Mattie Jo, was that the voice was male and there were no male guides on duty. Mattie Joe taps her walking cane on the floor for emphasis. "She was about to shake it off as just her imagination when the voice called more insistently, 'Kathleen!' She got annoyed because she couldn't see anyone; he wouldn't show himself, yet the voice kept calling her name, demanding her attention."

Mattie Jo tilts her perfectly coifed head sideways and gives a nod of approval at Kathleen's refusal to allow any further ghostly interference. "She just turned, looked over her shoulder, and said, 'Mr. Stanton, you can have it.' And she went on down stairs back to work." Months afterwards, Kathleen Butler still insists, "I just knew, I just knew it was him."

On another perplexing morning when the home was operating as a bed and breakfast, one of the managers reported to Mattie Jo that she smelled the strong odor of cigar smoke in the first-floor library—an area off-limits to guests during the night.

"I asked her if it could have been a guest, and she swore she turned the security system on." Mattie Jo stresses the alarm's effectiveness. "Stanton Hall has a very sophisticated alarm system with a secondary system between the first and second floors so that people staying upstairs could not wander downstairs during the night." The ghost of Stanton Hall, original owner Frederick Stanton, apparently feels the prohibition does not apply to him; for judging by the lingering smell, he continues to enjoy his imported cigars in the evening hours and easily circumvents the modern alarm system.

Chef Bingo Star returns to confirm Mattie Jo's dinner reservation for the upcoming holiday meal. The new chef has added a few Creole dishes to the staple of Southern fried chicken, tiny buttered biscuits, and mint juleps and is eager for Mattie Jo's approval. There is some good-natured banter, and then Mattie Jo remembers a less-than-pleasant visit just three weeks prior. The sinister overtones have nothing to do with the menu, but with a menacing presence who invited himself to lunch.

"This is strange and this has to do with me. I park in the lot for handicap parking on the side of the house over there." She brandishes her cane in the air, which is for balance after hip-replacement surgery. "There wasn't anybody else parked there." She clears her throat and resumes. "I started towards the Carriage House, and as I stepped on to the brick walk, I was aware that somebody was walking behind me. I didn't turn around, of course, and I wondered where they came from because there wasn't any car that had driven up, so I just continued on a regular walking pace coming to the Carriage House. The footsteps got closer, and I thought that this is really kind of rude for somebody to walk so close. By the time I got to the side door over there, they were really close, and I thought, *'How rude can this person be?'* So I turned around real quick because I was going to say, 'I beg your pardon,' and there was nobody there!"

Mattie Jo dismisses the notion that the stalking phantom might be Frederick Stanton, because he was always a perfect gentleman in life. She puzzles over the identity of this crude and sinister spirit now lurking on the grounds of Stanton Hall.

Stanton Hall is a magnificent and princely edifice. The property encompasses an entire city block bounded by High, Commerce, Monroe, and Pearl streets, just four blocks from the Mississippi River. The scale is huge; excluding galleries, basement, attic and observatory areas, the two principal floors and wing total 10,766 square feet. Four massive fluted columns topped with Corinthian capitals dominate the front entry. Lacy iron railings adorn both levels of the portico. Nine granite steps lead to the solid oak door. Five levels of opulence, including a belvedere. Upon completion in 1858, builder and architect Thomas Rose of Natchez presented a bill for $83,262.23. Frederick Stanton christened his stately creation Belfast, after his family home in Belfast, Ireland.

Stanton, a wealthy cotton broker and plantation owner, spared no expense on interior furnishings and embellishments—silver door knobs, keyhole escutcheons, hinges and lock plates, immense gilt mirrors from France, Carrara marble mantles, Greek Revival-style double arches, and

A portrait of Frederick Stanton, the ghost of Stanton Hall.

Hulda Laura Helm Stanton, wife of Frederick Stanton.

grand bronze chandeliers depicting Natchez's early origins: Indians armed with bows and arrows, wolves, rattlesnakes, corn, and etched glass shades. Frederick Stanton was often quoted as saying he wanted to build "a gem for Natchez." And in this glittering mansion, Frederick; his wife, Hulda; and their children could entertain guests in two double parlors and a back parlor. Upon his death in 1859, Frederick's estate inventory listed furnishings for the "library, dining room, pantry, kitchen, servants' hall, four servants' rooms, seven bedrooms, a nursery, an upper hall, card room and billiard room."

Frederick had but a short while to enjoy his creature comforts. He died only a month after moving in on January 4, 1859. His widow, Hulda Laura Helm Stanton, was more fortunate. She lived in the palatial residence with her children and grandchildren for thirty-four years until her death in 1893. During the Civil War, one errant shell rocked the family's peaceful existence. In 1863, a cannonball from the Union gunboat Essex landed in a soup tureen. No one was hurt. According to a history compiled by the Pilgrimage Garden Club, privates in the Union army did occupy one wing of the family home and were said to have "chloroformed daughters Varina and Elizabeth Stanton while they slept in their bedroom in order to steal some handsome large pieces of silver hidden under the beds."

From 1894 to1901, the home became the Stanton College for Young Ladies. It was then reverted to a private residence. Under the direction of the Pilgrimage Garden Club, the home reemerged as Stanton Hall.

This was never a home open to the common riffraff. So what rude spirit lurks out in the courtyard, nipping at the heels of visitors? If he is one of the pilfering Union privates out to gather more family silver, Mattie Jo Ratcliffe would be happy to see him banished from the property. This gracious lady does not have an issue with the supernatural hanging out; she would just prefer that they be a little more circumspect.

For more than thirty years, Mattie Jo lived with a very personal ghostly drama. "I believe in the supernatural because a former home of mine in Natchez is haunted; it's definitely haunted. It's called the Van Court Townhouse. It's an 1835 house on the corner of Washington and Union. My husband and I and family lived there."

What convinced this regal matron that her former home had ghosts?

"The reason I know they are there at my old house is because one of the owners after I sold it was a medium, and she saw the ghosts."

At a chance encounter with the same medium years later at Stanton Hall's Carriage House restaurant, Mattie Jo and her adult daughter gleaned some insight into the identity of the troubled spirits at the Van Court Townhouse. "My daughter, who grew up in this house, walked over to the medium and said, 'Well, have you seen any of our ghosts?' And she said, 'Yes.' I said, 'You have?' She said, 'They followed me up the stairs. It is a mother and three children. They all died in that house during the yellow fever epidemic in 1837.'"

Mattie Jo says that in their years living in the townhouse, her family never actually saw the ghosts. "With us it was noises, inexplicable. My husband, my late husband, was a very hardheaded surgeon who said, 'There is no such things as ghosts, don't be ridiculous.' So he was pretty hard to convince. I didn't convince him; he changed his mind on his own." One item that led to Dr. Ratcliffe's conversion was an antique mirror with a child's footprint.

"We had a large mirror over the mantel and the first time I saw what looked like a baby's footprint in it, it I said to myself, 'What is that?' I told the maid to clean the mirror with Windex, which she did, and it kept reappearing. And so a young doctor and his wife were visiting us one time, and I said, 'Jimmy, go and look at that mirror there and tell me what that spot is.' He was from out of town and knew nothing about our ghosts. After looking at it from several angles, Jimmy said, 'Well, I'd say that is a child's footprint. I imagine probably about two or something like that.' I said, 'That's one of our ghosts.'"

Mattie Jo chuckles, "And you know that young man was so scared when he and his wife went to bed, they kept the lights on all night. I told him, 'They are not going to hurt you, they never hurt anybody.'"

She admits that old houses creak and groan as floorboards settle in and wind rattles windows, but other sounds and actions are harder to dismiss. "On the wooden steps, you'd hear one step at a time as if someone was going up, when no one was on the stairs, and there were other times when there would be a sudden crash when there was nothing that crashed, or the sound of a door slam, when it didn't move, but it sounded like a slam."

Mary Jo did not want her children to be frightened, so she often made light of the situation. "My boys slept upstairs on the third floor. And they would run downstairs all hours of the night yelling, 'Mommy there's somebody up here, somebody just touched my face.' And I'd say, 'Don't be ridiculous, go to bed.'"

On yet another night of interrupted sleep, this harried mother simply threw up her hands over her restless spirits. "My daughter woke up one night right after her grandmother died, and the rocking chair that was her grandmother's favorite was rocking in her room. She asked me, 'Do you suppose it was Mimi?' All I could say was, 'I don't know. I just can't keep up with all the ghosts in the house.'"

Mattie Jo Ratcliffe has seen and heard a lot in her years living in Natchez—local scandal, local lore. As a member of the Pilgrimage Garden Club since 1948, as a first time Natchez Pageant participant in 1938, and a tour guide for the annual spring and fall pilgrimages, she has had an inside, behind-the-scenes-look at good times and bad and witnessed ghostly antics, pranks, and poltergeist activities. She embraces them all. "If you love history, you meet wonderful people from farmers in Idaho to politicians and presidents."

Mattie Jo has sat and chatted on the back gallery of Stanton Hall with Jason Roberts, met with John Travolta and Muhammad Ali. She has been intimidated only once. When the *Delta Queen* docked in Natchez, she greeted the passengers at the gangplank as they departed for a tour of Stanton Hall. When she spotted national radio guru Paul Harvey, she gasped and said a prayer, "Dear Lord, if I have ever been articulate, let it be today!"

And when asked why she accepts the idea that ghosts, like Frederick Stanton, still wander about Stanton Hall, she states in a melodic Southern drawl, "Since I experienced so much in my own house, it made me even more receptive, I guess, to the supernatural."

Postscript: Ghostly manifestations at this historic home include a playful puppy. In a family photograph dated 1888, Frederick's widow, Hulda, is seated in the back parlor surrounded by her children and grandchildren. Jet, the family's favorite dog, appears in the lower right, curled up in the arms of granddaughter Cecil Rawle. Mattie Jo Ratcliffe identifies the breed. "They had a black cocker spaniel who raced up and down the stairs after the children." Various contemporary accounts report the dark shadow of a longhaired dog charging up the inside staircase and the clicking sound of paws coming back down. Mattie Jo confirms the presence of the four-legged phantom. "Obviously the feet of a dog and not a person."

Mattie Jo has her own visions. She strolls down the baronial hallway and stops at the bottom step of the stairwell. She hears footsteps and girlish giggles. A line of little girls in long, flowing nightgowns creep down the steps. Memories flood back. "When I was a little girl, my friend's mother rented Stanton Hall for a sleepover." Her voice wavers. "I still see us sneaking out of our bedrooms and coming down right here." For one brief magical moment, this delightful woman is a child again. The ghosts of her youth have returned and she cavorts with her playmates.

Longwood, the unfinished, octagonal mansion known as Nutt's Folly.

6

Longwood

NUTT'S FOLLY. Two centuries later and the ridicule still rankles the spirit of Haller Nutt. A rogue gust of wind blows the gaunt figure through a windowless arch of the observatory. He waits for it to pass, then drifts out on to the tin-lined walkway of the parapet some ninety feet above the ground. The narrow parapet surrounds the base of Longwood's onion-shaped dome. So much frustration. His transparent hand reflexively clutches his chest. Residual spasms of phantom coughs from a fatal bout of pneumonia are ever-present. Returning in spirit form has taken monumental concentration and effort.

As a doctor and a scientist in life, Haller Nutt's paranormal alter ego applies the same serious study to unraveling the mysteries of the afterlife. There have been a few missteps. The day he startled the groundskeeper was a shock to both of them. He had no way of knowing that his current embodiment was visible. He had been roaming undetected for so long throughout the interior floors of Longwood with little impact on the living that he had nearly given up on getting anyone's attention. On that beautiful spring morning, he had finally mastered a technique that would launch his spirit from the confines of indoors to out. A straightforward leap and he was hovering over the grounds. A few practice runs and he could rise or lower at will. There were disappointing drawbacks. Aerodynamics was a troubling factor; winds wreaked havoc with his navigational skills. Broad, open spaces made him nervous. What if his spectral self, so insubstantial, got lifted and pushed away from Longwood? But innate curiosity trumped fear.

About fifty feet from the front entrance, a man in coveralls walked behind a strange mechanical device. He propelled it forward by pushing a tall handle, extending from the top of a rectangular-shaped box on wheels. Thin blades of grass spewed out of the side. The man and machine repeated a straight-lined, back-and-forth pattern, which greatly pleased Haller, for both he and his father, Dr. Rush Nutt, were strong advocates of horizontal plowing to preserve hill land from washing away. The ghost of Haller Nutt surmised that there had to be a series of rotating blades hidden at the bottom of the box on wheels. The challenge became how to slip underneath the roaring machine for a more thorough examination. Anchoring himself with his back to a stately oak, he probed for a solution to his dilemma and forgot that his presence might have an adverse effect on the male human intent on his task. Haller Nutt knew the precise moment he'd been spotted. The grounds keeper paused to pull a stained, blue bandana from his rear pocket. He swiped at his sweaty brow. His mouth opened and he gulped air. His enlarged Adam's apple bobbed up and down. He abandoned the machine as fast as he could set his leaden feet in motion. He ran. Ran hard. Too frightened to risk looking back.

In 2009, Lynn Bradford corroborated the paranormal encounter between the long-deceased Haller Nutt and the startled lawn man. Lynn is the niece of Louise Burns, the resident manager of Longwood for almost thirty years.

"There was a gentleman who was part of the grounds keeping crew; he was mowing the grass. My Aunt Louise was inside, but she could hear the steady drone of the lawn mower. After some time had passed, she and my uncle thought he should be finished with his job. They waited. Didn't see him, but they could still hear the lawn mower. They went out looking. He was gone. Nowhere in sight, but the lawn mower was left in the middle of the lawn, still running. Of course, they thought that quite strange. The man didn't come back the next day either. On payday, he was still a no-show. When they finally tracked him down, my Aunt Louise asked what happened the day he ran off and left the lawn mower running. He said that while he was mowing the grass, he stopped for a minute, looked over, and saw a man leaning against a tree watching him."

Lynn stands up with her back to the wall, and crosses her arms over her chest. "This was the posture that my aunt showed me, and she also said that the lawn man claimed he got scared because the man leaning against the tree had on old-time clothes, period clothes. He was positive the ghost of Haller Nutt was staring at him and all he could think of to do was run."

Haller Nutt, the builder and resident ghost of Longwood.

If unfinished business keeps spirits tethered to the earth, then the ghost of Haller Nutt has more motivation than most. Haller Nutt died of pneumonia at Longwood on June 15, 1864, a man broken in heart and spirit, a visionary whose fairy-tale castle rises majestically on a gentle slope set within a forest of giant magnolias, towering pine, cedar, pecans, poplar, and live oak trees. Dogwood, locust, mimosas, wisteria, and crepe myrtle dot the landscape as if an artist dipped his brush in a riot of colors and spattered it over the green canvas.

Haller Nutt commissioned famed architect Samuel Sloan to design an "oriental villa." Sloan oversaw the building of the largest octagonal house in the United States. Work began in 1858. The five-story architectural wonder would boast more than one million bricks in the foundation, pillars, and walls. In all, 120 Corinthian columns, 8 verandas, and 4 porches graced the exterior. Planned for the 30,000 square feet of living space were 115 doors, 125 windows, 26 fireplaces with marble mantles, 24 closets, and 13 stairways. The 32-room mansion was designed with 9 bedrooms; a bathroom with running water; nursery and playrooms; formal drawing, dining, and banquet halls; a smoking room; a billiard room; private office; sunroom; a fifth-story solarium; and a sixth-story observatory. Longwood was designed as an elegant, extravagant home. The idea of a haunted house never entered its creator's mind.

When work began on Haller Nutt's dream home in the fall of 1858, the pressure was on. By early 1861, he urged a small army of carpenters, brick masons, plasterers, and tinsmiths to work faster and faster. Although he was an avowed Unionist, abhorring the very notion of Southern states setting themselves up against the North, he was powerless to stop the inevitable. April of 1861 saw the start of the Civil War and work on Nutt's dream, *Nutt's Folly* locals called it, came to an abrupt halt. The craftsmen and artisans, many of them from the North, packed up what tools they could and left. "So Haller hired local workers to plaster the brick walls here in the above-ground basement to make Longwood habitable for his family," explains hostess Gay Guerico. In 1862, Haller; his wife, Julia; and their children moved into nine basement rooms. Windowless openings on the upper floors were boarded up. "He thought it was going to be a short war, and they could wait it out at Longwood."

Recently, members of the Pilgrimage Garden Club uncovered a new piece of information on those who labored to bring Longwood to life. Gay describes what happened. "They found this card in the newspaper from the last workmen to leave, the bricklayers from Philadelphia. In the paper, the bricklayers thanked the people of Natchez for their hospitality and hoped they could come back and finish the house after the *current excitement* was over." Time proved otherwise. Today, on the second floor, in what would have been a bedchamber, buckets, saws, and cut timber sit coated with the dust of the ages. Longwood remains virtually an empty shell—magnificent on the exterior but minus interior floors, walls, and upper windows.

Today, many visitors, as well as guides, claim to see Haller's ghost, shoulders hunched in despair, floating up interior stairs that lead to vacant rooms. Penniless and unable to provide for his wife and children, this once prosperous planter died in the basement, his dream an unfinished nightmare.

The workmen's abandoned tools on the upper floor of Longwood.

Following her husband's death, Julia Augusta Williams Nutt remained at Longwood and raised eight children. The presence of Julia and the children also lingers on.

Gay stands in the rotunda. Over her shoulder hangs a large portrait of Julia. The Mistress of Longwood keeps a watchful eye. She's dressed in a pale-blue frock trimmed with lace at the neck and arms, with thick, dark hair; oval face; aquiline nose; and chin jutted slightly forward.

"I have not *seen* Julia," begins Gay, "but I have read so many of her letters, so much of the history of the house, that to me, she *is* a presence here, because she is a survivor. A lot of days I'll come up the driveway, and I'll have some kind of problem, personal problem, and I'll think to myself, 'You know, Julia could do this; the way she was raised,' and then as soon as I think of her, somehow I know I can deal with whatever is bothering me. She had strength of character that stood her in good stead when she was left with no money, without the love of her life, and eight children to raise, the youngest only three."

Lynn Bradford feels her Aunt Louise and Julia shared a similar mindset, which perhaps explains a paranormal encounter between these two women who are separated by nearly a century. "Louise was a very strong Southern lady, both in body and mind. She was not a person who spent a lot of cerebral time thinking about ghostlike or supernatural things, or just the eeriness of living in an old home. She was not like that. She and my uncle lived here together for the first seventeen years. After he passed away, she stayed on and slept at Longwood by herself for another dozen or so years."

In 1971, Longwood opened its doors to the public as a historic home and architectural marvel. A small den and modern kitchen were carved out for use by the resident manager, but at night, the family slept in the same bedrooms used by Haller, Julia, and their children. Louise Burns chose to sleep in a room with two massive beds, each of which has elaborate canopies that barely clear the basement-level ceiling.

Lynn Bradford describes how her aunt received a middle-of-the-night wake-up call. "My Aunt Louise said she was asleep and was awakened by, what felt like to her, two hands that cupped under her head, tilted it from side to side a couple of times, and then gently laid her head back down on the pillow. No one could have been behind her because

The widow Julia Nutt still wanders through the house.

the big headboard is against the wall there and the pillow was touching the headboard. My aunt said she was positive she was awake and not dreaming when it happened. I remember her saying she looked around the room to ground herself in reality, and said out loud, 'Okay, now there is my purse in the chair. There's my robe hanging on the door,' just things that would convince her she was fully awake."

Lynn Bradford cannot prove whose spectral hands lifted her Aunt Louise's head, but she feels it is likely they belonged to Julia Nutt because both women had so much in common. Both were married when they moved into Longwood, and both became widows during their residence. Both shared the responsibility and burden of serving as caretakers. Kindred spirits in many aspects, these two, Louise McNeely Burns and Julia Augusta Williams Nutt, did not waver from their duties.

Mattie Jo Ratcliffe served as a guide during Louise Burns's tenure. "I would bring a group to Longwood, and Louise and I would stand outside and chitchat, so I had many, many opportunities to talk with Louise and

The bedroom where the ghost of Julia paid a visit to a sleeping Louise Burns.

she convinced me. Louise said it was as if Julia Nutt were inspecting her, wanted a close look at her and that was the end of it."

Gay Guerico speaks to Julia's character. "She actually was a remarkable woman, very strong-willed. One time Haller did not stand up for her. There was some kind of confrontation that she had with one of the servants, and when Haller didn't back her up, she got in the buggy and went to her family home, Ashburn, not too far away."

Nineteenth-century women, explains Gay, did not often pack up and take off on their own. Haller found himself in the socially awkward position of writing a letter to his wife to ask her to come home. Haller was not merely embarrassed by his wife's absence; he truly loved her. "When Haller met Julia, she was eighteen and he was twenty-four. She was in love with someone her family considered unsuitable, so they sent her to Evergreen, their country plantation in northeast Louisiana." Haller was immediately enamored with the beautiful, vivacious daughter of Mr. and Mrs. Austin Williams. Family legend says that he courted her so ardently that he soon won her heart and her hand. "In fact," states the tour guide, "he was just crazy about her." Gay admits that "Julia was a little spoiled in the beginning. When she expressed a desire for him to buy this piece of property [the ninety-acre tract of the present-day Longwood], Haller did so as a surprise to please her. Julia's childhood best friend, Mary, had grown up in a previous home on the property, so she had very fond memoires. Haller absolutely adored her, so anything Julia wanted he tried to get."

The existing Colonial-style home on the property, also called Longwood, was simple and unpretentious, not suited to Haller's grand vision. One of the first things Haller attended to while the "new" Longwood was under construction was planting a garden. Gay tilts her head in the direction of the portrait and then points to the single, long-stem red rose clasped in Julia's right hand. "Haller planted ten acres of rose bushes on the property for her because roses were her favorite flower."

At the staircase leading to what would have been the principal floor of the house, Gay attributes the reputed haunted spot to the lovely Julia. "This is where they say you can smell the scent of Julia's perfume. It has the scent of roses."

Lynn Bradford often visited her aunt and uncle at Longwood. They both had encounters with Julia's spirit. Lynn balances her slight frame on the arm of a brown leather couch in the den area adjoining the staff kitchen. "My uncle used to sit right here and drink his coffee and watch television. I remember on more than one occasion that when he would sit here alone, he'd say later that . . . just a whiff of perfume would go through the room. It happened enough times that he would jokingly comment, 'Oh, Julia just passed through.'"

Mattie Jo Ratcliffe is on the board of directors of the Natchez Pilgrimage Club, which owns and operates Stanton Hall and Longwood. This lively matron with her coif of gray curls is happy to have the ghost of Julia and her wonderful perfume in the house. "Julia's presence is always with the scent of rose. Louise told me she always knew when Julia was around because she would smell roses."

Mattie Jo reveals a compassionate side of this Southern woman whose husband was a Union sympathizer. And it is a tale that leads to yet another lost soul. "At night, in the back of Longwood, Louise told me that she was aware that there was a ghost couple who appeared there. The lady, the female, was saying good-bye to the male in uniform; he was leaving for battle. And I asked Louise, 'Do you know who they were?' And she said, 'No.'" Mattie Jo leans over and shares her thoughts behind the mysterious appearance of the clandestine couple. "Mr. Nutt didn't go to the war. But during the war, Julia received and took care of Yankee soldiers." Mattie Jo has proof. "There is a wicker coat rack made of wisteria vines that was on the brick porch as you go into the house and it was made by a wounded Yankee soldier who Julia befriended and ended up nursing him until he was well enough to leave. So I kind of think maybe it was him leaving to go back to war." Apparently the soldier lost his way, for his transparent figure returns over and over to say his good-byes to his kindhearted hostess.

Gay Guerico's sympathies lay with the mistress of the home. "Imagine poor Julia living here with four unfinished floors over her head, worried about young children running around in the scaffolding, stairways with no rails, and balconies with no doors."

Due to the inherent hazards posed to inquisitive and rambunctious children, Julia Nutt encouraged her children to play outside. In *The*

Legend of Longwood, written in 1972, author Margaret Shields Hendrix describes one specific site dedicated for the children. "Between the big mansion and the servants' building there is a low mound on which five graceful live oak trees are growing. Legend tells us that Julia planted these trees so that the little girls would have a shady playground near the house, and here Mr. Nutt planned to build for his children a lovely gazebo."

In the present day, this same site is forlorn and bare, dominated not by a gazebo, but an immense, rust-colored sugar kettle. The younger spirits don't seem to mind. Lynn Bradford confirms that little ghosts still come out and play. "My aunt and some of the maids that were helping in the house would often hear what they thought were little girls playing out near the servants' quarters, but there was no one out there they could see. And the dogs would start barking as if they could hear something too."

Gay offers insights into the lives of the children who grew up in the basement of Longwood. "These are their bedrooms; they open on to the playroom." Gay waves her arms like a fairy godmother over the

Children's voices are heard playing near the sugar kettle.

Fanny's grave in the family cemetery on the grounds of Longwood.

miniature kingdom, comfortably furnished with cribs, rockers, and toys. Gay identifies eight children through portraits and photos scattered about the rooms. "The four boys were Sargent Prentiss, John Ker, Haller Jr., and Calvin Routh. The four girls were Mary Ella, Carrie, Julia, and Lily."

Three other children did not survive: Fanny died at age two in 1848. Her four-foot cross is the most prominent in the family cemetery. Seven-year-old son Austin was accidently shot. The last child, Rushworth, was born and died in 1863.

In one large portrait, Mary Ella, clad in a deep, wine-colored dress, kneels at the lap of her older sister Carrie Routh. Gay forms her own opinions on which spirits roam the rooms. "Carrie Routh ought to haunt here because she died in childbirth in the house in 1867, and she's buried in the cemetery."

Daughter Julia Augusta appears as a somber spinster in a black-and-white photo displayed on the table. The seasoned tour guide shakes her

Mary Ella Nutt kneels at the feet of her older sister Carrie Routh.

head and laughs as she reveals how modern-day children interpret the sad plight of the unmarried sisters, Mary Ella and Julia. "I ask the school children on tour, 'Why do you think they never married?' And this little boy points to Julia Augusta's face and says, 'Cause she's ugly.' Gay concedes, "She does have the Nutt nose; it doesn't look so good on her."

But it was not a lack of physical beauty that impeded a marriage proposal. Again, Gay sets the story in the context of the times. "I think Julia and Mary Ella wanted to marry, but there was no one. There was a whole generation of women who didn't have an opportunity to marry

The somber spinster Julia Augusta Nutt.

because most of their potential suitors were killed in the war." Gay picks up Julia's geography book from the table and reads from her handwritten notes in the margin: *"I don't know what's wrong with me tonight. I can't seem to concentrate on my studies."*

Of all the girls, baby sister Lily seemed to fare the best. "She was married to James Ward at St. Mary's Basilica. She had nine bridesmaids and," says Gay with pride, "the reception was here at Longwood." Lily and James had five children. During the 1930s, their bachelor son Merritt William Ward was the last of the immediate family to live in the house. The neighborhood children often taunted him, saying that the deteriorating old house was full of "ghosts, goblins, spirits and spooks."

An unsolved mystery linked to Merritt Ward started even more rumors and conjecture. In the bedroom where this lonely bachelor slept, a faded landscape painting hung over the marble mantle. Merritt would often complain that there were eyes in the landscape staring at him. No one paid much attention to the ramblings of an eccentric man. "Merritt was right all along," says Gay. "When the painting was sent out to be cleaned, a painted-over portrait came to light." Merritt's "eyes" belonged to an exotic dark-haired beauty wearing an evening gown with revealing décolleté. "This is our anonymous lady; no one knows who she is," announces Gay. There are no family records documenting the painting's origins. The woman with the enigmatic smile has been dubbed Longwood's "Mona Lisa." "Some people say this was Haller's mistress." But Gay has serious doubts. "Haller and Julia had eleven children in twenty-two years, so he didn't have a lot of time for extracurricular activities."

Tour guides at Longwood have more than enough to keep them occupied. Reciting the particulars of the house—with its great octagonal rotunda open to the entire six stories, a Byzantine-Moorish dome with a twenty-four-foot finial, and original family furnishings, each with their own history—is sometimes a challenge. Gay Guerico says that when fellow guide Sandra Frank "didn't get the statistics right, a light would blink. She felt it was Haller Nutt's way of correcting her, letting her know she made a mistake."

In 1968, the surviving heirs sold Longwood to Mr. and Mrs. Kelly E. McAdams. In 1970, the McAdams donated Longwood to the Natchez

Longwood's mysterious "Mona Lisa" who hid behind a landscape.

Pilgrimage Garden Club with the stipulation that the house remain unfinished, as is. On Valentine's Day 1971, Longwood opened its doors to public tours. As a National Historic Landmark, the home is to be treasured. For the ghost of Haller Nutt, his workload has taken on new dimensions. His former home is filled with a steady stream of visitors. From tour guides to caretakers to housekeeping staff, the number of employees is a supervisory overload, taxing for any human; for a dispirited spector, it is all consuming.

Postscript: Before the final approach to Longwood, along a single-lane county road that threads through the forest like a child's lost hair ribbon,

The Longwood family cemetery in a secluded glen on the grounds.

is a small clearing on the left. The family plot is on a knoll tucked into the woods. For all who desire a more intimate connection with the past, pause here and reflect. The love of Haller for Julie with their side-by-side headstones, the heart-wrenching tragedy of children lost too young, the knowledge that life is brief, and the soul's need for solace are emotions keenly felt within this wooded glade.

7

Linden

A bed and breakfast with a few phantom guests can spice up any overnight stay. Linden, set on a gently rising slope on the outskirts of downtown Natchez, does not disappoint. Built in the 1790s, with a front doorway copied from *Gone with the Wind*'s Tara, and occupied by six generations of the Connor family, this is a home whose history and lineage encompass enough tales to sway even the avowed disbeliever.

Jeanette Feltus welcomes her ghosts as warmly as her human guests. "I am not afraid at all here." Although they pop in and out minus the required reservation, Jeanette boasts that her ghosts are very civilized. "They don't move furniture around and they don't break things." The ghosts of Linden provide exemplary service. "I know this sounds funny," admits Jeanette, "but there have been times when I have heard things like human footsteps on the front porch or back galleries, and I don't ever get up and see. If there is a real person out there trying to do harm to the house or get in, the ghosts appear and the intruders leave. Everybody knows we have ghosts, so they are afraid of them. And I think they protect me."

Jeanette Feltus does augment her ghost patrol with an alarm system. When it was first installed, Jeanette found out it needed an immediate upgrade. "The big horn is on the upper gallery. One of my bed-and-breakfast guests accidentally set it off." With a drawl as thick as the honey set out for morning tea, Jeanette mocks herself. "I was asleep in my bedroom, and honey, I didn't hear a thing. I am so deaf; it takes a lot to wake me up. The police came and the firemen came and all the guests were outside, but they couldn't find me. Finally, one of the guests told

The Linden Bed & Breakfast mansion is haunted by a family of ghosts.

the police, 'I think she might still be in her room.' So they came around to the front gallery where my bedroom is and rattled and banged on my shutters. I always lock my shutters at night." Concerned that the hard-of-hearing owner didn't respond to the screeching alarm, the security company quickly installed an effective remedy. "The next day, they came in and put a horn *inside* my room."

She is also a firm believer in buzzers. Listed on the National Register of Historic Homes, Linden is a large and rambling structure. The two-story center section dates to 1790, and the east wing was added in 1818. In 1849, widow Jane Gustine Conner purchased Linden. Mrs. Conner oversaw the further expansion of the house. The new west wing brought a more harmonious symmetry to the front façade and created an interior courtyard in the rear. When Jeanette moved in with her husband and two daughters, they were the sixth generation of Conners to reside there, but not without a few problems. Due to the configuration of the home, there was a communication issue.

"When we were first here as a family, I didn't do bed and breakfast. So we gave the girls the two upstairs bedrooms in the main house so they could have their stereo and all that noise. My husband, Richard, and I, our room was on the ground floor in the east wing. Because it was such a long way from them to us, we had buzzers put in each room; so if the girls got sick or frightened and needed us, they could buzz us." Jeanette takes a sip of wine and settles in on the high-backed Federal sofa.

"One night, Richard is out, Margie has gone to spend the weekend with a friend, and Celice, our younger daughter, is getting ready for bed. She is in her bathroom brushing her teeth. The bathroom door and the door to her bedroom are open. When both doors are open, you can see into the second-floor hallway that leads to the upper gallery. All of a sudden the buzzer in my room goes off." Jeanette reasserts the house rules. "The girls were not allowed to buzz the buzzer unless it was something really serious." Believing this was the case, this protective mom leapt into action. "I got the gun where Richard told me it was. It was left from the War Between the States, and it had no safety, and so Richard kept the first chamber empty as a safety precaution. I started up the steps, and I thought to click the gun to make sure my bullet would be where I needed it." Jeanette tucks an errant strand of hair back into in her pale bouffant hairdo. "Thank goodness it didn't go off; I never used it before. The door to the top of the stairs stood open. The only way you can open it is from the inside; it's got an eighteenth-century lock, and the girls were taught to lock themselves in at night. So I stood there surprised to see it open, and there is poor Celice. She is about the color of that white cabinet. She says, 'Mother, somebody walked down the hall and the door was open to the gallery.'"

Jeanette scrunches her narrow shoulders inward and describes how she handled the frightening situation. "I peep out the door. I don't see a soul. So I just yell out, 'If you all are on this gallery, you'd better jump or run like hell because I've got a gun, and I don't know a damn thing about it!'" Jeanette confides that she had called the police before going upstairs, and by the time she'd finished giving her version of fair warning, she "had about ten policemen with those big lights. They didn't find anyone, but it had to be somebody because the doors couldn't open by themselves; they are always locked and bolted at night."

In hindsight, Jeanette is now convinced that the *figure* Celice saw was simply one of her ancestors taking a stroll down the hall. "Normally, the girls were used to ghosts in the house, but I guess that night, this one appeared so real that for a second Celice thought it was an actual human intruder."

To emphasize her daughters' usual comfort level with living in a haunted house, this mother expands on their experiences with family ghosts. "When we first moved into Linden, there were no bathrooms upstairs. During the renovations, I could hear something in the attic. It really didn't bother me because if it was a ghost, he could stay up there and I could stay where I was. I could hear him, but I never saw him. Celice and Margie saw him several times." Jeanette offers a reason why her daughters had the ability to see the ghostly figure. "I am not a member of the family." Jeanette married into the family and is not a Conner descendant; she feels family ghosts are more likely to appear to kin.

The present owner's attention drifts across the room to a portrait of the first Mrs. Conner. The woman in the gilded frame has a kind face, large brown eyes under arched brows, finely shaped lips, and a strong chin. Her midnight-black hair is tucked under a gauze veil. In keeping with her widow status, the harshness of her black dress is broken only by a white eyelet collar and a short, white scarf pinned with a small, round cameo. The portrait stirs up memoires of a séance held in the home.

"When Margie was in college, she went to Louisiana Tech and her friends used to come to Natchez for the White Formal, and we'd have champagne parties before the event, and some of them would stay overnight here. One weekend, some of Margie's close friends wanted to have a séance. I called Margaret Marshall who'd led séances before. The girls sat around the dining room table, turned out all the lights, and Margaret did whatever she did. When it was over the girls came and found me and said they saw a lady, a dark-headed lady, and the lady was so excited there was a party in the house." Jeanette connects with the portrait that hangs to the right of the grand piano in the parlor. "I told them it was probably Mrs. Conner, Margie's great-great-great-great-grandmother."

After her grown daughters moved out, Jeanette opened the large home as a bed and breakfast. The girls' former bedrooms offer the largest

Jane Conner, the first woman to own Linden, stares out from her portrait.

accommodations. "I had two double beds in each of the children's rooms if they had company." The two rooms also tend to be the most haunted. "I have many guests, especially in Celice's room," comments the innkeeper, "come back down the next morning and say, 'Mrs. Feltus, there was a strange thing last night; I woke up and there was this man with a top hat looking at us.'" To this, Jeanette gives her standard reply, "That's our ghost who lives in the attic. He is a family member. I don't know which one, but he comes here often."

Jeanette is even less sure of the identity of the ghost who occupies Margie's former bedroom. "I had a couple and their daughter who were staying in Margie's room upstairs. In the middle of the night, both the mother and father were awakened by someone singing in the room. At first, the father thought it might be his daughter, Carolyn, who was musically gifted. He even asked his wife, 'What in the world is Carolyn doing singing in her sleep?' The wife checked on their daughter and said, 'That is not Carolyn singing, I can tell you that.' They came down the next morning and told me about it." Jeanette frowns. "This is the first time I heard about a ghost singing in the room. We don't know who it is."

The most widely circulated ghost tale associated with Linden shines the spotlight on a flying female figure and a conflagration.

"When my husband lived here as a child," Jeanette explains, "there used to be a pool table upstairs." With a wave of her arm, she indicates the room above the parlor in the oldest portion of the house. "I don't know a thing in the world about pool." Her shoulders rise and fall. "I've been told that if one person is shooting, the other players stand around and wait their turn. When Richard was a teenager, he and his friends were playing pool one day. Three or four of them went out on the upstairs back gallery. They looked across the courtyard and saw a form of a lady jump off the two-story west wing and float across the courtyard. Just before she hit the ground, she disappeared. These same boys have talked about it ever since they were in high school. They've debated whether it could have been a cloud or the shadow of a plane, but they all saw her. They all still say it was a woman. She started off on the roof and jumped. It was afternoon. Daytime. They hadn't been drinking or anything."

Because she had been questioned so often about this tale, Jeanette has done a little research. "I don't know if this has anything to do with it, but

Linden's inner courtyard where Richard Conner saw the ghost leap to the ground.

when the Reeds lived here, they had gone to visit friends at Monmouth Plantation nearby. They left the mother or mother-in-law in the end room alone. She got too close to the heat and her gown caught fire and she burned to death. Some people say it is probably her ghost, her spirit, that Richard and his friends saw floating or jumping off the roof."

Jeanette moves on to act two in the family drama of haunted tales; the paranormal activities in these scenes all swirl about her father-in-law, Dick Feltus. "Dick was a wonderful storyteller. Some true. Some not true. A big grin sweeps Jeanette's face as she recounts one early episode in Linden's legendary past. "The original road to Linden came to the front door and circled around where we still have the mounting and dismounting steps for carriages, and then went all the way to the back of the house." This explains the odd, gray, three-tiered formation anchored in the front lawn. "The road is still gravel, and we could always tell who was coming by the way a particular car traveled through the rocks. The same thing was true of buggies. Back then, the family used to sit on the rear gallery. There was a cousin named John who had died a few weeks before. They heard his buggy pulling up, and they didn't think too much about it; just someone bringing his buggy back. They heard the horse and buggy stop and waited for whoever was driving it to walk in. Of course, back then, they left everything wide open. No one locked the doors. Finally, when no one came through to the back gallery, one of the other Conner relatives got up and went out front to see where the driver was. But there wasn't a soul out there. No driver. No horse. No buggy. Dick swears that is the truth."

When Jeanette and Richard were newlyweds, they lived in another house in Natchez. Richard's aunt resided at Linden. When she died, the Conner ancestral home became the property of four heirs. "Dick wanted to come home. So forty years ago, we bought the other three heirs out and that's how we got it."

Dick Feltus, along with his son's family, settled into Linden. Jeanette sums up their living arrangements, "Dick by this time was divorced from Richard's mother. Dick's room was the last one on the east wing, our bedroom was next to his, and the girls' rooms were upstairs. Dick was asleep one night. A Conner cousin had just died. Dick woke up and saw his cousin standing at the foot of his bed. Now, Dick was a personable person. He always wanted to shake your hand or hug you. So when he saw his cousin, he said, 'How are you doing,' and he reached out his hand. And the cousin said, 'Oh, no, you can't touch me. I just came back to see how things were going.' Dick didn't listen. He leaned over more to try and shake his cousin's hand and with that the ghost disappeared."

Jeanette's fondness for her father-in-law shines through every word of every story. She gathers his talents, his eccentricities, and his flaws into a bouquet and presses it to her heart. "Dick liked his toddies. He'd get up every night, fix his milk punch from a little refrigerator in his room, and go out to sit on the gallery. After he had had several strokes, he needed a cane to get around. He'd wander all over the grounds during the day, and I was so afraid he'd fall and we wouldn't know it. Fortunately, after my daughter Margie left for college, her little dog Tara adopted Dick. Tara slept under Dick's bed and every time Dick got up to wander about, Tara followed him. One day Tara came to the side door and kept barking and barking and barking, and he would start back down the road, so I followed him. And sure enough Dick had fallen and couldn't get up." All of this is Jeanette's prelude to her favorite ghost at Linden.

"Dick died in October; he died on my birthday. By the following March, I was in full swing with the bed and breakfast." Jeanette tackled the monumental task solo; her husband Richard had died shortly before Dick. "I moved into the front bedroom and rented out the other two rooms in the west wing, including Dick's old bedroom, as well as the girls' rooms upstairs and the two in the east wing. I was the only one left in the family, so Tara adopted me." Jeanette pours another glass of wine from the cut glass decanter. The curtain opens on act three.

"That particular night, Tara kept barking and barking and barking. I told him to hush because I was afraid the dog would wake up my houseguests. At breakfast the next morning in the dining room, several of my guests asked who was on the gallery last night. Jeanette replays both sides of the conversation around the breakfast table.

"We heard someone walking with a cane, like *step, step, thump; step, step, thump.*"

"Oh, that was Dick."

"Well, where *is* Dick?"

"He's in heaven most of the time. He comes back now and then to see about us."

Jeanette arrives at the grand finale. "I'll tell you a funny story about Dick." She pauses. I nod my head. She nods back satisfied that she has my full attention. "I rented his room out to a couple; it was their second marriage, both of their previous spouses had died. We were in the parlor discussing ghosts; everybody likes to talk about them. I was telling them about the different ones we have here, and the gentleman said, 'You know my wife just tossed and turned all night long.' I said, 'I am so sorry. Was something wrong with the mattress?'" Jeanette interrupts her own tale. "Someone has to tell me something is wrong, so that I can go and get a new mattress; I can't go around and test all of them." I nod in agreement once more, hoping we'll get back to the story. No problem. My hostess returns to the scene and now quotes the wife who's had trouble sleeping. "'No, it wasn't the mattress. I woke up because there were people in the room—two men, a woman, and two children standing at the foot of my bed.'" An amused Jeanette says she had no problem identifying the ghostly visitors. "That was Dick, his brother, his sister Margaret, and her two children. All deceased."

The sleepless guest then swore things got a little more peculiar. "Well, after a minute or so, they all left, but one; he got in bed with us."

"I told her," said Jeanette, "you shouldn't have worried. That was Dick and he's a perfect gentleman."

Jeanette has been giving tours of Linden for several decades. She believes her devotion to the home, with its enclave of family ghosts, will continue through advanced age, senility, and beyond. She has it all worked out. "I don't really care about having to be put in a casket and stuck under the ground. First of all you run out of places to bury people in a cemetery; our family plot at the Natchez cemetery is so full that I want to be cremated." Squaring her shoulders, she insists she wants her ashes placed in an urn and brought to the Natchez cemetery. "Dick's there and Richard's there, so I am going to be sitting right between them." Jeanette Feltus also plans on a busy afterlife. "I know when I die I will probably haunt Linden too. I really believe my spirit will come back here."

Puzzling postscript: During the research for the book, I spent one memorable night at Linden. Mrs. Feltus gave me the key to the South Room, the last room on the second floor of the west wing. The first Mrs. Conner used it as a schoolroom for the children. Although small, it had a lovely canopied bed, an antique dresser, nightstand, original plank flooring, and a fireplace. As with all the other rooms at Linden, the South Room has a private entrance accessible only by an exterior staircase in the courtyard. That weekday evening, I was the only guest. Jeanette retired to her room at the front of the west wing; we were as far apart as two bedrooms could be in the house. The night was chilly but not cold enough to turn on the heat. I climbed into the high bed, turned out the light on the nightstand, and pulled up the quilted coverlet.

Creak. The distinct sound of a floorboard as someone steps on it. I dismissed it as just the weathered wood rising back up after I clamored into bed.

Creak. Creak. I sat up and looked around. The moonlight pouring through the mullioned window was sufficient to see there was no one in the room but me. The creaking sound continued at irregular intervals as if someone was tiptoeing across the room. Eventually, I fell asleep. At 2:00 a.m., there was no creaking. Just a voice. A quiet little voice. A child's voice. *"Hello!"*

Upright, I surveyed the room. *"Hello to you too."* I waited. No response. No ghostly presence, child-size or otherwise.

In the morning, Jeanette joined me in the formal dining room for a Southern-style breakfast complete with homemade butter biscuits. I sheepishly shared my story. The gracious hostess of Linden poured another cup of tea and smiled a satisfied smile.

Chalk up one more spirit to the ghostly entourage at Linden.

Fluted ionic columns grace the front entrance to haunted Magnolia Hall.

8

Magnolia Hall

The ghost of Magnolia Hall has a loyal and diverse fan base. Sightings and paranormal activities have flourished for nearly half a century. Thomas Henderson, the original owner of Magnolia Hall, died at home on March 6, 1863. He appeared to rest in peace until the late 1970s when something got him all stirred up.

"It started with the bed, Mr. Henderson's bed. It was after the house was refinished and opened up again." Elizabeth Boggess speaks in a clear and concise manner befitting a cultural historian and classical archaeologist for the Lower Mississippi Valley. Boggess sits on the board of the Natchez Garden Club, which acquired the house in 1976. The members orchestrated a full restoration and an in-depth study into the history of the home.

In the aftermath of the Civil War, Thomas Henderson's family could no longer afford Magnolia Hall. For a short while, it operated as a boarding house, and then in the twentieth century, it served as Trinity Episcopal Day School. Henderson family descendants generously donated original furnishings, including the four-poster bed where Thomas closed his eyes for the final time. With his bed back in the house, Thomas, the grateful ghost, lays his head down repeatedly. Indentations in the bed coverings and impressions in the pillow the size of a man's head are a regular occurrence.

Former tenant and night caretaker Kay McNeil remembers opening the house for tours one morning and assisting senior hostess Judy Grimsley by turning on the lights room by room. "We got to the back bedroom where Thomas Henderson had died and there was an indentation on the pillow. I saw it," Kay declares. "We both saw it."

Judy is equally as emphatic. "We knew something wasn't right. Miss Myra Jones, our housekeeper, never would have left a pillow that was not as *smooooth* [she elongates the word for emphasis] as it could be." Judy says, at the time, she couldn't help blurting out to Kay and Myra, "I wonder if he has come back?"

Myra Jones resolutely refused to acknowledge the possibility of a ghost at Magnolia Hall. "I've known Myra since I was fifteen," says Judy. "After we fluffed the pillow back up, she said to me, 'Miss Judy, you know there ain't no haints up here.' Haint is how Myra refers to ghosts. I said to her, 'Oh, you think not, huh?' And she said, 'If there were any haints around, I wouldn't be here.'"

Hostess Patricia Taylor volunteers to take visitors on a tour of the home, which is on the National Register of Historic Places. Her experience kicks the pillow phenomenon up a few haunted notches.

Pat is British and her English accent adds a continental flare to the tale. "I had about ten people, mixed male and female, and we went through to Mr. Henderson's bedroom." Pat stands to the left of the canopied bed as she reenacts what happened. "I was in this room explaining about his death, standing here as I usually do and people were arranged in front of me."

There are two pillows on the bed. Pat reaches over and places her hand on the pillow closest to her. There is a slight tremor in her voice. "Now this pillow, I tried every conceivable logic and explanation for what is going on. I'm standing here, and we have a group of people in front of me, and a lady on the tour says to me, 'Am I just seeing what I think I am seeing?' And I turned around and this pillow, it was like someone had placed their head on it, and it was just sinking in like that."

Pat takes her hand and gently pushes down on the pillow to mimic the action she and her visitors witnessed. She raises her hand and taps at her lips. "For the first time in my life, I didn't know what to say. You could see the center of the pillow actually move in while we were watching it, and there were eleven people in this room. . . . We all saw it. And one man's jaw dropped, and he blurted out, 'God, I've never seen anything like that before in my life!' And it just stayed there."

To prove how incomprehensible the phenomenon, Pat again pushes down on the pillow with her hand, leaving a temporary impression.

Hostess Pat Taylor with the "sinking pillow" in Thomas's bedroom.

Slowly, the fluffy pillow puffs back up. "Even if you pushed your hand in hard, it comes back eventually, but what we saw was the pillow going down and staying down."

Pat picks up the offending pillow off the bed and turns it over, examining it as she did that daunting day. "I thought, *'This is a joke.'* I've got the pillow, and I'm thinking, *'Okay, so where is the trick?'* The hostess stutters, "I haven't, I can't come up with a logical explanation for it. And the room was chilly, but I can't say it was particularly cold, not like you are supposed to expect when you see ghosts or anything like that."

Pat said she and her visitors were frozen in their places, mesmerized by the movement on the pillow. "One man finally told me to 'get out of there,' and I said, 'I can't.' After a few minutes, everyone on the tour started to nervously joke about it. 'Do we have to pay extra for the ghost?' And I said, 'I have no idea what that is, maybe it *was* Mr. Henderson.'"

Pat volunteers her time at several historic properties in Natchez during the annual Spring Pilgrimage. The day after the incident, she was assigned to Rosalie, another home on the tour, and to her surprise three men showed up who had been with her at Magnolia Hall and witnessed the "sinking" pillow.

"I'm receiving at Rosalie and they look at me and they say, 'Did he come back?' Of course that got the conversation going, and one man announced, 'I never believed in ghosts, but I do now.' He said, 'I saw that as plain as day.'"

This bewildered docent is certain that while she can't offer a satisfactory rationale, there is no way that so many people could be wrong about what they saw. She pauses and considers the alternatives. "I want to dismiss it as just someone had been playing with the pillow before we got there, but the pillow was actually moving down while we were watching it."

Pat swears that until that incident, she had no knowledge that there were "issues" with the pillow. "It's only recently that I've learned that this is not the first time that this has happened, but I knew nothing about it at the time." Nor did Pat realize that there would be more poltergeist activity upstairs that would test her patience.

Passing through the doorway of the second-floor master bedroom, Pat approaches a bed cordoned off with red-velvet ropes strung between brass stanchions. "This was Thomas's bedroom prior to his stroke. This bed has a little bit of history with me. At the time, I was responsible for the whole of upstairs. I had just come upstairs and had a walk around to make sure everything was okay before the guests starting coming in, and the bed coverlets were all *ruched* up." Pat sits on the bed and messes the covers to demonstrate just how slept-in the bed appeared. "I have to get on it to make it happen; you can't do it by just running your hand over it." She gets up and points to the deep wrinkles made by the weight of her body. "You see, it was just like that. This was first thing in the morning. So I straightened it, went downstairs, and started the first tour, but every time I came in this room, the barrier would be in place [the red ropes to keep visitors off the furniture], but the covers would be disturbed again. I kept tidying up, but it did no good."

Late in the evening, Pat sought out Rose, the housekeeper. "I said, 'That darn mattress, I don't know what is going on; it keeps *ruching*.' Rose said, 'Show me, quick.' So we came upstairs, and it *ruched* again. Rose told me that that it does happen quite a lot and that the staff thinks

Mr. Henderson comes in and sits on the bed because he forgets this isn't his room anymore." Pat mocks herself. "And I thought, 'Yeah. Sure.'" The English woman apologizes for her early skepticism. "This is before I saw the pillow sink. So now it seems every time I walk though the room, the cover needs straightening, and presto, I'm doing it all over again. It happens whenever I come anywhere near it. I joke that we should just leave it messy and see if the ghost or ghosts would pick up after themselves." Pat's smile is broad. "They obviously don't." In a soft aside, she adds, "Actually I do have an affinity for the supernatural, but this is just peculiar."

Elizabeth Boggess separates the types of ghostly activity at Magnolia Hall by floor. "We know when there is an ambulatory manifestation; it is upstairs. It's as if he is walking around looking for something."

Natchez Garden Club president Cheryl Morace concurs. "I've heard the walking. I've been here late at night and closed up the house and heard walking upstairs. I felt weird going up there to check when I knew no one was there."

At the turn of the millennium, a Jackson, Mississippi, radio station held a Halloween contest. The prize? An overnight stay in Natchez's most haunted home. A group of lucky winners curled up in sleeping bags in Magnolia Hall's front hall to find out for themselves if ghosts were out and about. The sounds they heard kept them up all night. "It was six young people in their twenties and thirties—not teenagers," reports Judy Grimsely, who was still working at Magnolia Hall. She found the amateur ghost hunters' morning-after account highly credible. "They heard that distinctive ping that silverware makes when it's tapped on fine crystal."

It would be extremely challenging, according to Judy, to mimic the sound of a toast by either a disembodied spirit or human hands. Although Magnolia's banquet-sized dining room table displays full place settings of china, wine goblets, and silverware, a closer inspection reveals that each of the knives, forks, spoons, and serving pieces are tethered to the table by monofilament fishing line, a precaution to prevent theft. On the morning after the sounds were reported, there was no evidence of tampering with the antitheft fishing line or signs that the crystal glassware had been shifted out of its properly aligned position on the table.

There is also a hint of admiration in Judy's voice when she speaks about the second disquieting sound heard by the visitors—the tinkling of piano keys. "During the night, the square grand played in the front parlor. It has never played. It is terribly out of tune, but somehow that night it made magical music, and they all heard it."

Despite cameras rolling, the group was disappointed they didn't capture an image of a ghost on tape. "But," declares a magnanimous Judy, "all six heard the same sounds, so we have to believe them."

At Magnolia Hall, the ghostly antics extend beyond pillow ploys, footsteps, and musical interludes. Paranormal manifestations include a chair that walks, lights that flicker and send Morse code from the beyond, a scorching hot Bible, and a mysterious message.

Elizabeth Boggess has a wry sense of humor when it comes to all things supernatural. "I know that whatever goes on in the downstairs bedroom, there are certain things that you find in a different place. If you move stuff, the next morning you may find it somewhere else, but that may be because the housekeeper came in and put it back."

Lou Ann Jordan, another member of the Garden Club, is passing by the kitchen on her way to setup for a special event. She overhears the conversation in progress and pokes her head in. "That is so funny you said that because twenty years ago when I was Candlelight Dinner chairwoman, I turned the light off in the bedroom and it came back on. I knew that room was supposedly where the ghost was, and when I came back through the bedroom, I started talking to myself, saying, 'The light is on, and I know I turned that light off.'"

Lou Ann is momentarily distracted by a droning sound coming from the left side of the kitchen. "What is that?" She is drawn to the automatic coffee machine on the counter. "Is it the coffee pot?" She leans over the coffeemaker and checks the switch, which is in the *off* position. She announces to Dr. Boggess. "It is not on." However, the low-decibel noise continues like bees buzzing about a hive.

Elizabeth, curious, also begins to scan the room. "Is it the microwave?"

Lou Ann checks the microwave, shakes her head from side to side, and makes her way back to the unplugged coffee pot. Her dark eyebrows pop up as she places her hand on the lid. "It's the coffee pot. The sound is coming from here."

Elizabeth offers a tongue-in-cheek *raison d'être:* "Guess the ghost wants a cup of coffee." She gives the room a thorough appraisal. "Thomas, go back. We're fine here." She looks over at Lou Ann. "Oooooh, I just felt a cold breeze."

Lou Ann's eyes widen, and she backs into the kitchen counter.

Elizabeth, who is having a bit of fun, announces in a deadpan voice, "The new ceiling fan works."

Lou Ann, realizing she has been had, refuses to be dissuaded that there is a ghostly presence in the house. She confesses that the bedroom makes her nervous, and rather than go in alone when she needed to retrieve some tablecloths, she brought her adult daughter, who does not buy into the whole haunted house theme. "So I said, 'Come here. I want to show you something.' . . . I wasn't going to dare tell her that I was afraid. . . . I just wanted her to walk with me because I was scared. I've heard all kinds of things about that bedroom. And that time when the light went back on . . . I swear to you that I turned it off."

Elizabeth throws in an odd twist to the spectral equation. "There is a chair. It has to be to the left of the bed as you are facing the headboard. If you put it on the other side, it comes back."

Lou Ann is intrigued. "I never heard . . . I never knew that. I've got to go see." She leaves the kitchen on a quest to see the chair with a mind of its own.

Elizabeth calls after her: "I think it's the only chair beside the bed. Come back and tell us which side it is on."

A confused Lou Ann returns from her inspection and announces, "Well, I'm no help. There was a chair on both sides of the bed." The revelation elicits laughter from those assembled in the kitchen.

Elizabeth advances a theory as to why there are so many ghost stories swirling about Magnolia Hall after the death of its owner. "There is enough independent reporting of phenomena here that is consistent with an untimely death that something is going on. Whether Thomas Henderson fell—it might have been that he fell and hit his head rather than having an epileptic stroke or apoplexy—he did live for awhile after he was brought home."

Katherine Blankenstein, a silver-haired woman dressed in a pale-blue ensemble, joins in the discussion. Kathie is related to the Hendersons by marriage and has done extensive research on the family's genealogy. "And the diary is there and it's explicit," states Kathie.

The diary under discussion is that of Julia Henderson, Thomas's eldest daughter, who began a journal on January 27, 1863. Julia's account tracks the events and visitors who came to see her father during the three months leading up to his death.

Elizabeth Boggess notes, "That's a legitimate diary because that was written at that time as opposed to some of the Civil War accounts, which weren't written down until thirty or forty years after when memories are cloudy."

In her journal, Julia writes that her father is paralyzed on his left side; he can only turn his head to the right. To comfort her stricken parent whose paralysis has rendered him speechless, she reads to him daily.

From her years working at Magnolia Hall, Kay McNeil is familiar with Thomas Henderson's daughter and her habits. "Julia would sit and read to him from the Bible. I'm sure. Dr. Stanton, the minister for fifty-plus years of the Presbyterian church, would come and sit there as well."

Today, the cane-backed chair with its gold upholstered seat and arms is protected by a ribbon of rope to discourage curious visitors from sitting down. *Someone* else seems to look out for the chair as well.

If during regular, evening-hour house-cleaning duties, such as dusting, sweeping, and vacuuming, the housekeeping staff inadvertently moves Julia's chair to the opposite side of the room, the stubborn chair is found in the morning back on the left side of the bed. The repositioning is most often attributed to Thomas, but there are those who also believe it is the determined spirit of the dutiful and pious Julia settling in to read another passage of the Bible to her dying father.

Judy Grimsley may be retired, but she cannot forget the family Bible used by Julia. "It was the prayer book of John Henderson, Thomas's father and Julia's grandfather. It wasn't any bigger than the palm of your hand. Tiny little print. Leather bound with the name Henderson embossed on the red cover."

In the twentieth century, this small religious artifact became "too hot to handle." Kay, who now serves as the historian at Jefferson College in Natchez, relates the events leading up to the book's scorching effect. "It was quiet, the last day of the Natchez Fall Pilgrimage, October 20, 1986.

Thomas's daughter, Julia, who still sits and reads to her dying father.

Julia's chair that moves at will.

I had on my hoop skirt, and I was standing on the staircase of Magnolia Hall. A couple from Illinois arrived. They introduced themselves as the Goodmans. They said they had been driving around trying to decide which home to visit when, according to the wife, Magnolia Hall called out to them. I let them tour the two front parlors, and then they moved on to the back bedroom. Billie Ann, the hostess back there, started yelling, 'Kay, come here. Quick. Quick. Quick!' I ran back and stepped in the doorway, and the light beside the bed where Mr. Henderson died was blinking on and off."

Judy backs up Kay, recounting, "When the Goodmans stepped across the threshold, the lamp went on and off three times."

Both Kay and Judy agree on what transpired next. The wife, Marcy Goodman, said in a very calm voice, "Something happened in this room; something dreadful happened here," and the light commenced to blink on and off, faster and faster. Judy further confides that later, after the couple left, the lamp and the electrical outlet were examined for shorts in the wiring. "There was nothing wrong with the lamp."

Much to the astonishment of the hostesses gathered in the room, Marcy Goodman claimed to have psychic abilities. She asked to hold something personal that belonged to the Henderson family. Kay complied.

"I ran and got the little tiny Bible that belonged to Thomas's father, John, from Glasgow, Scotland. I handed it to Marcy. The Bible fell open to a passage from Exodus where Moses is told by God to give a message to the people. Marcy read the passage. And then she closed the Bible and said, 'He is trying to convey a message. You've got to listen to him.' She meant Mr. Henderson."

Kay speaks rapidly, one word tumbling over another as if she needs to release the hold that this peculiar tale has on her. "Marcy Goodman handed that little red Bible back to me. It was so hot, I couldn't handle it. It was like it was on fire, and I kept going, 'Hot. Hot. Hot.' It was all I could say. I couldn't get out, 'The Bible, it's hot.' I dropped it on the table. Marcy looked me in the eye and said, 'Don't be afraid. Mr. Henderson is trying to tell you something.' And I still kept going, 'Hot, Hot, Hot.' It was all I could say. It was just unbelievable, and everybody kept looking at me. Finally, I was able to say, 'The book. Hot.'" Kay shakes her head, and her voice drops to a mere whisper. "It was so weird that I could not form the words. I thought, 'This is not happening, but its real and I'm here. I'm here.'"

Judy Grimsley swears she could not pick the book up either. "That did happen." Judy rules out extreme heat from the sun warming up the leather cover. "It was a dreary day, and the shutters were closed so no outside light came in, no sun rays at all."

According to Kay, psychic Marcy Goodman firmly said, "This is really important if you are interested. He is trying to say something, a message. It begins with the letter *M*."

Kay continues, "We start guessing: *Money? Money . . .?*"

Judy describes their excitement, "We danced in the room. We shrieked, 'Dig up the floors. Find the money.'"

The group soon came back down to Earth when the psychic shook her head unable to confirm their hopes. Instead of providing a map for hidden treasure, Marcy Goodman pulled out her business card and began to write her phone number on the back, but as she went to hand over the card, she stopped. "This is not my handwriting. This is a man's handwriting. This is not mine." She took out another card and wrote her phone number again. Holding up the card, she announced, "*This* is my handwriting."

The psychic left with one parting warning: "He's not going to rest until he tells you something."

After much discussion, Kay and Judy believe there are other options for the *M* word. "He was very ill," Judy explains, "and it could have been 'medicine.' We have had people on the tour, and unknown to us there would be a doctor or a nurse in the group, and they would say they could smell a medicinal odor in that room and on the second floor where the master bedroom used to be. We thought maybe they smelled Pine-Sol cleaning fluid, and they would disagree and insist it's more of a painkiller medicinal smell."

Thomas Henderson's doctor had been prescribing laudanum, a derivative of opium, a common nineteenth-century treatment for pain. Judy also thinks that instead of the psychic hearing the beginning letter of the word, the *M* sound might have been for the end of the word. Perhaps Thomas was asking for more laudanum.

Kay states that Julia wrote in her diary about her father's struggle to speak. "It was like on the tip of his tongue . . . it must have been so frustrating." Fortunately for Thomas, his final moments were peaceful. Devoted daughter, Julia Henderson, closes the chapter on his life with this deathbed description: *"He stretched out his hand to those who stood at his bedside, suffering no one retain it very long. It was evident to all who saw it that he meant goodbye . . . Oh, the beauty of his countenance the moment after he was gone. Surely a glimpse of heaven must have been vouchsafed to his departing spirit, to leave that indescribable sweetness on the clay tenement. March 6, 1863."*

Kay O'Neil feels Thomas's tranquil countenance might be the result of a little medicinal intervention. "Apparently he had had laudanum to calm him down after he had had a frightening episode. That's powerful stuff. With a stroke, it would be so scary. . . . He probably had things he wanted to say, but he knew he couldn't." Kay theorizes that at the end Thomas became resigned to his paralysis and inability to speak.

Thomas Henderson was unable to communicate his message in the days prior to his death, but he might not be as hampered in the afterlife. His presence is felt by many, yet Kay says sadly, "We still don't know what he wanted to say."

Others in Natchez have no such doubts. The *M* word Thomas Henderson struggled to speak was *murder*. A murder mystery at Magnolia Hall.

Eric Williams of Natchez Ghost Tours explores the city at night. On the weekend before Halloween, Williams pulls his bus loaded with tourists up to the front steps of Magnolia Hall. On this night, the moon casts diabolical shadows; the evening breeze lifts the branches of the trees; and one bare limb rises and falls, pointing fingerlike at the bedroom window. Williams regales his patrons with a lurid tale: Thomas Henderson was poisoned by his two greedy sons who were tired of waiting for their father to die. After Thomas's death, his doctor became so suspicious that he tested his patient's bedside drinking glass and found traces of arsenic. Thomas's angry ghost prowls the halls at night.

Elizabeth Boggess cautions, "You have to be very careful. A lot of our ghost tours are made up out of *hole* cloth. Nobody in Natchez heard those stories before."

Henderson genealogist Kathie Blankenstein rolls her eyes. "Those kind of stories are tourist bait." She feels that present-day Henderson descendants would be "appalled" to hear that Thomas' sons poisoned him. If further proof were necessary, Kathie adds, "Thomas' sons were away at war."

Military records confirm that John Waldo Henderson joined the Confederate forces in August of 1862. These same records list a "leave of absence—father ill" granted to John on February 15, 1863. He arrived in Natchez on February 22, 1863. His father died on March 6. After the funeral, John left Magnolia Hall on March 15 to rejoin his unit. According to Julia Henderson's diary, both her brothers, John Waldo and elder son Thomas Alexander, *were* at their dying father's bedside, but there is no proof they hastened his death.

Kathie is dismissive of spurious allegations of patricide. "No one would have ever dreamt of doing such a thing. The entire Henderson family was pillars of the community, staunch Presbyterians."

Elizabeth Boggess is in full agreement. "There is absolutely no indication that Thomas Henderson was poisoned." While her next statement may seem contradictory, this historical expert finds it necessary to clarify her position that traces of poisonous substances were likely already in Thomas Henderson's system. "Given what some of the medications [were] that were in common use, yes, some of them had mercury, the blue pill. Everyone was given chamomile for this and that; that's mercury. Laudanum is opium, the green medicine. It was in the cough syrup. It was in the digestive meds. It was known that it was poisonous. It was known that it was addictive, but they thought that if they cut it with enough other stuff, it wouldn't be. Thomas's doctor would have prescribed it for pain."

Elizabeth is adamant. "Since we have very good contemporary death bed accounts, we know exactly what happened when he died. We know what sermon was preached at his funeral. For me the truth is always much more interesting than the fiction. Here is a man who died in the full sanctity of his religion, deeply convicted Christian . . . really in the best possible spiritual shape, so the question is 'Okay, why is he back here? What unfinished business might he have?'"

Kathie retorts, "His religion would not hold for his coming back. Presbyterians believed that the souls of believers at their deaths, their souls go to greater glory and their bodies remain in their graves till the Resurrection."

"So," Elizabeth reasons, "the in-between stage does not pertain. It contradicts his religious beliefs. If his spirit, his ghost is here, he's back because he has something to do. It's got to be that he's here because he has some good to do, not because he's failed to do something."

Judy Grimsley is one of the rare few who has seen the ghost of Thomas. "It was a cold, dreary, miserable October morning during Fall Pilgrimage. I walked from room to room turning on the lights and getting ready to open the house, and I had a funny feeling. I was at the front door and the hairs on the back of my neck felt like I needed to scratch, like somebody was looking at me. So I turned and I looked up the staircase, and midway of the stair was a form. I did sort of a double take and looked back and the form had disappeared, so I told Kay what had occurred. I definitely saw a form of a man in a black suit, white shirt with a long, sort of hanging black tie that men wore back in the 1850s. We concluded that it was Thomas Henderson, and he was just checking to make sure that everything was going well. We had no feeling of fear, just that things were comfortable in the house. There are some strange things that happen at Magnolia Hall. They did happen. I guarantee they happened, and most people that know Kay and me believe us."

Kathie sits at the kitchen table listening with little enthusiasm for the unfolding ghost stories. When pressed if there might be some truth to the tales, she responds with as much diplomacy as she can muster. "I am not much of a believer in that sort of thing. Those who claim to have seen it or heard it I don't dispute."

Judy speaks up for Kathie's views. "Now, Kathie Blankenstein is my childhood friend and grew up with all the stories of the Hendersons, and they were staunch Presbyterians and not one of them will accept it because it is family. I told her, 'Well, Kathie, none of us believe that our loved ones are walking around clanking chains scaring everybody, but there *are* paranormal experiences that no one can explain.'"

To illustrate her point, Judy describes a more recent manifestation. "We had a young volunteer one Spring Pilgrimage, and she was in the hallway in front of the massive mirror. In her group were a young girl and her husband. And all of a sudden, the young girl turned as white

Thomas Henderson.

as snow. And the docent asked, 'Are you all right?' The young girl said, 'No. I just saw a gentleman sitting in that large chair next to the gold mirror.' She described a man who was dressed like our Mr. Henderson, with the black coat on, the white shirt, strange string type of a tie. So then the docent said, 'Well, is he still there?' The shaken woman said just one word, 'No.' In the blink of an eye, he was gone. So other people do see and hear things." Judy smiles. "I think Mr. Henderson is just very pleased that things are going so well. He is still enjoying his house. Absolutely and totally, but you won't get Kathie to agree to that."

Kay McNeill has no such reservations. She not only worked at Magnolia Hall, but the part-time hostess was also a resident tenant and night caretaker. Kay's apartment was on the second floor of the L-shaped wing in the rear of Magnolia Hall. Sitting at a long wooden table in the former Jefferson College, Kay glances out the window. Her memories of her days and nights at Magnolia Hall are vivid.

"It was almost midnight. I was getting ready to go to bed. I had gone to the bathroom and I smelled that sweet medicinal smell. Directly behind me was a locked door. My apartment and the main house have a shared wall, but there is no access. I heard a picture sliding down the wall in the connecting room and hitting the floor. My cats were right there too and their eyes got as big as buttons. I decided to wait until the house opened the next day to check and see what had fallen. So when Jean McConnell, the head hostess, came in the morning, I told her what happened. We walked up that main staircase to look in the room where I heard that sound." Kay pauses, still disturbed at what they didn't find. "There were no pictures on the floor. There were no pictures hanging on the wall anywhere. I don't know what happened, but I heard the sound of a picture or a painting falling and so did my cats."

The following night, Kay had a surprise visitor. "On that Monday, I was in the same position coming from my bathroom, and it was about eleven thirtyish, almost midnight. I had my back to the main house with the locked door right there, and I smelled the laudanum smell again. I remember it very vividly. All of a sudden I was like this." Kay stands and freezes in position. "I couldn't move. The hair on my neck and my arms stood up, and I thought, *'What's happening?'* I moved my eyes around, and my three cats come running into the room, and they stood right in front of me, one, two, three: Neffy, Hatshepsut, and Gwin. They were looking over my shoulder and their tails puffed up and that strip of fur running down their backs stood up in a line." Kay delivers her tale in a rapid-fire staccato. "I kept thinking to myself, *'I know he's here. I want to see him. I want to see him,'* but I couldn't move my feet. Then I felt a light tap on my right shoulder. So I kinda tried to move my eyes and the minute I did, he was gone, and the cats took off in the other room."

Kay believes her slight movement broke the spell. She remains implacable that the supernatural event occurred, and she has witnesses. "My cats saw something. I wish they could have talked and told me. It was there. I felt so full of electricity. I still feel the hair on this arm standing up, just this one arm, standing up. Mr. Henderson's stroke paralyzed his left side. He could only move his head to the right and move his right hand. And I thought about that when I felt the finger, one finger, tap me on the right shoulder; I knew that was him."

Of all the reputed paranormal occurrences at Magnolia Hall, none is more bizarre than the case of the roving rocks. Judy Grimsley speaks of their mysterious appearance and discovery by the grounds keeper for Magnolia Hall. "Cleveland is always earlier than the rest of us, making sure the heat is correct and things like that. He came in one morning, and there were three rocks lying on the rug in the downstairs bedroom. As soon as the rest of the staff arrived, he told us about the rocks. I said, 'What did you do with them?' He said, 'I threw them in the trash.'" Judy said that sounded like a reasonable solution to her, except the problem escalated. "The next morning, there were three different rocks on the floor, not little pebbles; these were good-size rocks. We said, 'Gosh, did someone play a trick on us trying to put more rocks here?' Cleveland said, 'I don't know.' Cleveland threw them away, just like the others. On the third morning, the same thing. And so we all gathered, and we threw those rocks away. And someone told me later that if you find rocks on the floor in the bedroom, not to be frightened; it means the paranormal wants you and anyone else to sleep like a rock." Judy has a good laugh at that notion.

After three mornings of the unusual poltergeist-like rock display, the paranormal activity appeared to take a breather. "We, the hostesses who were there then, never saw them again," says Judy. "Cleveland has never said that he has seen any haints or anything unusual, except the time about the rocks."

While the appearance of the rocks on the bedroom floor did cause quite a stir, Judy remains convinced that life at Magnolia Hall is wonderful. "There isn't anything frightening about it. We've always felt [that] the paranormal presence of Thomas Henderson is a friendly one, and he's just happy that the Natchez Garden Club is maintaining his home so well."

A housekeeping footnote: In its present reincarnation as a historic home, stately Magnolia Hall appears far too grand to be a haunted house. When sixty-year-old widower Thomas Henderson moved into the lavish home, with its library, double parlors, and banquet hall, he was all too-familiar with death. Of his five children, only three survived to adulthood. First-born son William lived a mere six months, and baby daughter Selah never made it to her second birthday. Bathsheba Putnam Henderson, his wife of twenty-four years, died on June 11, 1844, never to enjoy the splendor of Magnolia Hall.

From the time the first brick was laid in 1858, odd aspects have surrounded its construction. For Thomas Henderson, it was all about location. This immensely wealthy planter, merchant, and cotton broker did it the hard way. To get the site he wanted, he had to move an existing home on the grounds and level the hill it stood on. Rather than demolish Pleasant Hill, Thomas had the house raised on log rollers and pulled by teams of oxen one city block away. The arduously slow process took more than a year to complete, but the transition was smooth. Smooth enough for the family to live in the house as it rolled along and for Thomas's niece, Mrs. A. J. Postlethwaite, to deliver a baby as the home inched forward through the intersection of Pearl and Orleans streets. Back at the now vacant lot at 215 South Pearl Street, Thomas oversaw what has been deemed the "finest Greek Revival style townhouse in Natchez."

If this was a game of one-upmanship to outrival the significant accomplishments of his prosperous father, then Thomas, the second son and fifth child of John Henderson, won the largest house contest. With a front portico supported by massive Ionic columns, wrought-iron banisters, and brown stucco over brick exterior, Magnolia Hall made Pleasant Hill seem like a country cottage. Thomas Henderson invested so much of his passion, energy, and wealth into the building of Magnolia Hall that even in death he retains a proprietary sensitivity to this jewel of Natchez architecture.

9

Glenburnie: A Tangled Tale of Murder, Goats, and Ghosts

The attacker keeps coming. He takes aim with a .32-caliber pistol. The blood from the hole in her head drips down in thick red rivulets, streaking her nightgown. It splatters on to her slippers. Jennie stumbles into the dining room. Another shot flies past her and makes a sharp crack as it splinters a window frame. She slips on her own blood. In a painful half-crawl, half-walk, she reaches the side porch and escapes into night. But the bullet wounds are fatal. Sixty-eight-year-old Jennie Merrill dies barefoot in a thicket of woods one hundred yards from her home.

Today, Glenburnie is the lovely home of Carolyn and Gary Guido. No trace remains of the brutal 1932 murder that rocked old-line Natchez—unless a ghost or two wafting in and out could be linked to the crime scene. For the Guido family, and for the others who have lived at Glenburnie over the years, the speculation, the scandal, the mystery remains unresolved. The murder of Jennie Merrill careens around two aging lovers, feuds and lawsuits, goats and gardens, debutantes and dandies, elegance and decay, and accusations and cover-ups.

Carolyn Guido's mother-in-law, Margaret Guido, is visiting for the afternoon. "My husband and I lived here for thirty years. I was fully aware when I purchased the house of what happened here. I had no problems with it, but my housekeeper did. When I told her we were going to move to Glenburnie, she said, 'To that ghost house?'" Margaret laughs. "And I said, 'I don't know if it's a ghost house or not; it's a beautiful house.'"

Beautiful now, but prior to Jennie's murder, Glenburnie and its closest neighbor, Glenwood, were both in shambles. The oddest of odd couples, Jennie Merrill and Duncan Minor, and Olivia Dockery and Dick Dana,

Glenburnie, the site of Jennie Merrill's murder.

were feuding and fighting like the Hatfields and McCoys. And some swear that they are still at it.

If one of the ghosts haunting Glenburnie is the murdered Jennie Merrill, then this is a conflicted spirit indeed. Born in 1864 to Ayres Phillips Merrill Jr. and the well-connected and wealthy Jane Surget Merrill, Jennie grew up at Elms Court, another fabulous Natchez mansion. At the onset of the Civil War, Jennie's father sided with the Union to the outrage of the Natchez citizenship and, conversely, to the pleasure of his distant cousin Gen. Ulysses S. Grant. Grant provided the Merrill family with safe passage to New York City. Jennie lived a lavish lifestyle in Manhattan and at a summer estate in Newport, Rhode Island.

In 1869, President Grant appointed Jennie's father ambassador to Belgium. Jennie's mother had died, but along with her sisters and brother, she sailed with their father for Belgium. Teenage Jennie traveled through Europe and was presented to Queen Victoria at the Court of St. James. Petite, intelligent, and, by all accounts, quite ravishing, Jennie was

Jennie Merrill as a young debutante.

considered an American princess. After her father became ill and resigned his ambassadorship, the family split. Jennie's siblings returned to the East Coast while she and her father headed south to Elms Court.

In 1883, Ayers died, and Jennie began a downward spiral. She sold Elms Court in 1890, and then moved restlessly from mansion to mansion: Glenwood, Gloucester, and finally Glenburnie in 1904. The once social and flirtatious young woman became a recluse. She clung to late-Victorian clothing, shunned electricity, posted "No Admittance" signs, and allowed only one visitor into her home.

Second-cousin Duncan Minor became her sole confidant and companion. Duncan, with a dashing similarity to movie star Clark Gable, was the great-grandson of Don Estevan Minor, governor general of Natchez; son of John Minor and Katherine Surget Minor; and grandson of James Surget, brother of Jennie's grandfather. Considered eccentric even by Natchez standards, Duncan was one of the richest and stingiest men in Mississippi. In the book *The Goat Castle Murder*, Duncan's penny-pinching is underscored. He used a ladder to reach the second floor of his home rather than repair the rotting steps. He decided that nails for the leaking roof were too expensive, and the cook held an umbrella over her head in the kitchen when it rained. Yet, every evening, rain or shine, he rode his horse from Oakland, his mother's home, to Glenburnie to visit Jennie. And on that hot August 4 evening in 1932, it was Duncan Minor who discovered the bloody trail outside Jennie's home.

Shortly after Margaret Guido moved into Glenburnie, she threw a dinner party for a few select guests, and one uninvited phantom party crasher. Backlit by the late-afternoon sun, Margaret describes the event. "I had some company. We were in the family room, and my friend Catherine Meng was looking through the doorway and turned to me, and she suddenly asked, 'Who else, is someone else in here in the house?' I said, 'No.' Catherine said, 'Yes, there is. I just saw somebody walking from the dining room through the parlor there.'" Margaret clasps her left hand tighter with her right, a little sigh escapes. "My heart stopped, and I questioned, *'What is this? What is Catherine seeing?'* So I got up and went in there to look. We all did. We never saw anybody. To relieve the tension, I said, just teasing, 'It must have been Jennie Merrill.' And Catherine said, 'No, because it was a man.' Margaret's hands flutter open.

Jennie Merrill prior to her downfall.

Duncan Minor, Jennie's cousin and constant companion.

"So I said, 'Then, it must be Duncan Minor looking for Miss Jennie.'"
Margaret leans in and confides, "Duncan was her friend, actually her
cousin, her second cousin."

The local rumor mill often speculated that Duncan and Jennie were
more than "kissing cousins." Jennie came back to Natchez because she
and Duncan were childhood sweethearts, but cousins, even second
cousins were not suppose to marry. When asked if this is why Duncan
and Jennie tried to hide their relationship from prying eyes, Margaret
reveals a more pragmatic reason. "Well, that, and I think Jennie's family
was hoping that she would marry someone and bring in new money.
That wasn't always part of the story. It didn't always get told. Everybody
knew it, but it wasn't politically correct to talk about it."

More gossip points the finger at Duncan's mother Katherine, who
threatened him with disinheritance if he dared to marry Jennie. Margaret
manages a half-smirk, half-laugh. "Well, Duncan came every night after
dark—whether they were secretly married or not." And if the ghost
who came to dinner is male and might be Duncan, then ghost number
two, who all agree is decidedly female, may be his beloved Jennie. If it is
Jennie, she remains as reclusive in death as she had been in life.

"After my old housekeeper passed away," says Mrs. Guido, "my new
housekeeper, Bessie, would hear the doorbell ring and would go to the
door, and there wouldn't be anybody there. And for me, it was like I
would feel something and I would look around and it would seem as if
there was someone in the room. And my daughter, Janice, who slept in
the front bedroom, she was here visiting, she saw a white apparition, like
a woman."

Margaret's daughter-in-law, Carolyn Guido, attests to a female
paranormal presence. "I have never seen her, but I definitely felt her, and
I smelled her. Perfumey, wonderful, and I am like, 'Where is that coming
from?'"

Carolyn's daughter, Megan, also speaks of the ghost in the female
gender. "We know there is a ghost here, but this ghost isn't a bad ghost,
and this ghost doesn't really bother us. I can just feel her. I can just
tell that there is a spirit in here." Megan, whose bedroom was in the
refurbished lower level of the house, has had a few close encounters. "I've
heard her in the basement, in that closet in the basement." Megan refers

to a large storage room where hoop skirts and antebellum dresses are packed tightly together. The rustling sounds Megan hears could be a curious Jennie, known as a pack rat in her later years, rifling through the colorful pastel costumes. "She is just looking around at things in the house. I don't get scared."

In 2007, Megan's grandmother, Margaret, swapped homes with her son and daughter-in-law. It is evident as her eyes sweep the grounds through the floor-to-ceiling windows of the renovated sun porch that she misses her life here despite the home's grim past. "My husband passed away and this was too much for me by myself, and so I decided that I was going to sell it, and my children didn't want me too. Finally, my son, Gary, and his wife, Carolyn, who lived over by the river, said they would trade houses with me. So I am up on the bluff overlooking the Mississippi river, and it's been perfectly gorgeous up there. I miss being here, but it was overwhelming."

Built circa 1835, Glenburnie was a prime attraction on the Natchez Fall and Spring Pilgrimages. But most of those who came to the house were more interested in the details of the shocking murder, not the stunning architecture. "My friends helped me put the house on the tour, and Carolyn was always here, but it was a chore. People would always ask about the murder and I would tell them as much as I could, but you have busloads of people coming at the same time, and you couldn't tell the whole thing. My daughter, Janice, would come from New Orleans; she is a history teacher, who loved telling the story, and she would keep them forever, and the tour guides would be mad because they wanted to keep them moving along. We had it on tour for two years after I moved, and Carolyn had some little flyers printed up to tell about the murder so it wouldn't take so long."

What made the murder mystery so long and involved centered on the people accused of the deadly deed. Even more bizarre was the alleged motive—goats.

Not far from Jennie' Merrill's home at Glenburnie, the other odd couple, Dick Dana and Octavia Dockery, were camped out at Glenwood. Dick was the son of Rev. Charles Backus Dana, the rector of Natchez's Trinity Church. In Natchez, it's all about connections, true, loyal, and faithful to the Southern cause. The Reverend Dana was close to Gen.

Robert E. Lee, who generously bestowed enough Lee family heirlooms upon the Danas to furnish Glenwood, the Danas' home in Natchez. Young Dick went to college in New York with aspirations of becoming a concert pianist. While there, a window sash fell on his hand and crushed two fingers; his dreams died with the freak accident.

In 1890, twenty-two-year-old Dick Dana returned to Natchez to live the life of a talented *bon vivant.* He befriended Nydia Dockery Forman, a cousin by marriage of Varina Howell Davis, wife of Confederate president Jefferson Davis. Mrs. Forman and her late husband also were the beneficiaries of many fine antiques courtesy of Varina and Jefferson Davis. Into this mix, arrived Octavia Dockery, younger sister of Nydia. In 1893, near death and destitute, Nydia begged the young Dana to allow her sister Octavia to move in with him. A peculiar request given that Dana had little money, although he had inherited Glenwood from his father. The bigger issue of why Nydia chose a single man barely in his twenties to care for her twenty-eight-year-old sister defies logic. The arrangement tittered on the brink of insanity for this noncouple.

Describing herself in one letter as a "miserable creature," Octavia is also quoted in *The Goat Castle Murder* as saying, "I have stuck it out at lonely, deserted Glenwood with nothing but ceaseless drudgery . . . because I hoped better days would come." This forlorn Southern beauty tried to augment their income by writing poetry and magazine articles. Due to the small fees generated, Octavia made an astonishing choice, "I decided to establish a chicken farm on the property of Dick Dana." Soon chickens, pigs, and goats overran the grounds and the house. Octavia could not contain them. Her housemate Dick descended into madness, spoke in riddles, no longer washed, and spooked at human contact. He spent two nights on the roof of Glenwood after local teens played a practical joke. They taunted him as the "Wild Man," and Octavia as the "Goat Woman." The marauding goats not only destroyed the house, but also its contents. They feasted on leather-bound books once owned by Robert E. Lee and manuscripts belonging to Jefferson Davis. Dick and Octavia lived in squalor. And their neighbors began to feel the impact.

Octavia's goats, in search of fresh tidbits to destroy, crossed from Glenwood to Glenburnie; harsh words were exchanged between Jennie and Octavia. Jennie bought a rifle and a pistol.

In 1917, when Dick and Octavia failed to pay their property taxes, a disgusted Duncan Minor bought Glenwood at a sheriff's sale. He intended to evict the pathetic pair and relieve his cousin Jennie of the burden of dealing with them. However, Octavia was clever. She hired a lawyer who found a loophole in the law; "Infants and persons judged insane" could not be evicted for failure to pay taxes. When Natchez sherriff C. P. Rogers got the call that "something terrible has happened" to Jennie Merrill, two prime suspects emerged.

Margaret Guido sums up the scandal, "They went immediately to arrest the couple, Dick and Octavia. They never admitted they did it, but there was a lot of evidence."

Octavia denied all knowledge, while letting slip that she *might* have heard "noises" coming from Glenburnie. Police found Dick upstairs at Glenwood attempting to wash blood off a shirt. The unkempt man claimed it was pig's blood. The shirt was sent off for analysis, and the results came back as animal not human. Some still shrug in disbelief.

"What amazed me is when they went over to talk to the Goat Man and they found blood on a piece of clothing," states Carolyn Guido. "They claim they tested it and that it was goat's blood. I always think that could have been a cover-up."

Margaret is in complete agreement. "That's what I always thought. I can remember when Dick Dana died, I thought he'd confess on his deathbed, but he didn't."

Carolyn reveals a little-known Natchez secret. "A friend of ours who just passed away, she was kin to his family. She went to her grave knowing the true story. She would never tell."

Margaret turns immediately to face Carolyn on the couch. "Is that Dunbar?"

Carolyn allows that Dunbar Flinn's claim is only hearsay, Natchez hearsay. And those in Natchez are fiercely protective of their own.

Margaret admits a cover-up is likely. "It was such a scandal because it involved four prominent families. And then the sentiment kind of turned. You know, back then, everybody was so closely related and interconnected; they started feeling sorry for Dick and Octavia, so they thought, 'Oh, those poor people didn't do that.'" Margaret is ambivalent. "Possibly they didn't, but possibly they did."

So if it wasn't Dick Dana and/or Octavia Dockery, then who murdered Jennie and set her ghost off on a walkabout for all eternity? One candidate comes to the forefront—the devoted cousin. After all, Duncan was in Jennie's will. She left him her entire estate, including Glenburnie.

"A lot of people in Natchez felt that Duncan Minor had killed her," says Margaret with a sad smile, "but I'm too much of a romantic to think that after all that courting, all those years, thirty-something years, that he would have. He inherited her property, but he didn't need it. He had money of his own, but he didn't spend it. So there was talk, of course."

After the initial buzz, the next suspects are almost anticlimactic. Initially, the crime scene is riddled with bullets and blood but no body. In the dining room, investigators note a bloodstained bedroom slipper. Outside, fifty feet from the house, they find a bloody hair comb and the other bedroom slipper. A pool of blood congeals further ahead. The search continues through the night. Bloodhounds are called in. At 5:30 a.m., a searcher pulls back a branch and spots a woman's body in a shallow ravine. The discovery sweeps through Natchez. Newspapers across the country pick up the lurid soap opera of Duncan and Jennie, and misfits Dick and Octavia. Derelict Glenwood is dubbed "The Goat Castle."

Over in Pine Bluff, Arkansas, Police Chief Maurice O'Neill reads the sensational accounts and picks up the phone. He informs Sherriff Roberts in Natchez that on the previous evening, August 7, 1932, his men shot and killed a black man, George Pearls, when he pulled a .32-caliber pistol on them. Papers on his body purport to show that he had recently been in Natchez. It is four days after Jennie's murder, and the two law enforcement officials connect the dots.

A lab test verifies that the bullets fired from the gun in Pine Bluff match those found in the walls of Glenburnie. Pearls's fingerprints also are a match for a set found in Jennie's home. Emily Burns, owner of a Natchez boarding house, confesses that she and her roomer, George Pearls, went to Glenburnie to ask Jennie for money. Jennie refused, and Pearls shot her when she went for her gun. In light of this new evidence, Octavia and Dick are set free. Emily Burns is tried and convicted as an accomplice and sent to the Mississippi State Penitentiary. The case is officially closed in November 1932.

"I think the poor man up in Arkansas was a scapegoat," Margaret Guido deadpans. "He was already dead when they said he did it. The woman, Emily Burns, underwent a lengthy, grueling interview, and after she's sentenced, and goes to prison, she gets pardoned. It was kind of a screwy, messed-up tale actually."

And a tale that will not die. Gossip and innuendo flourish. The former miser, Duncan Minor, uses his inheritance to travel and trades in his horse for a car. At his death in 1939, he leaves the remainder of Jennie's inheritance to her side of the family, adhering to the stipulations in his cousin's will. Meanwhile, Dick and Octavia lead a three-ring circus. Capitalizing on the very first Natchez Pilgrimage Week in 1933, the enterprising pair hand out leaflets and sell tickets to Glenwood.

> *HISTORIC GLENWOOD*
> *FAMOUS GOAT CASTLE*
> DANA AND DOCKERY MUSEUM
> OPEN TO PILGRIMAGE TOURS
> PIANO RECITALS
> ROUND TRIP FARE 20 cents

The curious arrived in droves. Dick and Octavia do not disappoint. Dick bangs away on the piano, Octavia reads poetry, and the goats cavort through the house devouring priceless antiques, books, and letters.

"People used to pay twenty-five cents to tour the house. I remember going with a friend and her mother after church one Sunday," recalls Margaret Guido. "I was in eighth grade. Dick was still playing the piano. He was a mess. The house was a mess. They still had goats and cats and everything else just roaming around. Dick got kind of crazy and would spend all his time like," Margaret hesitates, "I don't know if he was in the trees or on the rooftop. He just escaped from life. As kids, we talked about the 'Wild Man.' Glenwood was separated from Glenburnie by a bayou and . . . woods." And these very woods spawned new tales of paranormal activity.

Dick Dana died of complications from pneumonia and asthma in 1948. Octavia Dockery continued to live at the Goat Castle until her death, a few months later in 1949. An auction of the salvageable contents of the house generated a surprising thirteen thousand dollars. By 1955, Glenwood is deemed unsanitary and unsafe and is torn down. A new subdivision of modest homes surfaces. Two street signs intersect with history and chronicle the past—Glenwood Drive and Dana Road. Children in the subdivision begin to report the sounds of an off-kilter piano coming from the woods.

"When we moved here," explains Margaret, "it was a jungle out there, a forest. It was kind of creepy, but I didn't know if it was supposed to be haunted or not. We cleared all the yard." She points to the well-manicured and landscaped backyard. "All those kids that live in that subdivision over there, lived in those bayous, they'd tell tales," and she adds with a chuckle, "and make up things, I'm sure."

Carolyn has been listening intently to her mother-in-law. "You know, it is strange, but I have heard music, but I've never heard the story about the kids before. One day, as I was taking a walk, I could hear music, and I was trying to figure out where it was coming from, but it could have been coming from the nursing home or from a house back there, but . . ." Carolyn suddenly rubs her left hand vigorously up and down her right arm. "Oh, I am getting chills. The music I heard, it was piano music."

One paranormal group alleges that the melodies increase in volume at night because the tormented specter of Dick Dana is trying in vain to drown out the moans and groans of the murdered spirit of Jennie Merrill.

Margaret Guido has been sipping freshly brewed tea. She lowers her porcelain teacup to its saucer. China meets china with a delicate tap, a poignant refrain to a tragic affair. "That was such a sad thing that she was killed for no reason that we knew."

Postscript: A key comes back. Pewter gray, heavy, five-inches in length. The type required to open the bulky nineteenth-century locks found on exterior doors. The key's only other distinguishing feature is that it is twisted as if someone was working hard to unlock an unfamiliar door and used too much force.

Carolyn retrieves the key from a bookcase filled with mementos and places it on a padded footrest in the center of the sunroom. It gleams in the sunlight like an offering on an altar. Still puzzled by its mysterious

The crooked key that arrived without a return postmark.

arrival, Margaret gazes down at the key. "I've had a lot of people knock on the door of Glenburnie that had known somebody in the past, and they would ask if this was the Goat Castle. I would tell them, no, this is the place where the murder took place; the Goat Castle business is across the bayou, and you won't find it anymore. Then more people came who were very into ghosts and they wanted to touch something connected to the murder."

Margaret takes another sip of tea and resumes her story. "One day, I had this group from Texas. I was explaining how after Glenburnie sat empty for a number of years, vandals came and stripped it of everything—mantles, doors, locks, everything was gone. The house was wide open. Not long after that, around Halloween, I walked down to get the mail from the mailbox. Inside was a box about this long." Margaret spreads her hands about eight inches apart. "The address on the box read 'Goat Castle, Natchez, Mississippi.' I don't know why the postman delivered it to Glenburnie, but I guess because Glenwood doesn't exist anymore, this was the next best thing. I was scared to open it." Margaret confesses that curiosity won out. "I opened it and there was this big key, and that was all there was. No note. No explanation. It was spooky. I couldn't try it in any of the locks here, because none of them are original to the house. They all had to be replaced along with the missing doorknobs. The return postmark was from Texas, and I wondered if [in] that group . . . was maybe someone who had stolen things from here long ago, felt guilty, and wanted to return it."

Alternatively, if conjecture and speculation are allowed a little more latitude, is the twisted and bent key a crucial piece of evidence in the murder of Jennie Merrill? Is there someone still out there who knows more but is unwilling or afraid to come forward? Is the key, literally, a clue to what really happened the night a person or persons entered Glenburnie and shot Jennie Merrill to death? The spirits of the dead are said to linger on when there are unresolved issues. Jennie, Duncan, Dick, and Olivia are all buried in family plots in the Natchez Cemetery. All have sufficient reasons to return to Glenburnie and the woods once bordering Glenwood, the infamous Goat Castle.

Carolyn Guido's childhood home prior to restoration.

10

Homewood

I've lived among the ruins, walked among the dead
loved among the wreckage beneath a flag of red.
—Virgin Steele, "Life Among the Ruins," 1993

Most of us never see a ghost. Others like Carolyn Guido of Glenburnie in Natchez can't seem to get away from them. Dark-haired, petite Carolyn grew up at Homewood, having moved there at the age of two, and the spooky apparitions that populated her childhood made a big impression.

Homewood is known as the Lost Plantation. Once the stunning showplace of David Hunt's vast antebellum plantation empire, this magnificent mansion burned to the ground in 1940. All that remained after the ravages of the fire were two brick, two-story dependencies—a slave quarters and a kitchen. One of these stand-alone structures evolved into a family home rife with phantoms.

"After the main house burned, my grandfather, Alvin Laub, purchased the property." Carolyn's grandparents moved into one of the dependencies, and in time, they adopted the name of the original plantation for the smaller surviving structure. Alvin and his wife Lillian Laub found themselves at the center of attention. "The ruins were still standing, but there were so many tourists and Natchez people going out to look and pilfer through, my grandfather was afraid they would get hurt and sue. So he had the walls pushed in."

After her grandfather's death, the property was deeded to Carolyn's mother, Margaret Laub. What may have been one man's nightmare became another's dream. "My daddy arrived in Natchez and fell in love with my mother at the Burn, another family property." J. Wesley Cooper also fell in love with Homewood. Soon he persuaded his new wife that life among the ruins would be romantic. "My daddy, being this historian and Civil War buff, couldn't wait to move in." Carolyn recalls her mother describing the conditions there as "deplorable." "There were tenants living there who were doing farming on the land. It was squalor, chickens in and out." Carolyn's parents set immediately to work. "The house wasn't totally finished when we moved in, but it was livable."

J. Wesley Cooper labored daily on improvements. "The ruins of the main house were in the side yard. My daddy would get the brick, clean the brick, and then use them to lay brick floors inside, on the porches and patios." With a quick smile Carolyn adds, "We would find treasures— silverware, goblets, coffee cups." She retrieves remnants dug from the ashes of the once palatial mansion—a bundle of ornate blackened silverware and a charred pistol, its wooden handle missing.

A childhood spent digging for and finding buried treasure in your own backyard might seem like something right out of a movie, but J. Wesley Cooper had yet another passion he shared with his children— ghosts. "My father would take my mother; his mother; his good friend Betty Walsh, who called herself a witch; and my sister, Deborah, and I on these ghost hunts. We would go out on the Natchez Trace, have a cookout, and then he'd whip out the Ouija board, and he would ask it, *'How many ghosts live at Homewood?'* . . . The thing would just zoom to *five.* Then he would get someone else to ask it. Always the same number. And I would think, *'Please, don't take me home tonight.'*"

Some might say, given this strange upbringing, any child would be predisposed to believe that there were ghosts at Homewood. Carolyn shakes her head, wishing she could attribute what she has seen to an overstimulated childhood imagination. "I heard and saw them in numerous places at Homewood. It was scary. They were adult ghosts. I never could decipher who they were except one time. I saw a man in the doorway between the kitchen and the dining room with a suit coat and tall hat on."

Carolyn's cousin, Richard Metz, heard the ghosts, but they were mostly of the female variety. "He would sleep in the big living room, and my grandmother would sleep in the back bedroom. He would be terrified

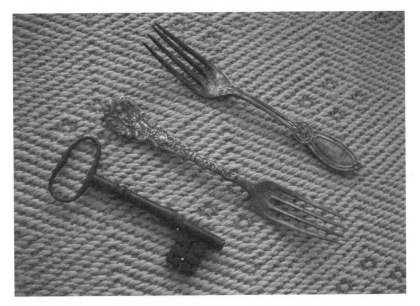

Knives and forks found in the ashes.

A pistol dug out of the ashes by Carolyn and her sister.

because he always said he heard a woman in bedroom slippers walking, scooting across the floor. And he would wake up my grandmother who never heard anything."

Carolyn shivers. "There were also five children's ghosts. . . . Five children died in the main house. They all had yellow fever. They were the children of the Balfours."

Catherine Balfour was the daughter of David Hunt, a man who possessed so many plantations he earned the moniker "King David." When Catherine Hunt married William Suggs Balfour in 1850, her father hired Scottish architect James Hardie to design a magnificent residence for the newlyweds. Homewood, a five-story brick mansion with a façade of iron columns, porches, and balconies encased by lacy-cast-iron filigree and capped with a widow's walk, had a Spanish-style architectural flair. Despite living in such a luxurious setting, Catherine Balfour paced the lofty hallways alone.

While William Balfour served in the Confederacy, the bereft Catherine endured a mother's ultimate tragedy. In *Lost Plantations,* author Dr. Marc C. Matrana writes that "Catherine mourned as she watched four of her beloved children die over the next years." This does make for a ghostly discrepancy, but ghosts by their very nature are hard to quantify. Four little ghosts? Five little ghosts? If ghostly behavior mimics the nature of their human counterparts, then counting the ethereal forms of tiny tots as they go cavorting by could prove challenging.

Given Carolyn Guido's unconventional childhood living in the Homewood dependency, it is surprising to learn that she returned. Not only returned, but she moved back in with her two daughters in tow. "After my parents divorced, the house was never fully restored. So I twisted my husband Gary's arm to buy it from my mother." Driven by her father's passion for the historic site and its bucolic acreage, Carolyn had her own dream. "I wanted to move out there and finish the house, live with my girls, have a horse, pond, ducks, and do all the country stuff."

Before moving in, Carolyn did a test run. "I was so freaked out; part of me wanted to raise my kids there, restore the house, make it beautiful, and the other half of me was like *'I don't know if I should do this. It's spooky out there.'* Momma had moved out. There wasn't hardly any furniture left in the house. I stayed all night just to see if I could handle being

The original Homewood mansion before the fire.

there by myself with the ghosts." Carolyn beams with pride. "I made it through the night, and we moved out there."

During the renovations, a few of the workmen had reservations about the Homewood site. One worker spotted an apparition in the same place and eerily wearing the same style of clothing as Carolyn had seen as a child. "He saw a ghost, a man in the den with a hat on. The guy never came back to work." Another continued on the job but kept his ears tuned for more. "One of the painters, Johnny Seale, swore he heard a little girl screaming, *'Help me!'* Carolyn believes it was likely one of the ghosts of the Balfour children still trapped inside.

Carolyn's daughters, Megan and Kari, were quite vocal in their opposition to the relocation of the family. "I pitched a fit when I was told by my parents that we were moving to Homewood. We moved there when I was in seventh grade." Megan, now a slender, soft-spoken young adult, speaks about what happened one night about a year after settling into their new home. "It was dark. It was a school night. . . . I was by myself. I remember being freaked out. I was so scared that I went and got under my mom's bed covers and just hid out because I felt like something not real was in the house."

Megan's aversion to Homewood began long before the family actually moved in. "We had to stay out there a lot because it was my grandmother's house before it was ours. We spent weekends out there. My younger sister, Kari, was scared too."

Megan sums up her feelings toward Homewood and its creepy after-dark residents. "I didn't enjoy it. It was constant. I hated being there by myself at night." For Megan, moving out of Homewood at age seventeen was cause for celebration. Carolyn says there was a very practical reason for leaving five years later. "I knew my children were going to grow up, go off to college, and with Gary working, I thought, 'I am going to be stuck out here on seventy-five acres all by myself.'" And Carolyn couldn't necessarily count on a multitude of friends to fill in the void. "Some of my friends would come out and visit me, but they would be just petrified."

The Guidos sold Homewood to another family. A family with a little girl. A little girl quite content with the ghosts. "This wonderful doctor lives there with his wife and a daughter who is nine or ten. Her name is Ashley. She doesn't appear to be frightened. Her reaction is not the same as ours," says Carolyn. Megan's assessment is similar to her mother's. "Ashley talks about the ghost like it is no big deal."

Carolyn nibbles at her lower lip as if she still can't quite believe how the story unfolded. "It was most peculiar," says Carolyn, who also claims they never informed the current owners of any reputed hauntings at Homewood. "One day, this little girl and her parents come into the furniture store where my sister-in-law, Gale, works. This little girl did not know Gale, and Gale did not know this little girl. While her parents are walking around looking at furniture, Ashley approaches Gale." Carolyn repeats the strange dialogue between adult and child verbatim:

"I want to tell you something," announces Ashley.

Gale, politely responds, "What is it?"

"I have ghosts in my house."

"You do?" replies a stunned Gale.

"I do. And don't tell my parents I told you."

When Gale introduces herself to the potential customers, the doctor and his wife, she is shocked, for this is the family now living in Homewood. She phones Carolyn.

"She calls me immediately. I can't believe this little girl has discovered the ghosts, and not only that, she tells a stranger who just happens to be connected to me."

The saga continues. "Three weeks later," says an amazed Carolyn, "I see this same little girl at a Halloween party. She is visiting another good friend of mine's child. My friend tells Ashley that she is sleeping in my old bedroom. And the little girl just opens up to me."

"You know we have ghosts," Ashley blurts out.

"No," says Carolyn feigning disbelief. "You don't have ghosts."

"Yes, we do. I hear 'em and I see 'em."

"Really?"

"I'm psychic," states Ashley. She giggles.

Carolyn tries a different tact. "Well, my little bedroom was upstairs, and it was painted blue when you moved in."

"It's my room now."

"Where do you hear and see these ghosts?"

"Mostly upstairs in the hall," replies Ashley. She follows up with, "Is that where you saw them when you were little?"

Carolyn says that at that point in this bizarre conversation, all she could tell Ashley was that she had seen a vague *them* in numerous places in the house. Carolyn's reluctance to reinforce the idea of Homewood as a haunted house stems from her own childhood. "My dad was always trying to conjure a ghost. After doing the Ouija board, we'd go down the old road on the Natchez Trace and he'd turn out the headlights. I'd be slinking down on the backseat. You know, I'm a kid. They shouldn't have had me in the car doing that." Carolyn winces at the memories. "His friend Betty Walsh, the one who said she was a witch, she'd pluck a piece of daddy's hair out, and she'd wrap it around a white candle, around the wick of the candle, and she'd get out in front of the car, and she'd do some *mojo* talk over this candle, and they would see things. I wouldn't look."

Through a quirky twist of fate, Carolyn now lives at Glenburnie, the scene of Jennie Merrill's murder, some say unsolved murder. Nevertheless, whatever haunted souls linger on at Glenburnie, Carolyn is at peace with their presence. Unfortunately, she never came to terms with the aberrations that populated Homewood.

Postscript: The Conflagration. After the destruction of many a great Mississippi mansion, the abandoned sites often retain an illusive vestige of the past that haunts the present. The original Homewood Plantation was a Natchez landmark. The blazing fire that brought the house down did little to eradicate its history or the evolving tales of its former occupants. After the last of the Balfours left Homewood in 1907, the plantation passed through a series of owners. Oil wells replaced cotton fields when "black gold" was found on the property. By the end of the 1930s, a new owner, a foreigner, moved in.

"She was a Yankee. She came from New York, and when she came to Natchez, she was wearing these slinky pants, and people were going, 'Who is that woman? We've never seen anyone from Natchez dressed like that.'" Carolyn and her mother-in-law, Margaret, share a hearty laugh. Carolyn fills in more details gleaned from local gossip. "Her name was Ann Swan, Mrs. Kingsley Swan. She had these huge German shepherd dogs, had a brick doghouse built, and she fed them steak every night. She ended up living at Homewood for several years. She put the home on tour."

Margaret interjects, "And she burned it. Everybody said she burned it."

"But they never proved it," cautions Carolyn. "That's what everybody said because she locked the firemen out. They were late getting there so that made her mad. She locked the gate." Mrs. Swan, according to Carolyn, refused all offers of help. "The Homewood property was adjacent to an old dairy. And even before the firemen got there, the men from the dairy came running with pails of water, but they couldn't get in. She held a shotgun on them." Carolyn's assessment of the known facts brings her to the same guilty verdict as Margaret. "So I agree; she burned her house down."

Black-and-white photographs from the Historic American Building Survey show an impressive front entryway in which four fluted Ionic columns support a lofty triangular pediment shielding a five-bay structure. "Daddy always said they could have rebuilt the house. It was a grand house." Carolyn's father regretted Alvin Laub's decision to demolish what was left of the remaining brick walls. Fortunately, for historian J. Wesley Cooper, one of the ancillary brick structures survived intact. It is visible at the far left of the archival photo of Homewood, flanking the rear of the house. This structure would become the private home that in the present day retains the original Homewood Plantation name.

Carolyn and Margaret, like many in Natchez, believe that Mrs. Kingsley Swan let the fire rage to collect the insurance money. The inventory from her insurance claim became public knowledge and fodder for more gossip. "Her nightgowns she listed as fifty or sixty dollars each and that was expensive back then for a nightgown. She was a nut," declares Carolyn. "She didn't try to save anything." As proof, Carolyn brings out another bundle of silver forks, knives, and spoons retrieved from the ashes and a pair of silver pistols.

The dramatic fire on the night of January 2, 1940, destroyed an architectural jewel, burned through three-inch-thick mahogany doors, reduced handcrafted antiques to rubble, scorched silver doorknobs and hinges, and displaced a home full of phantoms. Prior to the burning of the original Homewood Plantation manor house, there had been no talk of ghosts. After the fire, through three generations of Laubs, Coopers, and Guidos, and now one little girl, the confused ghosts appear at random, uncomfortable with their new surroundings. Carolyn Guido is adamant when she says, "I always felt like someone at Homewood was watching me."

The Old Armory, now Washington County's Convention & Visitor's Bureau.

11

Greenville's Ghosts

Greenville bills itself as the "Heart and Soul of the Delta." Recently, a few old souls felt compelled to reappear. As the seat of Washington County, Greenville has a storied past, which is reflected in her historic homes, schools, churches, cemeteries, and commercial structures. There is a timeless quality to it all, a mystique, and a new restlessness that the long dead have not entirely left the premises.

Just a block off the Mississippi River, the old National Guard Armory has been repurposed as the offices of the Washington County Convention and Visitors Bureau. Unfazed by walls decorated with colorful posters promoting the area's cultural attractions, one former guardsman remains on duty.

Wesley Smith, the energetic new director of the convention and visitors bureau, has seen the soldier on patrol. "I got here in October of 2008; a month later, in November, I was leaving for the night. The rest of the staff was gone. I got up from my desk, closed the door to my office, went halfway down the center hall to cut off the light switches, and in a split second, there he was." Smith gets up to demonstrate. "I was heading forward towards the front of the building." He points to the double metal doors that serve as the entrance. Each has a clear glass panel in the upper half. "It was already dark outside, so with the light inside, the windows in the doors acted like mirrors. Just as I was thinking that I need to cut the lights out, I see in the reflection of the glass panels a man in uniform walk across the hall behind me." Smith's voice rises. "It wasn't a wisp or anything; it was a solid-looking man. He didn't look at me; [he] just kept going out of what I thought was a door at the end of the hall and into the wall on the opposite side." Smith admits the sight startled him. "My first thought was that my brain had somehow transposed something. I couldn't be seeing what I was seeing, and I'd gotten confused." Rushing to make sense of what was happening, he bolted for the front door. "I pulled it open and scanned the street up and down. We don't get much street traffic here, let alone someone walking after hours. It was dark, and there was a light rain . . . and the street was empty."

The youthful-looking director makes it clear that until that moment, haunted tales had not easily swayed him. "I had never seen a ghost before. I'd never even taken a position one way or another if spirits, ghosts can return." Smith is positive of two things: the figure of a man appeared *behind* him, and he was in uniform. "It was an early World War II style with a long, light-colored tunic belted at the waist, and the pants were baggy around his upper legs and then tapered below his knees." These tapered pants were first worn by cavalry units so there would be less material to tuck into their boots while on horseback.

As news of the incident spread, Greenville citizens came forward to share photos, souvenirs, and memories. "A man named Tommy Harmon, whose father was stationed here for years, brought us a commemorative book from 1938. When I saw the pictures, I got goose bumps. There in the photos was the exact uniform." The man who shared the book also shared another detail in support of Smith's ghostly visitor. "Oddly enough, when we walked to the rear of the hallway and I showed him where the soldier crossed, Tommy pointed out that where the wall is solid now, there used to be a doorway. You can see the outline where it's been bricked up. I thought it was kinda neat that the soldier could have come out of the old doorway."

Originally, the squat, solid structure on Walnut Street was part of a 1930 army base before becoming the headquarters for Battery A, First Battalion, 114th Field Artillery of the Mississippi National Guard. On December 13, 1959, it was rededicated as Fort Nicholson to honor Louis M. Nicholson Jr. of Greenville, killed in action in 1943. The armory served as headquarters for the Second Reconnaissance Squadron, 198th Armor, Thirty-first Infantry (Dixie) Division. Commissioned officers, noncommissioned officers, sergeants, corporals, and privates have all drilled here. The echoes of their footsteps have occasionally interrupted the daily routines of the current occupants.

The morning after Smith spotted the soldier, he checked in with the bureau's other staff members. "I said to Lisa and Catherine, 'Have you ever seen or heard anything strange?' And they both looked at me and then at each other. I go, 'I've only been here a month. Tell me, what?'"

Lisa Winters is Smith's executive assistant. Her charming personality bubbles over. She speaks frankly about the ghostly activity in the old armory. "The footsteps overhead sound more like the thuds that boots make rather than shoes." Winters leads a tour through the vacant second floor. Large metal cabinets, some resting on their backs, others propped on their sides; discarded wooden crates; and unidentified objects swathed in layers of dust, a graveyard of the forgotten, create a forlorn scene. Winters keeps up a running commentary. "We've heard stuff up here." She looks down on two parallel skid marks on the dusty floor. "See, those marks are fresh. It's as if someone dragged one of the cabinets across the floor. And we hear heavy thuds like the boxes are being picked up in the air and then dropped. Catherine and I both hear it, but she doesn't like to talk about it much." Winters stands with her hands on her hips and surveys the room. "Why would anybody want to be up here?" She wipes the sweat dripping from her forehead with the back of her hand. "We had some ghost hunters here awhile back and it was just like this—about one hundred degrees. They had these temperature gauges going in this room and immediately the temperature dropped like twenty degrees. There's no air-conditioning here. And you can see how the sun just beats through these large windows. The ghost hunters say cold spots are the sign that a spirit is around." Winters grins. "I don't know anything about that."

The front of the armory faces the old Greenville Inn and Suites. To the right is a parking lot. Winters looks out the window to her red car parked below. "When I'm the last one to leave, I lock up, and as I cross the street, it feels like someone is staring down at me from this upstairs window, but when I turn around, no one is there." Winters, her blue-green eyes shining under a cap of blond hair, is glad of one thing: "I'm not alone when it comes to hearing some of these things."

The executive assistant has rejoined the director in his office. She peers across the wide expanse of desk to Smith, seeking confirmation. "What really got both of us was the whistling." Smith stretches his slender frame back in his chair, and lets Winters begin.

"I was typing at the computer and there was this really loud whistling.

I thought it was Wesley, and I said to myself, 'Well, I guess Wesley is in a really good mood.'" As the whistling continued, Winters heard the outer side door open and close. Smith entered the building.

"I didn't hear anything outside," says Smith, "but when I stepped in, I could hear this melody. I couldn't tell you the song, but it had form, like a military tune. I got about halfway up the hall, and I called out, 'Lisa, is that you?' I turned into her office and she jumped."

"My heart sank." There is a quiver in Winter's twang.

"She thought it was me and I thought it was her."

And the ghost of the old armory probably had a good chuckle.

Another incident had a bit of an intimidation factor. On this day, Lisa Winters and fellow staff member Catherine Gardner were assembled in Smith's office. "Catherine was seated where Lisa is now in front of my desk, and Lisa was standing closer to the doorway." Smith relates the sequence of events as they occurred during the informal meeting: "I had my legs crossed and propped up on the desk. We had been in there about ten minutes, having this long conversation and all of a sudden, I hear over my shoulder 'Haaaar.'" Smith lifts his right shoulder up to his ear as if to banish the unwelcomed sound. "It was so loud, all three of us heard it at the same time, and we all jumped."

"I heard it over here by me, and Catherine thought it was coming from behind her like someone was breathing heavy," adds Winters.

"It came out like an explosion. 'Haaaar.'" Smith repeats the sound.

The staff at the Washington County Convention and Visitors Bureau are uncertain if they have one ghost or a rotating cadre of spirits. A veteran in the community votes for the single ghost theory. Reports of the on-going paranormal activity at the armory prompted retired S.Sgt. C. J. Coursey to write a letter to the editor of the *Delta Times Democrat*. In the letter, Coursey states that neither during his years of service nor his father's service was there was any talk of ghosts at the armory. The retired sergeant speculates that the hauntings did not start until after the armory was abandoned by the military. Coursey refers to a thank-you proclamation hanging in the city library. "It was signed by all or most of them soldiers. My father's name is there and so is the man I suspect to be the ghost." The letter writer goes on to say that the alleged ghost was a noncommissioned officer who rose to the rank of command sergeant major. In 1990, the National Guard unit at Fort Nicholson was activated for Desert Storm, but the senior noncommissioned officer was not deployed due to his age. "The state of Mississippi hired this old soldier to watch over the property," says Coursey. "He probably did not like being left behind after all the years of being in charge."

After the unit returned, the headquarters moved into a new facility and the old armory building was donated to the city of Greenville. Coursey feels his former commander never accepted the change. "I suspect this guy is in that building and really needs, big time, to report to the supreme commander." And, according to Coursey, the task will be monumental. "It may take . . . all of us living old soldiers to convince this man/ghost that his work is done on this planet."

At the former E. E. Bass Junior High School in Greenville, there is another old timer too dedicated to leave. Herman Solomon was the principal for more than twenty-five years from the 1940s through the 1960s. The school he presided over was a mammoth complex. Built in two phases, the original Greenville High School was completed in 1916. In 1929, the junior-high annex was designed by renowned architect A. Hays Town. Both schools became the educational center of Greenville. Death has not deterred a vigilant principal from making his rounds.

"Those who have seen his ghost say it strolls the halls, which he did." Warren Harper attended E. E. Bass from 1959 to 1964. His memories of Herman Solomon are vivid. "Principal Solomon was a gnomish figure, a real small man who made a big impression. To us middle schoolers, he was a holy terror." In the hindsight of age, Harper acknowledges that Solomon was a good old disciplinarian. "He was hands on, but he didn't whip your fanny; he just sent you to the coach."

In 1980, due to age and increasing maintenance costs, the school closed its doors. Members of the community banded together to form the E. E. Bass Foundation to salvage the auditorium for performance space and turn other portions into offices. The attempts were only partially successful. For the next fifteen years, the vacant red brick building with its Grecian-style columns took on a mournful appearance. Sections of the roof collapsed and rumors of hauntings began to circulate.

A former principal still walks the halls of E. E. Bass Junior High School.

"The first sightings were in the early to mid-1990s," says Harper. Harper is a founding member of Delta Center Stage, a local theatre group that began to restore the once lavish auditorium. "We came in here in 1991. The place was a maintenance nightmare. Beyond the auditorium, there was no electricity, and when you came down the halls, it was dark. It was like a cave, a very, very spooky place, especially in the evenings." Harper concedes that the theatre troupe members probably scared each other as they crawled all over the space not knowing who was where. "On the second floor," says Harper, "you always had the feeling that someone was watching you. When we first came in the building, there were feral cats who had taken over, so there were always these eerie scratching sounds." Harper remembers one evening when his hair "stood on end." "There was a costume party and I was late. I had to go upstairs to the costume room by myself and I had to use a flashlight. This soft, scratching sound starts. I couldn't figure out if the scratcher had four legs or two legs . . . or even a body at all, so I grabbed a costume and got out of there."

Warren Harper has never seen the ghost, but the two people who have both swear that when they spotted the short male figure in the hall, he was walking away from them, lost in thought as if he didn't even know they were there. Harper surmises that the former principal was probably more focused on finding his students. "If ever a spirit should be haunting this building, it's got to be Herman Solomon. He loved this place. This was his life."

In downtown Greenville in a red brick building once teeming with life, a despondent reporter decided that life was not worth living. His troubled spirit appears on the upper floor of the historic *Delta Democrat Times* newspaper office.

The *Delta Democrat Times* newspaper rose to fame under the leadership of Hodding Carter II. In 1946, Carter won the Pulitzer Prize for his

An unhappy spirit haunts the second floor of the original Delta Democrat Times building.

editorials advocating racial tolerance and his series lambasting the ill-treatment of Japanese American soldiers returning from World War II. Today, the newspaper operates out of new quarters on North Broadway Street. The original site, on the corner of Walnut and Main, is a hollow shell. The only living occupant is metal artist John "Puddin'" Moore.

Puddin' crafts fish, butterflies, and swamp scenes out of scrap metal found along the levee. He works in the garage annex attached to the back of the old newspaper offices. This skilled sculptor is familiar with the history of the building and has no issue sharing space with any of its ghosts. "I hear bumps and noises and all kinds of things up there, but I don't pay no attention to it. This place has been a lot of different things—newspaper office, funeral home, furniture company, paint store—so it's hard to tell who the ghost might have been." Puddin' works as he talks, shifting sheets of metal on two scarred, wooden tables. A crumbling brick wall separates his studio space from the main structure.

Puddin' is a wiry man who moves deftly through the years of accumulated debris. He leads the way up a back staircase into a barren, cavernous second-floor room. Bare light sockets dangle fifteen feet from the ceiling on black electrical cords. "The newspaper moved out of here in 1967. It's spooky up here. Used to be where they had the printing presses, typeset everything by hand." The trapped heat is oppressive. The artist saunters over to a large freight elevator along the rear wall.

Running gnarled fingers through the thick wedge of white hair splayed over his forehead, he spins off a tale of a gruesome encounter. "See, back when the newspaper was still here, there was a custodian. They usually worked in groups of two or three, but that night he was by himself. He came up the freight elevator, stepped out of the door, and the ghost was staring back at him. The old man ghost was in all white, like a shroud." Puddin' says the only color on the figure was a long gray beard. "That guy, after he saw the ghost, he dropped everything, flew out the door, and down the street. He called the editor and said, 'If you want the building locked up, you'd better send somebody else because I am not going back up there.' He said, 'I wasn't seeing things either because this old man just stood perfectly still and stared at me.'"

Puddin' gives a whirlwind tour of the building. The curving front stairwell ends halfway down. Skeletal pigeon and other unidentifiable

The entrance to the Delta Democrat Times.

animal remains, rotting steps, and fallen slates from the ceiling barricade the descent. Mold makes breathing difficult. Puddin' offers to hoist the freight elevator, which is operated by a series of ropes and weights. I give him a negative response, and we return to the ground floor via the relatively clutter-free rear staircase.

More detritus awaits. A sixteen-foot boat, complete with outboard motor, is parked on a trailer. In the back corner, broken pieces of furniture are piled to the ceiling. It is hard to imagine that the legendary newspaperman Hodding Carter ever worked out of this space. Puddin' waves his arms and draws a picture of a room once humming with the click of typewriter keys. "There were cubbyholes all over here, and the editor had his own office back there." He indicates another spot under a bank of windows. "One guy who worked here found out his wife cheated on him, and he blew his brains out. Might be that's his ghost upstairs." Puddin' delivers this bit of shocking news as he ambles off to the garage to point out the high water mark from the 1927 flood that inundated Greenville.

Back in his studio, this artist and collector shows off the bottles, arrowheads, and bones he has scavenged from the riverbanks. A true Greenville character, Puddin' is as comfortable with the ghosts of the old *Delta Democrat Times* building as he is with his artifacts. "Been here twenty-five years; nothing surprises me."

Postscript: Bragging rights to a teddy bear and a frog. At South Main and Crescent streets, a historic marker in the Live Oak Cemetery leads to the tale of a presidential bear and a former slave buried nearby. In 1902, Theodore Roosevelt arrived in the Delta for a much-anticipated hunting expedition. By the light of a campfire, Holt Collier, the "greatest bear hunter of all time," promised to capture a bear for the president. Collier delivered, but an empathetic Roosevelt couldn't shoot. Roosevelt's failure to shoot was satirized in a political cartoon. Inspired by the president's sympathy for the bear, a toy maker created the now immortal "Teddy Bears." The city of Greenville boasts that the origin of the cuddly bears began with Holt Collier and a presidential visit to the Delta.

Just down Highway 82 in Leland, another Mississippi native son created one of the most popular children's characters of all times. As a child, Muppet master Jim Henson played along the banks of Deer Creek. The frolicking swamp creatures captured the child's imagination. He ran home, tore up an old coat of his mother's, cut a ping pong ball in half for eyes, and Kermit the Frog arrived on the scene. The Washington County Welcome Center displays an original Kermit and offers an opportunity to pose with a larger-than-life-sized version of the beloved green Muppet.

Legendary characters, real or imagined, warm and fuzzy, or spectral and spooky, thrive in Greenville, the timeless "Heart and Soul of the Delta."

12

Lake Washington's Lonely Spirits

Eighteen miles south of Greenville lies one of the most serene and ancient lakes in the Delta. Seven hundred years ago when the mighty Mississippi changed course, it created an oxbow lake. Two separate bends in the river merged to form Lake Washington. Before the lake was formally named, Native American tribes, such as the Choctaws, camped on its banks and enjoyed its abundant hunting and fishing grounds.

One Choctaw guide is said to have shown this natural wonder to Indian agent Robert Ward. In 1825, Ward purchased two thousand acres for fifty dollars in gold. His transaction brought white settlers to the region. Wealthy planters with impressive lineages, including Hezekiah William Foote, Frederick G. Turnball, Scotsman S. M. Spencer, Wade Hampton, and Henry and Elizabeth Johnson, recognized the potential of the fertile delta soil. Cotton plantations spread out across the eastern shores and small villages emerged.

Today, the glory days are gone. Village stores are shuttered. The magnificent mansions of the cotton barons are reduced to a footnote in history. Along East Lake Washington Road—more shell pathway than paved roadway—two faded ladies are the last holdouts of an unprecedented era. Their haunted appearances fuel ghost tales passed from generation to generation in the tiny hamlet of Glen Allan.

On a searing hot day in late August, the mirrored surface of Lake Washington is stretched taut and still. The bluegill, crappie, and catfish have retreated to its cool depths. The parched brown branches of the cypress trees are scorched to their tips. Only the cicadas seem to take a perverse joy in the oxygen-depleted air. Their spirited singing is disorienting. As the males contract their internal timbal muscles, their hollow stomachs amplify the clicking noises, virtually drowning out the voices of the humans gathered below the trees.

Mike Jones, a local fishing guide and owner of Bait n' Thangs Tackle Shop, wipes the sweat raining down from his forehead. He is conflicted. Standing by a side entrance to the crumbling Mt. Holly Plantation house, he wants people to appreciate this lonely remnant of the Delta's history, but he won't cross the threshold. His fear does not stem from any physical danger inside the deteriorating structure. Rather it is a deep-down-gut-induced warning that whatever lurks inside is not warm and friendly. "I listen to my instincts. You don't have to worry about me going no further. Ain't going to happen."

With his broad, barrel chest; curling biceps; and bristly white beard, Jones could easily slip into frontier garb and walk among the early settlers. His physical presence is imposing; the unacquainted might hold back. Yet he speaks with a gentle voice, filled with genuine warmth. Jones

Mt. Holly waits to be rescued on the shores of Lake Washington.

checks up periodically on the condition of the abandoned plantation built in 1856 by Margaret Johnson Erwin. He has no idea if it was Margaret's annoyed spirit who slammed the door in his face on an earlier visit; however, he does take the action to heart.

The incident occurred when Jones had escorted two women to the site on the lake's eastern shore. Both women were interested in preserving the historic home described as one of the finest examples of Italianate Villa architecture. They had circled past the large side veranda and were near the old kitchen annex, which juts out in the back. An arched walkway runs along one side of the house. The covered passageway had been enclosed with panes of glass during its conversion into a bed and breakfast. Jones's eyes close into slits as he recalls the episode.

On that morning, a single wooden door leading to the kitchen space is ajar. The two women enter first. Jones steps up to follow, only to have the door fly into his face with a vengeance. He stumbles backwards. As he makes his retreat, he spies the fleeting shape of a woman running down the passageway next to the kitchen.

Jones is firm in his conviction that the figure he saw was not human. Although the apparition was transparent, there was enough of a form for him to know that the door-slammer was female. Despite the ghost's rejection, Jones rarely turns down requests to guide interested parties to Mt. Holly. "History is a big thing with me. I hate having this place run down like this."

Mt. Holly is fading fast. The carved balusters on the balconies have been battered by the elements; those that remain are nearly stripped of their decorative paint and bleached to a dull gray. Windowpanes are broken or missing entirely. Most alarming is the condition of the slave-made, red clay brick. Chunks have disintegrated, undermining the integrity of the columns and the exterior walls. One preservationist source attributes the loss to "incorrect maintenance by a previous owner in the 1970-1980s." In an attempt to repoint the brick, the original lime mortar, which naturally breathes with the soft bricks, was replaced with a cement-based mortar that can't react to the change in seasons. The missing sections of brick look as if some monster hand has reached in and clawed out random chunks.

Also at odds with the historic façade are the more contemporary screen doors that hang off-kilter. The radical angle of the screens make the double front doors behind them appear as if they too are leaning away from the house. On the roof, the leftover scraps of dingy white tarp finish off the distressed, haunted house appearance. The tarp fragments dangle limply from the eaves—torn shrouds pierced with nails—offering no function other than to add another layer of disgraceful neglect. On moonlight nights, with a light breeze lifting the tattered scraps, the effect is that of a thousand shrouded spirits dancing on the roof.

Mike Jones had also visited Mt. Holly in its waning days of human occupation, when the family of Margaret Johnson had moved out, the thirty-two rooms were renovated as an upscale bed-and-breakfast retreat. After this commercial enterprise failed, the then-owners rented it out for weddings and special occasions. A few area businesses—caterers, florists, and rental supply companies—benefited from the large mansion's continued, if sporadic, use.

In addition to his tackle shop and RV campgrounds on the lake, Jones also operates a Christmas tree farm. The last time he actually ventured inside Mt. Holly was the day he delivered Christmas trees as part of the décor for a wedding ceremony at the mansion. "They were setting up right inside the lobby there, by that front parlor, and that's as far as I've ever been." Jones says that he set up his trees on stands as quickly as he could and got out. When asked why he was never curious to see more of the home, and why he planned on a quick exit, his reply is succinct: "You get that eerie feeling that someone or something is watching you, and you get out. If you're uncomfortable somewhere, you leave."

Other curious souls, who happen to come upon the neglected home, have described more pleasant encounters. One traveler from Louisiana wrote on her blog that after poking around and peering in windows, she is positive she heard music coming from the old piano and the soft sounds of laughter.

Reports have circulated that the current owner, who purchased the house in 2001, lives in Texas and his plans for the property are uncertain. Within the past few years, a house trailer was moved to the grounds. It sits at the edge of the front lawn, obscuring the view of the house from the lake. Workers lived there temporarily, started repairs, and left. The trailer, like the grand lady behind it, also shows signs of vandalism and neglect.

Visitors have heard music coming from the abandoned piano in the parlor.

If the ghost of original owner Margaret Johnson does return, she would likely be appalled. Floral wallpaper hangs in ragged strips. The stunning rosewood staircase with its trumpet balusters is littered with debris, making passage upwards impossible. Sections of the intricate plaster friezes, lining the fourteen-foot ceilings, and the carved medallions over the chandeliers have crashed to the floor. Curiously, the glass-and-bronze chandeliers and the marble mantels in the dining room and parlor have survived. The library's floor-to-ceiling shelves are lined with books, their condition unknown. In the pink front room, a massive antique mahogany piano is shoved against the interior wall. In such unstable conditions of heat, humidity, and cold, if ghostly fingers do run over the warped keys, as has been reported by a few visitors and backed by local rumors, the resulting sound would have to be horrific.

Recently, reporter and Webmaster Woodrow "Woody" Wilkins of CBS-affiliate WXVT-Delta News arrived on the scene to file a report. Following interviews with Mike Jones and me, Wilkins shifted the camera

Peeling wallpaper inside Mt. Holly.

to his shoulder and circled the grounds to shoot additional footage of the exterior. Upon completing his circuit, Wilkins returned and stood underneath the Palladian-style front archway. He lowered his camera to the ground and made two announcements. While shooting in the rear, he turned around to get a shot of the wooded area in back. As he did, a sudden sound, like a thud or a crash, came from the second floor of the house. He aimed the camera at one of the upper windows, zoomed in, and saw nothing. Wilkins grew up in the Delta and lifts his broad shoulders in dismissal. "I used to visit my sister in Jackson. We'd come up from Rolling Fork, and we could see Mt. Holly from the highway. As a child, it always had the look you'd expect from one of the old Scooby Doo cartoon haunted houses."

Jones, who has remained in the front, is staring at the wrought-iron balcony directly above Wilkins's head. Jones tells the assembled group to watch the faded curtain panel in the left front window. It is pinched

An unseen hand shakes the curtain in the window above the balcony.

about a third of the way down as if a hand has grabbed on to it. Although the air is still, the curtain moves back and forth in a rapid shaking motion. Suddenly, a welcome gust of wind lifts the strips of torn tarp on the roof. They flap in the breeze, blowing from left to right. The curtain panel stops its shaking motion and then is pulled from right to left, hugging the doorframe.

Mike Jones turns his back and heads for his black pick-up truck. He lets the bronze National Register marker have the final say.

MOUNT HOLLY
CIRCA 1856
Steeped in the history of the Mississippi Delta

It should, perhaps, more accurately read *"Steeped in the mystery of the Mississippi Delta."*

A short ride down the road from Mt. Holly is the Susie B. Law House. Even Jones is shocked by its appearance—or near disappearance. An insidious, tangled mat of creeping vines envelops the entire front of the house, from ground level to hipped roof.

Now hidden by the dense overgrowth, the main architectural elements of the house are a two-story, columned portico over the front entrance; a black, wrought-iron balcony separating two sets of matching double doors, each with oval glass inserts and glass transoms; and identical bay windows on the ground floor. There is nothing left of the rear of the house. No repairs are under way. The lawn is mowed sporadically, creating a wide expanse of yellowish-brown scorched earth facing the lake. To the right, nearly crushed by the weight of the heavy vines, a miniature playhouse cries out to be rescued. The playhouse is identical in design to the big house and, in happier times, must have delighted some very pampered little girls.

Five years ago, Jones was returning from Glen Allan on the way to his bait shop. "It was right before Halloween and it was raining. Nobody had been in that house since I've been here, and I've been here since 1997." Jones pinches the bridge of his nose with two fingers and shakes his head. "I was coming down the road, and I could see light inside the house. It's all dark except for this little light going up, so I eased down.

Vines creep over the front of the haunted Susie B. Law house on the lake.

A playhouse is barely holding up under the weight of the vines.

There wasn't even electricity hooked up to the house at that time. When I got to the front, there was a little ole bitty, frail lady holding a coal oil lamp. She was climbing up the steps."

Jones is leaning against the side of his truck, arms crossed and wrapped around his chest. Back then, he explains, the vines had not spread across the house, and he had a clear view of the woman through the windows on both floors. "You could see in as plain as day. There was a real tiny lady, wearing a white dress, a nightgown kind of thing, and as best I could tell carrying an oil lamp in her hand. She had a little bun on the back of her head. When I first saw her, she was at the bottom, and I watched her go slowly up the steps all the way to the top."

"Initially, I thought it was a real person. I mean, you see the light inside a normally dark house, and you assume somebody's broken in. I am sitting there thinking, 'Who is this?' I was fixing to call the sheriff's department, and then I got to looking at her some more and I said, 'Uh, uh. Something about her ain't right.'"

Jones decided that reporting an apparition to the sheriff might not be the best idea. "So I went on and got myself away from there. Later, I told a good friend of ours, who is kin with the people, with the actual granddaughter of Susie B. I described the lady in the house, and she checked with the family and told me that my description could fit that of the last owner—Miss Susie B." Jones nods his head sagely. "Folks have always said it was haunted. It's had that reputation every since Susie B. died."

Postscript: The families who lived at Mt. Holly Plantation and the Susie B. Law House have strong interconnecting ties to Lake Washington. Indian agent Robert Ward deeded his lakefront property to his eighteen-year-old son, Julius Ward. The young Ward built Erwin House at the head of the lake in 1830. One mile north of Erwin House, landowners Henry and Elizabeth Johnson ran a cotton plantation on more than two thousand acres of land with 103 slaves. In 1855, Henry sold part of his increased holdings of four thousand acres to his daughter Margaret. Margaret Johnson Erwin built Mt. Holly and settled in to enjoy the expansive lake view. In the 1880s, former Confederate officer Hezekiah William Foote added Mt. Holly to his extensive holdings of Delta plantations. State

The ruins of St. John's Episcopal Church on Lake Washington.

senator Huger Lee Foote inherited Mt. Holly from his father. Noted author and Civil War historian Shelby Foote used the family plantation as the setting for the fictional Solitaire in his novel *Tournament*.

By Mike Jones' reckoning, the Law family story falls along similar lines. "The Laws have lived on the banks of Lake Washington since before the Civil War." The family and their descendants are buried a short pace down the road at Evergreen Cemetery. The approach to the cemetery is marked by the ruins of St. John's Episcopal Church. Built around 1830, St. John's Episcopal was one of the first churches in the region. During the Civil War, desperate soldiers melted down the lead frames around the stained-glass windows to make Confederate Minié balls. In 1907, the church took a direct hit from a tornado. A partial wall, the cornerstones, and a short portion of the belfry are the sole structural survivors.

The ruins of St. John's and the crumbling tombstones in Evergreen Cemetery bare witness to a complex settlement history along the lake, consisting of Native Americans, African slave labor, Civil War soldiers, and settlers rich and poor. "This is the heritage of the Delta. This represents who we are here in Washington County." Mike Jones views it all with profound sadness imbued with stubborn Southern pride.

13

Jackson's Capitol and Madison's Chapel

Voices from the past can convey a message, a thought, an emotion, or even a warning. At the Old Capitol Museum in Jackson, one dedicated spirit invested his entire life trying to improve the health of his fellow citizens. Twenty miles north of Jackson, another spirit risked a life of love for honor. The one he left behind mourns his passing at the Chapel of the Cross in Madison.

Following his death on January 9, 1959, Dr. Felix Underwood continued to earn accolades as "the man who saved a million lives." Underwood was born November 21, 1882, in Nettleton, a railroad town in Northeast Mississippi. At ten years of age, Felix watched helplessly as his mother died of infection following childbirth. Underwood made it his mission to revamp the public health practices of his day. Many believe that the good doctor's haunted footsteps in the corridors of the Old Capitol Museum are a sign he has not given up his quest.

The former state capitol building on South State Street is a survivor. From 1839 to 1903, this grand edifice hosted the Mississippi legislature. After sixty-four years of glorious service, it was abandoned when a new government building was erected to house the needs of a new era. In 1917, a group of ardent preservationists proposed restoring the structure and repurposing it for use by state agencies, including the board of health. In January of 1921, Felix Underwood, M.D., was appointed director of the Bureau of Child Hygiene and Welfare. The former country doctor became executive officer of the Mississippi State Board of Health in 1924, a position he held for the next thirty-four years.

Ruth Cole works as the daytime hostess for the Old Capitol Museum.

The Old Capitol Museum in Jackson echoes with eerie sounds.

Dr. Underwood's portrait hangs in the Mississippi Hall of Fame.

Her personality is as cheerful and inviting as the floral-print linen jacket she wears. She is happy to share her years of knowledge of the history of the building and its occupants. She has high praise for Dr. Underwood. "Even after he retired, he was so dedicated that he'd come here to check on things on a volunteer basis. During that time, he had a heart attack while he was sitting at a desk and died."

Cole stands behind a large, half-moon-shaped welcome desk in the rotunda. To her immediate left, a museum security guard, in dark blue pants and shirt, sits and stares at a split-screen monitor. Cole leans over the glass counter and lowers her voice. "Some of our security police prefer not to be here at night. They think they hear somebody walking the halls when there is no one else in the building and nothing shows up on the security screens." One eyebrow arches sharply upward when it is suggested that the disembodied footsteps might belong to the deceased Dr. Underwood. "Well, he's the only one I know of to have actually died in the building."

Cole unfolds a brochure for a young couple just wandering in. The layout of the first floor is highlighted in blue. The two head off on their self-guided tour. Cole's smile is genuine as she watches them set out. "I'm never here at night. I'm lucky. When I hear footsteps, they all belong to real people."

Clay Williams is the museum's director. He is aware of the stories of the footsteps, along with another repetitive nocturnal sound. "I've had officers tell me that during the middle of the night, they hear kind of a thump coming from Dr. Underwood's old office on the first floor." At the time of Dr. Underwood's fatal heart attack, he fell forward and his head hit the top of the desk.

The museum takes a conservative stance when it comes to linking either the footsteps or the thumping sound to the good doctor. "We do get people who will ask if we have a ghost, and if they can do a paranormal investigation to prove who the ghost might be. The answer is no. The Mississippi Department of Archives and History would rather not be involved; we prefer that the emphasis be on the actual history."

Through the years, the paranormal sounds in the museum have struck a variety of chords. One incident involved Williams and his predecessor, Lucy Allen. "Back then, before Hurricane Katrina shut us down, I was in charge of exhibits. We were finishing up a temporary exhibit, and we were there pretty much every night to make the deadline," says Williams. "Lucy was my director at the time. She was in her office and heard a bunch of banging around and assumed it was us."

Allen now serves as museum division director over all the state facilities. She summons up the basic facts of that evening. "Clay Williams, my head of the exhibits, and his assistant, John Gardner, had been working all day on the ground floor. My office is on the second floor. We close at five o'clock. A lot of times, I would stay after five. It was close to six, and I was ready to head out. When I opened my door, I heard them, or what I thought was them, continuing to work downstairs. My first thoughts were 'my goodness, I am going to tell them that they need to go home. It's time we all go home and start over again tomorrow. They just need to take a break. They've been working way too hard.'"

Allen usually left the building by way of a back staircase leading to the parking lot. Due to her concerns about the staff, she chose to descend the grand staircase. "I wanted to be able to go past the exhibit room off the rotunda where they were working." Although she had just been listening to the distinct sounds of hammers and saws, "there was not anybody in the exhibit room. Not another soul in the building." Allen took a moment to assess the situation. "It did make me wonder why I was hearing as many noises as I was hearing, and how could that be?"

The next morning, Allen checked in with her staff. "I asked Clay and John had they been staying late? Had they just gone out the door before I had? They said no. They had gone at the regular time—five o'clock; they were exhausted. They looked at me strangely and asked, 'Lucy, are you hearing things?' And I said, 'As a matter of fact, I am.'" Allen has a comfortable laugh, unafraid to appreciate the humor of the situation. "The sounds were very, very distinctive. It was definitely hammering and shuffling of things around on the floor. I heard that." The identity of the helpful poltergeists may never be known.

Allen also agrees that one of the most powerful exhibits in the museum does inadvertently evoke a sense of spirits returned from the dead. In the restored, second-floor Senate Chamber, wooden desks are set inside a ring of fluted columns. Ghostly, off-white, life-sized replicas of senators sit, stand, and gesture. A debate is in progress. The passage of the 1839

The ghostly figures in the Senate Chamber.

Married Woman's Property Act sparks a heated exchange. A cacophony of male voices echo off the walls as advocates and opponents fight to have the final word: *"Women are worthy of being queens; This will sew discord and fraud."* A spotlight shines down on each of the spectral figures as he makes his argument pro or con.

"One thing we wanted to do was bring history alive, rather than just show a stagnant room." Allen offers an explanation in defense of the eerie effect. "The monochromatic mannequins give you a flavor of the period, but at the same time, they do not depict a particular person, decade, or style of dress. The time period for the three debates you hear is from 1839 to 1903; that's when that chamber was used." Allen adds that the audio component, the "speaking statues," helps instill a greater sense of the hopes, expectations, and challenges facing these early leaders.

Prior to the final installation, the statues arrived "bagged and tagged." It was a bizarre sight—humanlike forms encased in individual, clear, plastic shrouds. They reclined on their backs and sides; some had knees bent to be placed in chairs behind the desks. One anonymous staffer couldn't resist temptation. After unwrapping a standing statue, he positioned the "senator," with arm raised and finger outstretched, near one of the windows facing the street. Backlit by the lights inside the renovated Senate Chamber, passersby would do a double take at the six-foot-tall specter, standing in the window and gesturing down.

Clay Williams concurs. "I'm sure the sight of this all-white, humanlike form in the window at night spawned a host of stories that the museum is haunted."

Lucy Allen is unruffled at the prank. "There has to be some times when you have a little chuckle or fun with things . . . or it makes for some very long days."

North of the capital city of Jackson, in the rolling hills of Madison, a country chapel is forever haunted by a day that ended with the tragic death of a groom-to-be. A century and a half later, the ghost of the almost bride mourns at his gravesite.

The bride was the fair Helen, youngest daughter of John and Margaret Johnstone. Helen met her future fiancé, Henry Grey Vick, when his carriage broke down near Ingleside, her sister's stunning home. It was Christmas of 1857, and the dashing young man and the demur young lady fell immediately in love. At the insistence of Margaret, Helen's mother, Henry agreed to wait until Helen turned twenty before making her his wife. Henry courted Helen for two long years, traveling back and forth from Vicksburg to Madison County. At last, in the spring of 1859, wedding preparations were in progress. Helen and her sister Frances Britton helped their mother decorate the family's castlelike home, Annandale. The wedding ceremony would be held on the grounds of the Chapel of the Cross.

Local lore has it that during their courtship, Helen elicited one promise from her beloved: that he would never again use dueling as a means of settling a dispute. Four days before the wedding, Henry left for a trip to his family's ancestral home in Vicksburg and then on to New Orleans. While in the bustling port city, Henry ran into Laurence Washington Stith, a former classmate. Somewhere between the pleasantries and

The Chapel of the Cross in Madison.

reminiscing, a perceived slight escalated into a full-blown accusation of sullying a man's honor. Dueling was illegal, so both men agreed to meet in secret at Bascomb Course in Mobile and resolve the issue facing them by drawing weapons.

There are two prevailing versions of what transpired during the duel. The first is that Henry belatedly realized he was breaking his promise to Helen. To try to mitigate the circumstances, he kept to part of his vow; he would not kill. Henry shot his gun in the air and expected James to do the same, thinking the two men would walk off the field together with their lives and honor intact.

C.M. Stanley, in an article for the *Alabama Journal,* holds with a different truth. Both men were lousy shots. Vick aimed for Stith's forehead. The bullet missed and struck a tree behind him; Stith aimed for Vick's body, but shot him in the head instead.

Whatever the intent of the combatants, twenty-five-year-old Henry Grey Vick laid dead on the ground. Hours later, his body was placed on a steamer bound from New Orleans to Vicksburg. Also said to be on the steamer were a caterer with a crew of cooks and waiters and food for the much-anticipated wedding festivities to be held upriver at Annandale.

At Annandale, a servant announced that a courier on horseback was racing up the driveway. Mrs. Johnstone read the terse note: *"Henry Vick killed today. Duel in Mobile."* Helen screamed and fell to the floor. The wedding decorations were hastily pulled down and funeral preparations begun. At midnight on May 20, 1859, mourners gathered. Men were stationed with torches to light the long driveway leading up to the Chapel of the Cross. Digging commenced for a grave for the groom in the cemetery behind the rear altar of the chapel. Helen was said to have worn her wedding gown to the service. She cut off locks of her hair and placed them over the heart of the fallen groom-to-be.

Helen swore she would never marry another. A tombstone made to resemble the crossed limbs of a hewn tree trunk was erected at the head of Henry's grave. Helen had an iron bench installed next to it. Here she sat day after day, month after month, pining for her lost love.

Three years later, Helen's resolved weakened. In August of 1862, she married Dr. George C. Harris, a Confederate chaplain, who went on to serve as clergyman at the Chapel of the Cross. The couple lived at Mt.

Henry Vick's tombstone in the cemetery.

Helena, a grand home in Sharkey County. Helen Johnstone Harris died a widow in 1917, six years after her husband. By all accounts, it was a happy marriage, but Helen never forgot her first true love. In her final moments, she believed she was a young bride again about to walk down the aisle; she died peacefully with a vision of Henry waiting for her.

On balmy spring nights, the "Bride of Annandale" returns to the Chapel of the Cross. Light from the full moon catches in the folds of Helen's wedding gown as she steps lightly through the cemetery and sits on the bench next to Henry's grave.

Ruth Cole works at the Old Capitol Museum in Jackson and is a lifelong resident of the area. "I am a member of the Children of the American Revolution, and as part of service to the community, we'd help out at historic sites." Cole remembers excursions to the Chapel of the Cross. "This was a time when that area of the county was not as developed as it is now; it was very, very, rural. The setting itself, the woods, was a bit spooky. The chapel was only open once a month on Sundays. We'd go there to help with the cleaning. We'd sweep and dust."

Helen's ghost likes to sit on the bench near Henry's grave.

Cole says that as a child, she had heard the stories of Henry and Helen and that Helen's ghost returned sometimes to the cemetery. "It was all a bit eerie."

Postscript. The formal entrance to the cemetery is to the immediate right of the chapel. A pair of massive iron gates is inscribed with the family name—Johnstone. The gates are an intricate design of intertwined branches and leaves. Henry Vick's grave and Helen's bench are underneath the arched chapel windows. Scattered throughout the rural cemetery are other carved headstones and statuary. Most touching are the tributes by grieving parents for children lost in infancy. One headstone is capped with a stone pillow. Tassels hang from the four corners. In bas-relief, two little girls, one appearing slightly younger and smaller than the other, lay on their sides. The tiny replicas face each other, knees slightly bent. The inscription on the base of the tomb gives only their first

The little girl spirits like to swing on the cemetery gates.

Two sisters share a stone pillow.

The headstone of Helen and Anna.

names—Anna and Helen. One sweet tale relays that the spirits of the girls are occasionally seen playing and swinging on the cemetery gates.

Debbie Rayner, a tall, thin, pale, blond-haired woman, is a member of the Altar Guild at the Chapel of the Cross. She says she is unaware of who the ghost children might be. Spectral visitors don't bother her; the intruders she wishes would just find another home are of the furry variety. After the morning service, she helps to pull a large sheet of plastic over the altar. "We have flying squirrels that leave droppings; they squeeze inside through holes near the rafters." Rayner also has a problem with a few of the more lurid tales associated with the historic chapel. "This is still an active Episcopal church. There was an article in the *Northside Sun,* our local paper, and it talked about blood appearing on the floor like this was a crime scene. It bothered me. It's the opposite of how we feel about this place. More than anything, for most of us in the congregation, it is very peaceful here."

As a precaution, at dusk, the gates at the bottom of the hill leading to the chapel and the cemetery are locked. Visitors real or imagined are not encouraged after hours.

Rowan Oak deep in Bailey's Woods.

14

Rowan Oak

It is my ambition to be as private a person as possible, abolished and voided from history . . . that the sum and history of my life, which in the same sentence is my obit and epitaph too, shall be both:
He made the books and he died.
—William Faulkner

A peculiar genius, Nobel Prize-winning author William Cuthbert Faulkner reveled in a good ghost story. Hunkered down at Rowan Oak, his home and retreat on the outskirts of Oxford, Mississippi, he wrote about the darker side of human emotions in nineteen acclaimed adult novels and eighty short stories. He saved the tale of his favorite ghost for the children. She was the beautiful Judith Sheegog.

Faulkner delighted in repeating the supernatural yarn of a tragic spirit who haunted the gardens. "The one interesting thing about Faulkner's favorite ghost is that he never wrote the story down, so I've heard five or six different versions," says William Griffith, the curator of Rowan Oak. "One version is that the daughter of the original owner, Col. Robert Sheegog, fell in love with two soldiers and couldn't decide which one to marry. They killed each other in a duel, and Judith threw herself off the balcony because there would be no one to court her anymore. Another twist on the tale is that Judith was killed by a stray bullet when the two soldiers fought over her." A sly smile slips out as the curator delivers version number three. "One was a Confederate soldier, the other was Union. He was the one Judith really loved, and when he was killed in battle, she threw herself off the balcony." And for a final bit of drama, there is option number four. Judith was climbing down a rope ladder, tied to the balcony, to elope with her beloved Union soldier. She slipped and fell to her death.

Drew Chiles is a history student pursuing a master's degree at the University of Mississippi. He works as a part-time guide at Rowan Oak. Chiles is familiar with the saga of Judith Sheegog. "She had been unlucky in love, flung herself off the balcony, and her body is buried underneath the magnolia tree."

Griffith settles into a worn armchair in a back hallway of Rowan Oak. "They are all great stories with one common denominator—Judith dies in every one. She ends up buried in the garden in the front of the house and the garden is haunted." The curator's thin frame is nearly lost among the oversized chair cushions. Dressed in a rumpled white shirt and slacks, he is every inch the distracted scholar focused on facts, not fashion. "Faulkner may have created the different versions himself. At Halloween, he was known to tell the story with props, rattling chains . . . and another time he enlisted Cho-Cho, his eldest stepdaughter. While the other children were asleep, he had Cho-Cho slip downstairs and start playing the piano. Faulkner got the other kids up by telling them, 'Oh, the piano is playing by itself.' Of course, Cho-Cho ran and hid." Griffith realigns himself in the chair. "Faulkner loved ghost stories. Who doesn't? Especially in a house like this, you'd expect it to be haunted, have a ghost. You'd want it to have a ghost."

Faulkner certainly agreed, and he had an ulterior motive for keeping Judith's restless spirit alive. When he purchased the home in 1930, it was known simply as the old Bailey Place. The dense forest that surrounded the Greek Revival home was called Bailey's Woods. "It was pretty run down; the house had been abandoned for about seven years, and the pastures were rented out to a farmer who kept his herds on the grounds," says Griffith.

Faulkner was immediately enamored with the Gothic state of disrepair. While he updated the electricity and the plumbing inside the house, and later added an addition to the back, he wanted the gardens left as overgrown ruins. He concurred completely with second owner Grace Bailey, who called the entire grounds "a vulgar formality."

Estelle, Faulkner's wife, disagreed. She especially wanted to restore

Judith's burial site in Rowan Oak's garden.

Colonel Sheegog's antebellum maze garden in the front of the house. A circle of cedars ringed the perimeter. Inside the maze, concentric circles of raised brick beds contained sweet shrub and privet hedges. A magnolia tree grew in the center. During the Reconstruction era, and later by Grace Bailey's strict edict, the maze garden was left untended. "She just let the landscaping go. Volunteer trees—we call them that because they are self-seeding—grew up between the bricks and their heavy shade wiped out the hedges." Griffith says that Estelle argued with her husband and even tried to enlist the support of her children to restore the garden to its original splendor. Faulkner argued back that "only new money would ruin that garden." To ensure that nothing in the garden would ever be disturbed, Faulkner resurrected the ghost of Judith. "He said that if anyone messes with Judith's garden, where she is buried, it will anger her spirit. She'll come to haunt the house instead of the garden," states Griffith.

Faulkner won. Today, towering magnolia trees dominate the space.

Widespread branches, lush with iridescent green leaves and fragrant blossoms, cover the red bricks. "We maintain it the way Faulkner liked it, not as Colonel Sheggog and his family had it." Griffith admits, that just like Estelle, some contemporary visitors also object. "Yes, to the surprise, shock, and sometimes horror of many garden club members, we have not brought it back to the 1840s. We keep the property as Faulkner had . . . and that's all we'll ever do."

Rowan Oak was donated to the University of Mississippi by Faulkner's daughter, Jill, with the understanding that it remain as it was when her father was alive. The Do-Not-Disturb policy also guarantees that the alleged burial spot of the ghost of Judith Sheegog will remain untouched.

Faulkner lived on the property for two years before he gave it a name. "Faulkner loved legends. He was greatly influenced by Sir James Frazer's *Golden Bough,* a giant twelve-volume series about Celtic folklore, so he called his home Rowan Oak for the rowan tree of Scotland and the oak tree of America." According to Celtic legend, the boughs of the rowan tree, when placed over a doorway, ward off evil spirits. "It was kind of a joke and it kind of wasn't a joke," explains Griffith. "Faulkner's evil spirits were the tax man and the media. He felt compelled to have his estate have a name because of Southern tradition, and he also took those traditions and put his own spin on them."

Inside Rowan Oak today, Faulkner's personal belongings are scattered about as if the writer has just moved on to the next room. His glasses rest on a pile of books in the library; his favorite pair of riding boots are standing by a chair; neckties are flung over a dresser mirror in the bedroom; a pipe and cans of tobacco await the owner in his study; and the upper third of the walls bear the large script of his handwritten outline for a novel. Student guide Chiles says that it's the little things that cause some to believe in Faulkner's abiding presence. "People that have worked here say that they would walk into a room and it would smell like pipe smoke." Chiles, a tall, young man with curly, light brown, shoulder-length hair, expresses disappointment tinged with hope. "I haven't seen anything, but I'm waiting. I am looking forward to it. I'd love to see his ghost writing on the walls the way some have reported."

"I'm not against people who do believe that William Faulkner is still here. That would be just too good to be true," says Griffith, suppressing a grin.

Faulkner's glasses where he left them in the front parlor.

Faulkner's bedroom with his riding boots and pants hung over the chair.

The study where William Faulkner liked to write on the walls.

"But if we do have a ghost, it's not him. [Every] once in awhile we'll get psychics, and if what they are saying is believable, what they describe to me sounds more like Colonel Sheegog than William Faulkner."

In an upstairs bedroom, psychics report sighting a spirit dressed in a dark frock coat and top hat. "They say the old gentleman keeps asking why he has so much company coming into his house, and the spirit complains to the psychics that he doesn't have enough staff to accommodate them all." Griffith adds that the curator before him would say he did hear unusual sounds, eerie enough to make the surroundings feel uncomfortable. With a slight dash of cynicism, Griffith says, "Sure, I'm uncomfortable too when I am here by myself at night. Who wouldn't be? It's pitch black out here. No street lights make it back this far. The only illumination outside is the single bulb in the porch light . . . but nothing has ever happened to me."

Griffith rethinks his statement. His eyes are drawn to a revolving rack in the corner. Its shelves are crammed with magazines, newspaper articles, and one mysterious photograph. He gets up, digs through a pile, and returns to show off an eight-by-ten glossy. "It's a weird photo," he begins. "When I first took over as curator, there was a lot of renovation, a bunch of work needed to be done. Once we got funding, we stood in the center of each room and took photographs in order for us to put the furniture back in the right spots."

The photo Griffith holds is an enlargement of Estelle's room. Faulkner had the room, with its light-filled windows, added for his wife to use as both bedroom and painting studio. There is an easel set-up in the corner near the bed. Griffith directs the attention to the north window in the photo. "I didn't notice this at first, but my assistant did. Look through the three panes on the bottom. In the center pane, you can see someone sitting on a bench. In the pane to the right, you see a little cherry tree, and there is a child or a woman standing next to it." Griffith grasps the photo with both hands and gives it a little shake. "If you go up to Estelle's bedroom right now, you can look through that window; you'll clearly see a grape arbor and behind that a house, the old servant's quarters." He holds the photo up for inspection. "This photograph was taken in January, wintertime. No big, leafy trees to block the view. In the photo, the house and the grape arbor are gone. Where they should be is a black void, negative space. In the foreground, we have a woman on a bench and another woman or child to the right as if they are conversing." On the day the photo was taken there were no visitors allowed on the grounds "What is so shocking about this is that it is a documentary photograph for the purpose of expediting a move. We did not take it to try and capture a ghost or prove anything other than the location of the furniture."

Mammy Callie's house is the wooden structure that has vanished in the photograph. Visitors to Rowan Oak can go to the backyard and still see the house Faulkner built for his beloved family caretaker, Caroline Barr, better known to all as "Mammy Callie." The clapboard cottage was erected on the same foundation as the old slave quarters. Mammy Callie lived there from 1930 to 1940. "Faulkner brought her to Rowan Oak when she was around ninety years old. She had been his nanny, but she didn't come here to retire. She took care of his two stepchildren and his daughter, Jill," says Griffith. Faulkner never knew his nanny's exact age. Mammy Callie was born a slave. She remembered being in her

Mammy Callie's house on the grounds.

mid-teens when the Civil War broke out and around twenty when it ended. She cared for Faulkner's children until the day she died from a stroke. Faulkner held her funeral service in the front parlor. She is buried in the African American section of the cemetery. The epitaph on her grave reads *"Mammy Callie. Her white children bless her."*

When asked to speculate if the figure on the bench in the photograph might be Mammy Callie, Griffith replies candidly, "I would love it. It wouldn't surprise me if it turned out to be her because she was very dedicated to the family. She really was very much part of the Faulkner family lore and affections."

As for the other phantom figures standing near the cherry tree, theories are all over the place. Colonel Sheegog's wife? Faulkner's wife? The cantankerous Grace Bailey? Could the second figure in the photo be that of a child? Faulkner's first daughter, Alabama, only lived nine days and is buried in the Faulkner family plot at St. Peter's, so she would seem unlikely. Faulkner's second daughter, Jill, lived to be a healthy adult. Naturally, the speculation veers toward Faulkner's beautiful ghost, the haunted Judith Sheegog. On the day the photo was taken, was she restless enough to venture from her burial place beneath the magnolia tree and join another group of spirits near the grape arbor? It would be a lovely thing, indeed.

Postscript: A cemetery and a statue. On finishing his final novel about the inhabitants of the fictional Yoknapatawpha County, Faulkner said he was done. He had "broken the pencil," and wasn't going to write any more. "He wanted to buy this big estate in Virginia, teach at the University of Virginia, and spend the rest of his years with his daughter and his grandchildren." Rowan Oak curator William Griffith says that although Faulkner was ill, his death in 1962 "shocked everyone."

"He was sixty-four, fell off his horse, and injured himself more severely than he realized. He resorted to his usual whiskey therapy, which is how he often dealt with injuries, heartache, or disappointment. He'd go to his room, go on a binge, and wait for it to pass. This time it was taking too long; he'd been lying in bed a couple of weeks, drinking very heavily, eating very little, and he asked Estelle to 'take me to the clinic in Byhalia.'" Estelle complied. However, according to Griffith, "As soon as the family left, he had a heart attack and died."

Faulkner often expressed a desire to be buried at Rowan Oak, but he never put his wishes in writing. "Estelle buried him at St. Peter's Cemetery in Oxford, and later she was buried next to him." Their side-by-side stone slabs are etched with names and dates. On her husband's, Estelle had inscribed *"Beloved Go With God."*

In lieu of flowers, there are occasional tributes from those who come to bring sustenance for Faulkner's spirit. On one dreary, wet, summer afternoon, it's an amber-colored bottle of beer. "He preferred whiskey," says Griffith, "but they'll leave a bottle of bourbon too." When quizzed about his basic requirements, Faulkner wrote, "The tools I need for my trade are paper, tobacco, food, and a little whiskey."

Griffith corrects one misconception about the famed novelist's drinking habits. "He didn't drink to write; he needed it to let go. He had a hard time letting go." A prodigious drinker, Faulkner had rules when

William and Estelle Faulkner's graves in St. Peter's Cemetery.

it came to imbibing. Griffith ticks them off, "You shouldn't drink beer after sunset, that's tacky. Vodka, scotch, bourbon, and whiskey are inside drinks, and gin is an outside drink. Mint juleps are served in a metal cup; no other kind of cup will do."

The town of Oxford prefers to honor longtime resident William Faulkner with pipe, not drink in hand. In the historic Oxford Courthouse Square, a bronze statue of Faulkner sits on a bench in front of the red-brick Romanesque Revival Oxford City Hall. When the statue was dedicated in 1997, on the centennial of Faulkner's birth, family and some friends objected, saying they didn't get it right either. "Faulkner made it very clear how he felt about statues; he was against them," states Griffith. "The family felt it was a tasteless gesture. . . . He never would have sat on a public bench in a welcoming posture for you to sit next to him." In one newspaper article, his brother, Chooky Faulkner, wondered, "What effect a stick of dynamite might have on it?" A nephew was unhappy with having his uncle being reduced to a tourist attraction.

Faulkner's controversial statue in front of Oxford's City Hall.

A *Saturday Evening Post* article quotes the author on his wishes for life after death: "If I was reincarnated, I'd want to come back as buzzard. Nothing hates him or envies him or wants him or needs him. He's never bothered or in danger."

Elvis Presley's birthplace in Tupelo.

15

The King Lives on in Tupelo

They arrive by plane, tour bus, RV, car, and motorcycle caravan. Three decades after his death, they come not to mourn, but to connect. For these die-hard fans, there is no question that Elvis's spirit lingers near his childhood home in Tupelo, Mississippi. "We have an elderly woman who visits four or five times a week," says Dick Guyton, executive director of the Elvis Presley Memorial Foundation. "She sits on the front porch on that swing right there and talks to Elvis. She moved from Florida to Tupelo to be closer to him." Guyton, a tall man, wearing a green museum polo shirt and khaki slacks, hesitates before revealing more. "At first, we thought she might be a distraction to other visitors. She has these animated conversations as if she can hear him. We don't know what she sees; she's never described her vision. This obviously means so much to her, so now we just let her be."

The fifteen-acre Elvis Presley Birthplace and Museum complex draws both the curious and the loyal. Local resident Lisa Hall is amazed. "People turn up in Tupelo from all over Europe and the United States. Two ladies—one's from Montana and one is from Idaho—they meet here every year to be near Elvis." Not all claim to see his ghost, but the experience of walking in Elvis's footsteps is often overwhelming.

Sybil Presley Clark is a distant cousin. She keeps vigil perched on a stool just inside the door of the two-room, shotgun-style cottage where the young Elvis lived. As the hostess assigned to the birthplace, Clark has dealt with a wide-range of reactions. "There was an Elvis impersonator from Brazil here the other day." Guyton interjects; he prefers the term "Elvis tribute artist." An exuberant Clark shakes her streaked, steel-gray-and-white hair and continues as if there has been no interruption. "In walks this tall, beautiful, young man, a big artist in Brazil, and as soon as he steps in the room, he can't even talk. He's just crying, tears rolling down." The Brazilian artist's emotional outburst preceded Clark's poignant recitation of the King of Rock 'n' Roll's first moments.

"Elvis was born right here." Clark waves her hand over the handmade quilt, covering the iron bed that is set on a diagonal to the fireplace. "Of course, you all know he had a stillborn twin, and because of that, Gladys became the overprotective mommy. Elvis slept with her all his little life. There used to be a crib. They took it out because he didn't sleep there; he slept in his mother's arms. When he started school, she would walk him back and forth. The other children teased him and called him a momma's boy." Clark pauses to give the group, crowded into the small bedroom, time to absorb the details. She has grown accustomed to the fans' deep attachment to Elvis, but it's taken a little time.

The bed where Elvis was born.

This Presley cousin listens with polite Southern restraint while visitors regale her with tales of ghostly encounters. "Just the other day, it was so precious; some girls, who go to a church in Ohio, said that their pastor got in an elevator with Elvis. The pastor started to witness to Elvis, and Elvis stopped him and said, 'I gave my life to Christ when I was twelve years old.'"

Guyton is pleased that fans like to share their stories and remembrances, yet he is not fully on the ghostly bandwagon. "We'll joke about going into the house in the morning, and the picture in the bedroom will be crooked on the wall, and the staff will say, 'Well, Elvis must have been here.'"

Clark says she doesn't need ghost tales to be reminded of him. She pats the *"I-Miss-Elvis"* button over her heart. "Being here everyday, I do feel close to him. I was raised with Elvis. He was eight years older than me." Clark looks out the single window on to the street. "Within three blocks around here, this place could have been called Presleyville. Elvis's grandfather and my grandfather Noah were brothers. There were ten of those kids. My grandfather Noah raised his family on First Street and had seventeen kids. Elvis was just one of many, many cousins." She smiles and her blue eyes light up behind wire-framed glasses. "We didn't know he was going to be famous. My older sister was his buddy, and I was the pesky little sister, so he has always been part of my life."

And for a couple from Saranac Lake in upstate New York, Elvis will always be a part of their life together. Making a pilgrimage to his birthplace, they are convinced that the young Elvis has returned to Tupelo. Filled with nervous anticipation, Randy and Holly Miner are taking pictures of the 450-square-foot, white clapboard home at its original location on the southwest corner of the property.

"This was a surprise for me," proclaims a wide-eyed Holly. "Our anniversary is the twenty-sixth of August, and we've traveled over 4,100 miles to be here. My husband didn't tell me where we were going to celebrate our thirty-third anniversary."

"Elvis died ten days before our wedding," Randy Miner announces as he stands stiffly beside his wife. "We got married August 26, 1977."

"I always wanted to come see him, and ten days before we were married, he passed away, and I was like, I will never get to see him." Holly crosses her hands over her chest and rubs her arms up and down.

"It gives me goose bumps to be here. I've got chills. This is where Elvis started off, and now I get to be with him where he was at the beginning." Guyton does not find it at all unusual that a couple would link their wedding anniversary with Elvis's death. "Everyone knows where they were and what they were doing when JFK was assassinated, and Elvis fans around the world remember where they were and what they were doing when he died on August 16, 1977."

After his phenomenal rise to fame, Elvis built a grand mansion in Memphis and lived a lifestyle far removed from his humble beginnings in Tupelo. To Dick Guyton, this has little bearing on the true nature of the man whose music took on an iconic status. "Elvis came back to Tupelo a lot; he never forgot where he came from. He would drive down from Memphis in the evening and spend two, three, four hours visiting." To avid fans, this is proof enough that Elvis's heart and soul remain in Tupelo, not at his Graceland mansion.

Clark also emphasizes Elvis' strong ties to his birthplace. "Elvis's father, Vernon; his uncle; and his grandfather Jessie Presley built this house in 1934." Clark points to one of the rare photographs of the child Elvis with his parents. Father Vernon and mother Gladys appear uncomfortable, yet their impish, three-year-old exhibits no such qualms. The young Puck wears a scaled-down fedora-style hat, cocked sideways. His cherubic cheeks and full lips hint at drama ahead. Not long after the photo was taken in 1937, the Presleys lost their home when Vernon went to prison for altering the figures on a check he received for payment on a hog.

Sybil Clark remains indignant about the severity of the punishment, and she is pleased to be able to announce with a well-satisfied smile that "twenty years later, Elvis comes back here famous, and he bought the house and took it back. Then, he built a swimming pool and a ballpark and installed playground equipment for the community. He did it for the children, built a beautiful park so they could have what he never did."

Once the park was built, Elvis had a dream, a premonition of sorts. Dick Guyton, his voice in the lower register, explains what happened. "Not too many years before he died, Elvis and Janelle McComb, a dear friend of his from Tupelo, were walking the property and reminiscing. Elvis turned to Janelle and said, 'You know, it would be nice to have a sort of meditation place out here.' The story is that he used to go to the overlook on the backside of our property, take his guitar, sit, and look out over the lights of Tupelo."

When Elvis died, his fans were devastated. As the news of his passing spread, according to Guyton, "fan clubs from everywhere sent money for no reason, and the city fathers said, 'What are we going to do with this money?' And Janelle stepped forward and said, 'Elvis wanted a meditation place, why can't we build a chapel?' That's how it started."

The Elvis Presley Memorial Chapel is a contemporary design. "The chapel was dedicated in 1979, two years after he died. I think he would have approved," says Guyton as his eyes sweep the interior. "We play Elvis gospel music. And you walk in here and there will be someone sitting quietly, listening to the music, saying a prayer, tears in their eyes. We have a few local people who visit regularly and spend twenty to thirty minutes. Yeah, this is where they feel closest to him."

A woman in her late fifties gets up from one of the oak pews. She has been staring at a bank of five stained-glass windows that line the front wall. The brilliant purples, greens, lavenders, golds, and blues are arranged in a semiabstract mosaic pattern. The visitor adjusts her glasses and approaches the center panel. "I see him," she exclaims with delight. "There's his face and his arms are stretched up to the heavens." Elvis sightings in the chapel are a fairly common occurrence says Guyton. "Once one person sees the pattern in the glass, then everybody crowds around looking for more."

Other fans arrive with tokens of their love and respect. Pedestals are provided for the daily flow of fresh flowers: a dozen yellow roses, a spray of mums, a single red rose. It is a perpetual wake inside the chapel. Sharing a common bond, the mourners are unwilling to let go of their memories. Guyton knows why. "Even if they didn't know him, never saw him perform, if they came from the same kind of poor background, they can relate. The birthplace is all about the little boy. . . . These were the formative years that affected the rest of his life, so the fans by coming here, they can connect. His family didn't have anything, and yet, Elvis rose to be the greatest entertainer of all times. The gospel music that he sang in the church, music that he heard in Shake Rag, the black section of town, and the mixture of his music that made his a totally different sound, all came from his roots here in Tupelo."

Elvis sightings are common in the chapel's stained-glass windows.

In addition to the chapel, there is another house of worship on the grounds. The Assembly of God Church is where the Presleys attended services on Sunday mornings and Wednesday evenings. Visitors are ushered inside the actual wooden, one-room structure. A hush descends. All eyes are on the pulpit. The austere podium matches the stark simplicity of the country church. As if on angels' wings, three white screens silently descend from narrow slits in the paneled ceiling. During the multimedia presentation, the former congregation appears dressed in their humble 1940s-era Sunday best. Brother Frank Smith steps up to the pulpit and the spirit-filled service commences. There is a call to renounce evil, a laying on of hands for the fallen and repentant, and enough gospel music to cause hips to sway and hands to clap. Brother Smith calls upon the young Presley family to step forward. With eyes lowered, ten-year-old Elvis quietly begins to sing, "Jesus Loves Me," and the new congregation of twenty-first-century visitors join in. Many are so caught up in the fifteen-minute presentation that they forget it is all a reenactment, caught on tape and rewound for their benefit.

If all of this is not enough to evoke the spirit of Elvis, there is more—an opportunity to hold his hand. In the center of the complex, between his childhood home and the Assembly of God Church, thirteen-year-old Elvis waits impatiently. He is caught midstride. His oversized, hand-me-down coveralls bunch around his ankles. A guitar, purchased by his mother from the Tupelo Hardware store, dangles from his left hand. But it is his right hand that is a fan magnet. Avid devotees squeeze in for a photo op. They nestle their heads low on his shoulder. Then, trancelike, they slip their fingers into his right hand, curled ever so slightly upward. The physical contact, albeit with a bronze statue, elicits sighs, smiles, and pure joy. "We have 60 to 65,000 people a year. Almost 700,000 people have touched that statue," boasts Guyton.

From the elderly woman who moved to Tupelo to commune daily with Elvis to the couple who track their wedding anniversary by aligning it with Elvis's untimely demise to those who sit in the chapel and are moved to tears, finding Elvis in Tupelo is a spiritual journey. Here they have faith that the young, innocent Elvis Aaron Presley hovers close by.

Postscript: The centerpiece of the Elvis Presley Birthplace is the museum. Through exhibits and audio-video presentations, visitors see first hand the effects of the Great Depression. There are family photos of Elvis's maternal grandparents, aunts, uncles, and cousins. Gospel music, ballads, and the folk tunes of the era play softly. Every artifact bears witness to the theme—"We all know it ended. This is how it began." Much of the original collection came from Janelle McComb, who first met Elvis as a two-year-old in Tupelo. She later became his number one fan and often acted as a second mother following the death of Gladys Presley. Janelle saved everything.

Guyton points to a small glass case—a treasure chest of toys, including marbles, kites, and comic books. "Elvis loved comic books. His favorite character was Captain Marvel, who had a bolt of lightning on his costume." Guyton believes the design heavily influenced Elvis throughout his career. "If you'll notice Elvis's hair, it always hung in a point down his

The statue of Elvis as a young boy is a big draw.

forehead. It's quite the same shape. His jewelry, the TCB [taking care of business] necklace has a bolt of lightning."

One blue velvet costume brings a flood of memories to the museum's director. "Elvis was four years older than me, and I was sixteen when he performed a benefit concert at the fairgrounds for the city of Tupelo. Town boy makes it big," says Guyton with evident pride. "Everybody celebrated. It was so hot; it was in early September 1957. Elvis had on that blue velvet shirt, and he was burning up, and we were burning up."

The weirdest exhibit displays bed linens and towels from a motel room where the King stayed during a concert in Monroe, Louisiana. "Two ladies went in and collected everything he touched, including those two coffee cups and a wet towel. One of the ladies put the towel in her freezer for a number of years, and after Janelle opened the museum, she gave it to her, as well as the coffee cup which still has coffee in it." The rarest item is as personal as it gets. "If you look real close, there is a piece of scotch tape over a black hair on that towel."

Guyton repeats that the museum owes its existence to Janelle McComb. "Janelle often wrote the cards for the family—birthday cards and holiday cards for Lisa Marie and her dad. Vernon commissioned her to write the epitaph for Elvis's grave."

The epitaph reads in part "He became a living legend in his own time; earning the respect and love of millions." Above the tombstone is an eternal flame erected by McComb and nine other close friends and associates. On the base is a telling inscription, also penned by McComb. *"May this flame . . . serve as a constant reminder to each of us of your eternal presence."*

The haunted theatre in downtown Tupelo.

16

Tupelo's Lyric Theatre

His name is Antoine. He has been haunting Tupelo's Lyric Theatre for as long as anyone can remember. His past is murky, but his activities in the present day keep the staff in turmoil. Lisa Hall is the theatre's box office manager. Fringes of short dark hair frame her startling, near-turquoise-blue eyes. Wearing a bright-yellow blouse, Hall looks like an effervescent pixie who has just flown in from the shores of Neverland. Instead, her command post is the front desk and her archenemy is not Captain Hook, but the mysterious Antoine, a ghost with a penchant for mischief. Hall recounts a typical incident. "We were upstairs in the costume room, and we had moved some things around, and we left. We came back a little later and everything had been rearranged, and there was no one in the building but us."

Tracie Maxey-Conwill serves on the board of directors of the community theatre. Maxey-Conwill is a statuesque blond dressed in a simple white blouse and black pencil skirt. "I never had any problems with Antoine until our annual Fall Haunted House." As an all-volunteer operation, the Lyric Theatre Board relies on revenue from memberships, ticket sales, corporate sponsors, and an annual Halloween Haunted House fundraiser. Each year, members pitch in to transform the stately old theatre into a spook-filled, monster mansion.

Maxey-Conwill describes the huge undertaking and how one disgruntled ghost went for his own special effects. "We had hung large sheets of black plastic upstairs on every wall of the back hallway so all of our light switches were covered. We just put blue lights in, and we left those on 24/7 while we got ready for haunted theatre. We had cleared out everybody, and I was going back through checking on everything. I was at the corner, near the bathroom, and all the blue lights went off." Maxey-Conwill lets out an exasperated sigh. "I knew no one could get to the light switches, or would know where they were, so I had to assume it was him [Antoine], and I said, 'I have never messed with you. Do not mess with me.' Just as I gave him his marching orders, the lights popped back on. The next thing I remember was that I was in the lobby, and I don't know how I got there."

Executive director Tom Booth is standing in the office listening to Maxey-Conwill. He cocks his head to the side, surprised at her revelation. "I never heard about this. When was this?"

"That was two years ago."

Booth glances from Maxey-Conwill to Hall, inhales slowly, and then in a powerful, deep undertone decides to share. "I've had two haunted experiences, both late at night. We had an event here; I had left the stage area, closed everything down, came back, and came in this door." Booth indicates the entrance to the office to the right of the main lobby doors. "When I came in the door, I heard, I can only describe it as sort of laughing/singing, *La La La. Ha Ha Ha Ha Ha.*" And I replied back, sarcastically, 'Ha Ha. Very funny.' Being a volunteer organization, there is always a director, a production manager. A lot of people have keys. People come in at all hours. So when I heard the voice, I thought there must be somebody in the building; they heard me drive up late at night and were trying to scare me. I go throughout the entire building, upstairs, out the stage door, all the way around the outside. Of course, the place is empty. There is nobody here." Booth rolls his pale-blue eyes. "I got my keys and I went home. It was very creepy."

Booth shifts his stance. A black Lyric Theatre T-shirt molds to his well-toned upper body. Part two of his inexplicable encounters unfolds. "The other time, it was late at night. I came in my office door. We had had a party, a dinner with beautiful flower arrangements. They were just going to go to waste, so I was going to get them and carry them to my church so they could be used the next day." Booth folds his arms across his chest. "I got them. I loaded them in my car. I came back in and realized that some lights had been left on. I go through the building cutting out lights, checking air conditioning, and I get ready to go."

Booth hesitates, pats his pockets, and looks around, imitating his actions of that night. "I can't find my keys." His voice takes on a puzzled air. "I backtrack all my steps, go out to my car, search everywhere, [and] search the building; thirty or forty-five minutes later I give up." Booth throws two muscular arms in the air. "I go to the phone to call someone to come get me." As a theatre director, Booth slips easily into the role of actor and demonstrates. He steps over to the inside wall lined end to end with a narrow counter. It serves as desk and catchall for a myriad of office equipment: fax machine, printer, stacks of paperwork, and a black phone resting on a clear Plexiglas stand. The stand has a slot to the right to hold pencils and paper clips.

All eyes are on Booth as he continues with his recreation. "I start to punch in numbers on the phone and I look down in this slot and there are my keys, wedged in there tight." Booth stares at his audience and in a firm voice announces, "I have never put my keys in there. I would have no reason to put my keys there."

The issue of how his errant keys were jammed into the unlikely location still gnaws at him. "I spent about half the next week trying to bounce my keys in there and couldn't do it." His irritation is apparent. If the culprit is the illusive Antoine, Booth has no explanation for how the ghost pulled it off or even why. "I have tried to figure out some logic to it all. Once again, all I could do at the time was yank out my keys, lock the doors, and go home."

One theatre volunteer believes she has a photo of the ghost. "There's a lady here that works for the Haunted House Theatre event we do here every year, and she has this picture and she swears it is Antoine." Hall has seen it, but she's skeptical. "She showed it to us; there is a white shadow and these lights go out from it. I think it is just something that happened in the processing of the picture, but she really believes she caught him on camera."

What bothers office manager Lisa Hall more are the noises and the odors. She tries to justify it all and fails. "Now the slamming of doors could just be part of the old building and drafts, and the traces of smoke—we have a No Smoking policy here—so I guess that odor could be left over from before, but sometimes the smoke smell is awfully strong. And sometimes you hear shuffling coming from the stage area when no one is there." Hall leans in, her voice a whisper, and states, "There was a girl who came in from a nearby town. . . . She wanted to do one of those paranormal investigations, and I told her I couldn't give permission. I would have to check with our board and let her know. As soon as she left—there was nobody here but me and Claire who also works here— this door behind me that leads into the theater space slammed shut so hard it was like Antoine didn't want her here." Hall glances quickly over her shoulder as if fearful the ghost might hear her talking about him. "If Claire had not been here, I would have thought it was just the wind, but all the doors were closed." Hall adds that Claire will not go upstairs by herself. She refuses to enter the second-floor costume, prop, and dressing rooms without accompaniment.

Booth shrugs it off. "I've spent the night in the theatre, maybe three, four, five times through the years, working very late. It would be one, two, or three o'clock in the morning. I'd be just wiped out. I live thirty minutes from here. I'd find a couch or a bed on the set, go upstairs, get a blanket or a pillow out of our prop room, and go to sleep. Never heard a thing." He corrects himself. "Well, I shouldn't say *never* heard a thing. The floors pop. This is like an old building, over one hundred years."

Booth's nonchalant attitude gets a jolt. "Look at that!" A thick drop of water plops down from the center of the ceiling and makes a loud splat on the floor. The director goes for the punch line: "Looks like Antoine just spit at us." There is nervous laughter from the rest of the group in the room. "It's like if we leave and then come back in, we disturb him, and it annoys him."

Hall agrees. "People are convinced that as long as you leave him alone, he is not mean, except to slam the door to express his displeasure."

Why does this ghost prefer solitude over company, and where did the name Antoine come from? Hall offers a historical perspective. "A long time ago, someone gave our ghost that name. He could possibly have been one of the victims of the tornado that went through here in 1936, and he was brought here and never left. Almost three hundred people were killed or maimed. They used the Lyric as an operating room. They took the doors off the county courthouse across the street and used them as litters to bring the wounded and injured over here to operate on them." Hall passes on a few more grisly tales. "There are rumors that the limbs of the victims that were cut off during the operations . . . were thrown . . . under the stage." Hall's face compresses into a grimace. "I don't know if there is any truth to that. It does kind of smell kind of *off* down there."

On April 5, 1936, the fourth deadliest tornado in United States history slammed into Tupelo. The massive funnel skipped over the downtown business district, but to the town's horror, it zeroed in on the residential areas. There was little to no warning. The tornado leveled homes and wiped out entire families. The death toll hovered around 230, but this only accounted for white families. The actual number may be significantly higher as death tolls among African Americans were not reported or recorded until the late forties. Singling out Antoine from among the hundreds of dead, dying, or injured in the theatre that dreadful evening would be a formidable task.

Booth says that over the years there have been several potential characters cast in the role of the theatre's grouchy ghost. "Some people think he may be someone that died during the tornado, others believe it might be a previous caretaker of the building who has never left, never went away. No one really knows. I've been around for eighteen years, and he's always been called Antoine. I can't say anymore, except things happen. When the Tupelo Community Theatre bought the building twenty-six years ago, I guess we inherited the ghost."

Postscript: The sturdy Art Deco building at 200 North Broadway has always been in the spotlight. Built in 1912 by R. F. Goodlett, the Cosmos (the original name) was designed for live vaudeville acts. In the 1930s, as vaudeville took a back seat to "talkies," the M. A. Lightman Company reconfigured it as a movie theatre. Its popularity grew along with local lore that the town's most famous native son, Elvis Presley, stole his first kiss in the balcony of the Lyric movie theatre. Sadly, by 1984 the theatre fell into decline. It was abandoned, and its finale was to be a date with the wrecking ball. A reprieve arrived in the form of grants, gifts, pledges, and community and state support. The Lyric was restored and is now home to of one of the finest amateur theatrical venues in the South.

Feathers, a symbol of the ancient ones, dangle over the river.

17

The Singing River

My life
is as the waters of a river
and I cannot change my course.
Perhaps there was a time,
somewhere in the beginning,
but not now.
So I will take the path I must
toward whatever seas await me.
—Jim Metcalf, *Waters of the River*

As the waning, hazy days of summer turn into early autumn, as the sun dips into the horizon, a faint murmur floats across the waters of the West Pascagoula River. To the uninitiated, the disquieting sound is a buzz, rising like a swarm of bees in flight. For the residents of Gautier, Mississippi, the crescendo is a chant, the requiem of an ancient people.

Anola of the Pascagoula loved Altama of the Biloxi tribe. A détente existed between the two tribes who hunted and fished along the same riverbanks. Anola was already promised to another within her tribe when she secretly fled to be with Altama. The Biloxis, thought to be fierce and unforgiving warriors, sought revenge. The small clan of outnumbered Pascagoulas joined hands; they prepared to move from one world to the next. Led by Altama and Anola, they chose death over torture and enslavement by the Biloxi. Together their voices rose in a somber, rhythmic lament. Pascagoula men, women, and children stepped off of the riverbank into the swirling waters and disappeared beneath the surface. The chants of these lost people

The Old Place in Pascagoula sits on the west bank of the Singing River.

*were so powerful that their timeless echo can still be heard rising up in the
waters of the Singing River.*

The Singing River flows past the Old Place, a West Indies-style home
in Gautier. This hipped-roof house is surrounded by deep galleries on all
four sides, offering expansive views. Giant oak trees, limbs dripping with
Spanish moss, guard the water's edge. In 1867, Fernando Upton Gautier
and his wife, Theresa Fayard Gautier, arrived at this restful spot to
establish a homestead and begin operation for a sawmill on the river.

Aimée Gautier Dugger is a great-great-granddaughter of Fernando
and Theresa Gautier. Dugger feels strongly that the legend, in its present
form, was woven by her great-aunt. Josie Gautier, the ninety-year-old
matriarch, may have heard the story as oral history passed through
generations of the Gautier family.

"My great-aunt Josie did not get this out of a history book, she wrote
it down that Altama discovered Anola and they fell in love. The warrior
Biloxi tribe was incensed, and the peaceful Pascagoula had no way of
protecting themselves; so they joined hands, went down to the river, and

drowned. The river took up their song and sings it to this day." Dugger is quite proud that Josephine Gautier wrote music to accompany the legend, and she says, "The chords replicate the sounds the river makes." A little tugging at the threads of the Gautier lineage might explain why this legend had such an impact on Josie.

Josie Gautier lived at Westside, a raised home set three hundred feet back from the Singing River. Josie's father, Walter Gautier, built Westside in 1848. Walter was the second son of Theresa and Fernando Gautier, who continued to live at the Old Place on the river. Theresa Fayard was the granddaughter of Jean Baptiste Baudreau Graveline who took for his second wife "a squaw of the Indian Nation." Whether Josie identified with her Native American roots or was just enamored with a mythological love story that took place near her home, no one knows.

Positive of one thing, Aimée Gautier Dugger says, "My great-aunt Josie and my grandmother, Hattie Gautier, Josie's sister-in-law, both

A view of the Singing River from the gallery of the Old Place.

heard the river sing and both said that this [the Old Place] is where Anola and Altama walked into the river."

Even with her abundant admiration for all her great-aunt accomplished, Dugger is puzzled about the location of the legend. "The tributary of the Pascagoula River that passes by the Old Place is called the Singing River, but this has been debated, because at one time the main river and the west tributary both used this name." Dugger goes back to her childhood. "My parents and my grandparents showed me several spots where the river sang on the city of Pascagoula side of the river, the east river. In my lifetime, I have heard it sing on the east river. I was three or four the first time. My parents heard it walking along the wharfs on the east side."

Dugger tries to mesh the conflicting versions. "The main river was dredged early on, big ships came into the port, [and] shipyards developed. . . . Due to the noise of the shipyards maybe that is why it has not been heard on the east side from the 1950s on."

Al Allen, senior vice president of Blossman Gas in Oceans Springs sees the legend every day. A large six-foot-by-six-foot painting of Altama leading Anola and the remaining Pascagoulas into the river hangs in the corporate office on Washington Street. The mural-sized dramatic depiction was the last painting of noted artist William B. Steene. Company founder Woodrow Blossman commissioned it. Allen says he has never heard the river sing, but his third-grade teacher in Pascagoula would regale the class with firsthand accounts. "She would get calls from the bridge tender of the two-lane toll bridge that used to span the Pascagoula River. The bridge tender would tell her and her sister that the river was singing that day, and they would go up there to hear the sound coming from the middle of the river."

East side, west side, or midstream, the lure of the legendary chants of the Pascagoula people served as inspiration for Josie's business, Singing River Originals. Fifty-year-old Josie started mixing clay from the riverbank and made pottery molds based on nature and sea life. Some of her pottery creations, such as honeybee pitchers, blue crab seafood serving sets, birds, shrimp, fish, and oysters, now command hundreds of dollars at auctions.

Persistent reports of the ghostly moans rising from the West Pascagoula River continue to fuel the legend. A 2003 television documentary, *The*

Singing River: Rhythms of Nature, produced by the Mississippi Public Broadcasting in association with the Nature Conservancy, attempted to record the sound of the river and track the origins of the legend. On camera, Rosalie Steve, a storyteller with the Mississippi band of Choctaw, raises her voice in prayer and states that the river does "sing." Bill Shrimp from Poticaw Landing claims that he has heard the peculiar haunting sound five different times. "The sound is there, there is no lying about it."

Mark Wallace, a professor of religion at Swarthmore College, has vivid memories of the sound of the river. "It was a high-pitched undulating sound. It wasn't a keening; it wasn't a wail; it was more of a call, a lament, a longing. My mother's family called the entire Pascagoula River the Singing River." Wallace often visited his maternal family's homestead on Hastings Street in Gautier. "My grandmother, Winona, carried a picture of her mother in tribal dress. My mother," says Wallace, "would tell me about my great-grandmother, Francis Hawkins; she was a Seminole who migrated to Pascagoula, and the story of her migration was infused with the legend of the Pascagoula." Wallace states that link between the two were always confusing to him. "I suspect it was not clear because in the 1930s through the 1950s my mother's family had terrible anxieties about miscegenation, mixed blood lines between native and nonnative people, so my great-grandmother did not talk openly about her Indian heritage."

Nevertheless, Wallace came to believe in the legend of the Biloxi brave who fell in love with the Pascagoula maiden. "My mother told me that rather than be killed, the Pascagoula went single file into the river singing a community song." Wallace remembers seeing the sheet music and listening to the song of Altama and Anola, "The Singing River," which was composed by Josie Gautier. The impact of the legend and the music inspired a then seven-year-old Mark Wallace to take his first plunge into the river to find out for himself. In *Finding God in the Singing River: Christianity, Spirit, Nature,* Wallace writes about his transforming experience. "I swam in the river and heard the plaintive song of my ancestors. . . . I listened to the distant echo of the ancient river music mysteriously preserved in this underwater environment."

David Gautier, the younger brother of Aimée Gautier Dugger, runs a shrimp processing business where there is little room for myths and legends. Yet, he admits with no hesitation in his voice, "I have heard the river hum. I love to fish. I am always on the Singing River."

He has a ready explanation for the phenomenon. "It could be tidal flow." When pressed if he has heard this "hum" on any other body of water in the entire state of Mississippi, Gautier is forthright. "No, I haven't. I've only heard that hum in the West Pascagoula River, the Singing River."

If he had to choose between a scientific rationalization and a legend, Gautier favors the latter. While Mark Wallace makes it clear that "no one from my mother's family could ever vouch for the historical veracity of the legend." He feels the story has merit in other ways. "I think of it as a moral and spiritual message to have certain empathies for the land and for the river and its ecological impact on the Gulf Coast."

Postscript: Grayhawk Perkins, an elder of the United Houma Nation, who is also Choctaw through his father's lineage, affirms that the Pascagoula and the Biloxi had villages in the coastal Mississippi region, but he has issues with the legend. "I have never heard of Native Americans committing mass suicide. It would be against their spiritual beliefs." Grayhawk agrees that the Pascagoula no longer exist as an identifiable tribe, but not because of a threat posed by the Biloxi. "These people worked together, sold land together, and when the Biloxi moved to Bayou Boeuf around 1795, the Pascagoula went with them." Grayhawk's research indicates that over time the Pascagoula were absorbed by the Biloxi. Contemporary Tunica-Biloxi tribal members live on today in Mississippi and east central Louisiana.

Grayhawk translates the name of the Pascagoula, "*Goula* is a person or people; *paska* means bread, so Pascagoula would be the Bread People." He frowns at the names assigned to the legendary lovers, Altama and Anola. "Those names were not used among Muskogean or Siouan language speakers." Grayhawk also cautions that storytellers should be mindful of documented history. "For the most part, Native Americans did not name rivers or villages. This practice came into use after the Europeans arrived, and they named places for the tribes they met in any given area."

Native American feathers caught in the limb of a tree.

The impact of the legend continues into the present day. The city of Pascagoula has a Singing River Hospital, Singing River Mall, Singing River Federal Credit Union, and a Singing River Kennel Club, all emulating the Singing River designation of the west tributary of the Pascagoula River.

Legends, like the ghosts who inspire them, are tricky things.

18

Beauvoir

A formidable figure squares off, his sculpted face buffeted by the winds blowing in from the Gulf of Mexico. His right arm is raised, palm up, fingers outstretched. "He appears to be welcoming people to Beauvoir," says Richard Forte, the director of the Jefferson Davis Home and Presidential Library in Biloxi.

Like the man it was created to honor, the statue is a survivor. In 1998, sculptor Bill Beckworth's iconic image of Jefferson Davis, president of the Confederacy, greeted visitors as they entered the museum library. In 2005, Hurricane Katrina tried and failed to force him to step aside. "Davis' statue was the only thing left on the ground floor of the museum; everything else was gone," says the director.

The battered but unbowed figure, surrounded by a debris field of bricks and timber, was relocated to a temporary site on the front lawn of Beauvoir, just steps from the beach. Plans called for a new million-dollar museum and library on the northeast corner of the grounds of Beauvoir and the return of the statue. Some traditional cultural belief systems ascribe to the idea that everything on this earth has a spirit. If the same holds true for inanimate objects, then the stubborn spirit of Jefferson Davis' statue has swayed opinions. "Everybody likes it where it is out front, so that's where it's going to stay," states Forte.

In the aftermath of the Civil War, Davis retreated to Biloxi to write his memoirs and exorcise his ghosts. As he strolled along the sandy beach or sat in his favorite bench gazing out at the warm gulf waters, he was the living symbol of a lost cause—a man without a country. In March of 1899, six miles from Beauvoir in Mississippi City, Davis addressed a

Jefferson Davis's statue looks out over the waters of the gulf.

Beauvoir was the last home of the president of the Confederacy.

convention of young men. "Friends and fellow citizens," Davis began and then paused. "Pardon me, the laws of the United States no longer permit me to designate you as fellow citizens, but I am thankful that I may address you as friends." It would not be until nearly a century later that citizenship was returned posthumously to Jefferson Davis. Few men in history have suffered such an ignominious defeat in their public lives and faced such sorrow in their personal affairs.

In 1875, Sarah Dorsey, a family friend, heard that a haunted and haggard Jefferson Davis needed a quiet retreat. She offered her home, Beauvoir, as an "Eden by the sea." Sarah also offered her talents and literary expertise. Each morning, Dorsey met Davis at the east cottage on the estate and work began on the two-volume *The Rise and Fall of the Confederate Government.* During the early days at Beauvoir, twenty-year-old Jefferson Davis Jr. assisted Sarah in taking his father's dictation. Davis's wife, Varina, remained in Memphis with their daughter Margaret, vowing she could not live in the humid climate of the Mississippi coast.

Varina ultimately had a change of heart. Perhaps resentful of Sarah Dorsey, she journeyed to Beauvoir and, to her surprise, found the house and gardens amenable and peaceful.

The comfortable routine of days of writing and evenings spent strolling were shattered by the news of the death of Jefferson Davis Jr.; he died while visiting Memphis during the 1878 yellow fever epidemic. The city was under quarantine, and the distraught parents could not even attend the funeral. They had already lost three sons at young ages: Samuel Emory, two; Joseph Evan, five; and William Howell, eleven. Only their daughters, Margaret, married and living in Memphis, and Varina Anne "Winnie," away at school in Germany, remained. Beauvoir became the home of troubled souls.

With the quarantine lifted, Margaret "Polly"; her husband, J. A. Hayes; and their children, Varina Howell Davis Hayes, Lucy White Hayes, and Jefferson Davis Hayes, visited often. They were the Davis's only grandchildren. In *Beauvoir—A Walk through History,* there is a rare mid-1880s, black-and-white photograph of three of the Hayes children wading in the shallow gulf waters in front of Beauvoir. In time, the guest quarters to the west of the main house came to be known as the Hayes Cottage. The Hayes Cottage has been a hub of activity of both the human and paranormal kind.

The first owners, the Browns, offered it to the circuit-riding Methodist minister as a rest stop. During the Dorsey's ownership, Sarah used it for her office. Jefferson Davis enlarged the structure to make room for friends and family. The Mississippi Division, United Sons of Confederate Veterans bought the Beauvoir estate following Davis's death, and they offered the cottage to Beauvoir's official guests. Past and current administrators of Beauvoir agree the cottage makes strange sounds. One former superintendent swore that in the early morning hours he was awakened by a terrible noise that sounded like "a bunch of shelves falling down." Other overnight guests reported their sleep interrupted by the sounds of glass breaking and timbers cracking as if caught in a storm. "Dishes," corrects director Richard Forte, "the stories that I have heard about the Hayes cottage is that it sounded like dishes falling in the kitchen. Of course, nothing fell. I've been on the board of directors for thirty years, and I've heard a lot of different stories. I have never seen anything, but I have heard things when I stayed in the old Hayes Cottage. It's a typical antebellum home; it's got things that go bump in the night. You know, that's the way it goes," says Forte with a shrug.

Then there are the footsteps—*shuffle step, thud; shuffle step, thud*—two feet and a cane. "There was kind of a dogtrot between the old Hayes Cottage and the new one. The old one had a northward extension added on when it was the Confederate soldiers' home." Forte confirms that "a lot of guests heard footsteps walking between the two cottages, but no one has been identified. It's hard to say who it might have been."

Between 1903 and 1957, the state of Mississippi operated Beauvoir as a home for aged Confederate veterans and their wives. The first resident, J. R. Climer of Madison County, was admitted on December 2, 1903. The last two residents were Confederate widows—Mollie Lavenia Bailey, widow of Corp. Zachariah T. Bailey, and Mollie Cottle, widow of Pvt. James Cottle. State operation of Beauvoir ceased and control of the property reverted to the Mississippi Division of the Sons of Confederate Veterans.

Forte is clear, stating, "We're really into history. I've had ghost chasers who all want to come into here, but we are not into fantasy. We are not into something unless you can document it for a fact. The photographs are the only hard evidence I've ever seen of that."

Tourists posing in front of Beauvoir took the photos Forte refers to, and joining them are extra faces in the windows. "Three were taken in the 1990s and the last one was taken in 2001. In one, there is a female, another has a man and a woman, the third has children's faces, and the last has a man's face. There are four that I have seen," says Forte, "four different times, taken by four different people. Pretty convincing when you see them." He adds, "I have no idea who the people are."

The list of potential spirits in the haunted photos is long. The phantom children could be any of the young sons of Varina and Jefferson Davis. Three of their four boys died before reaching their teens. Many would love to think that ghostly couple was President and Mrs. Davis. They spent their final years together at Beauvoir.

In November of 1889, Jefferson Davis left on a trip to Brierfield, his family plantation on the Mississippi River below Vicksburg. He lay ill for four days. Mrs. Davis was alerted. She caught a northbound steamboat as Davis was transported downriver aboard the steamboat *Leathers*. The two boats literally were passing in the night when the captain of Mrs. Davis's boat realized his father, Captain Leathers, had Davis aboard his boat. The son brought his steamboat alongside his father's and Mrs. Davis crossed the gangplank in the middle of the river to join her husband. They made it downriver to New Orleans where Jefferson Davis died on December 6, 1889. The only peace the tormented president of the Confederacy ever found was at Beauvoir.

The single female spirit in one photo is a bit more problematic. Certainly, Sarah Ann Ellis Dorsey would be a prime candidate. She gave Beauvoir the name it bears today, which is translated as "beautiful view." She opened Beauvoir's doors to Jefferson Davis and later sold him the entire estate. What Jefferson Davis did not know was that Sarah was dying of cancer. In her will she left everything to the man she admired most: *"I do not intend to share in the ingratitude of my country towards the man, who is in my eyes, the highest and noblest in existence."* Sarah's love for her former home was such that she had a back-up proviso for Beauvoir's continued care: *"If Jefferson Davis should not survive me, I give all that I have bequeathed to him to his youngest daughter, Varina."*

The front bedroom of Beauvoir is a shrine to Varina, known to all as Winnie, the only Davis child to live in Beauvoir. If the spirit of Winnie, the "Daughter of the Confederacy," has returned to peer out of the windows, she has earned the right.

In the closing days of the Civil War, her father was imprisoned at Fort Monroe in Virginia. Except for two-year-old Winnie, the Davis children were sent to live with their grandparents in Canada. The toddler and her mother were allowed to stay with an ailing Jefferson Davis in his prison cell. After his release, Winnie was her father's constant companion, accompanying him on speaking engagements before Confederate veterans. And it was to Beauvoir that Winnie brought her first true love who asked for her hand in marriage. Jefferson Davis adored his youngest daughter and gave his permission with extreme reluctance. Winnie's beloved, Alfred Wilkinson, was the son of an abolitionist and Davis knew there would be repercussions. Patricia Ricci, director of Confederate Memorial Hall in New Orleans, says, "Confederate veterans were outraged that the daughter of the Confederacy would stoop so low as to marry a Yankee." Winnie called the engagement off. But after the death of her father, she reconnected with Alfred on a trip to Europe. This Romeo and Juliet became engaged again with equally vocal objections. Out of respect for her father's memory, Winnie parted with Alfred a second time. She continued speaking before veterans groups. A frail and brokenhearted Winnie died at age thirty-four. In her bedroom at Beauvoir, there is a large painting above the mantle. Winnie is costumed in glittering finery as the 1892 Queen of Comus, an elite New Orleans Carnival krewe. The painting captures one of the few truly joyous moments of her young life.

Two young boys are also enshrined on the grounds of Beauvoir. A statue depicts Jefferson Davis holding the youngsters' hands. But why show only two when Davis had four sons? The mystery deepens when Forte reveals that in the hearts of Varina and Jefferson Davis they had five sons—four by birth and one adopted. One small figure commemorates five-year-old Joseph Davis who died after falling off the balcony of the Confederate White House in Richmond. The figure on the other side of Davis represents his adopted son, Jim Limber. According to family lore, in 1864, Varina and one of her daughters were riding into Richmond when they saw a black man beating a child. They asked him to stop. His reply, "He's my child and I'll do what I want." Mrs. Davis prevailed and the boy went home with her in her carriage. When she asked his name, he said, "Jim Limber." Forte says, "The Davises more or less adopted him; they didn't have all the legal papers like they do now. He was raised as one of their own children. He was made a free black. He was with Jeff Davis when he was captured by Union troops in Georgia in 1865. Jim was taken away from Jeff Davis. When Davis was released from prison, he tried to find Jim Limber and never could." The statue was commissioned to commemorate the two hundredth birthday of Jefferson Davis and the lives of the two little boys who touched his heart.

Another monument at Beauvoir, a tribute to a beloved pet, is lost. "Traveler is out there, but we don't know exactly where he was buried," says Beauvoir's director. "He had a headstone at one time, but it's been gone since before Hurricane Camille." Gone but not forgotten, for some are convinced that the little phantom dog still runs around seeking his beloved master.

Jefferson Davis loved animals. Every morning at Beauvoir, he would fill his dressing gown pockets with grain to feed his large flock of peafowl.

Jefferson Davis with Joseph and Jim on the grounds of Beauvoir.

He would walk along a short pavement leading from the back steps of Beauvoir, which he would describe as "just the length of my exercise path in prison." Davis's favorite companion was Traveler, a mixed-breed bulldog, a gift from Sarah Dorsey. Traveler was a seasoned guard dog who had journeyed through the Arabian Desert with Sarah and her husband. Sarah felt he would provide the same loyal service to Jefferson Davis. Traveler was said to have "all the dignity and watchfulness of a squad of soldiers as escorts." When an absent-minded Davis would walk too close to the water's edge, or if big waves were rolling in, Traveler would bound between his master and the waves, or grip his trouser legs in his teeth. When Traveler died, Jefferson Davis was heard saying, "I have indeed lost a friend." Traveler was buried in the front yard of Beauvoir and his grave marked by an engraved stone. Richard Forte says no one has ever shared the story with him of a phantom dog at Beauvoir, but he announces with laughter in his gravely voice, "We have an alligator, Beauregard, and he's still there. I have never seen a ghost dog. I can tell you how well I know that place; I can walk on a moonless night every road, every path, and every trail here."

With his Southern drawl slowing to a crawl, Forte admits, "I really have felt a presence of Confederate soldiers or Jefferson Davis. There is just a feeling that you are not alone; that is for sure. I've had the feelings that they know who I am, and I think they appreciate what I have done. And if they didn't, they would let me know." The phenomenon happens most often when he is alone. "I don't have it all the time. I just feel like there is somebody, somebody with me. Friendly."

Forte also reveals that prior to his appointment as director, at least one paranormal investigation was allowed at Beauvoir. "Years ago, before I came here, they had a séance, and they said the spirits came, and they were friendly spirits." The presence of spirits is linked to specific locations. "Around the Hayes Cottage and the Beauvoir house, that's where I have had my experiences."

Hurricane Katrina devastated the entire Gulf Coast and may have also impacted the spirits at Beauvoir. "Somebody told me that storms release spirits. If that's true, the ones here had a good opportunity to be released because you could see the sky through the roof from the destruction that was done to Beauvoir."

Postscript: The phantom female face in the 1990s-era photograph taken in front of Beauvoir has been attributed to Sarah, Varina, or Winnie, but there may be one other person who had a vested interest in Beauvoir and is credited with the home's ultimate survival.

In 2005, Hurricane Katrina's fury ripped off the entire front porch of Beauvoir, including the brick support columns and parts of the slate roof. In spite of the Category 4 winds, the basic structure, reports the director, "came out pretty good. I tell people that Jane Brown picked the right spot because Beauvoir is the only national historic landmark left on the Mississippi Gulf Coast with the exception of the Biloxi Lighthouse."

Jane and her husband, James Brown, bought a tract of land on the Gulf of Mexico on September 2, 1848. The house was completed in 1852. Today, the white rocker on the front porch of Beauvoir will sway back and forth, lifted by the warm gulf breezes. Or, it may be Jane's proud spirit rocking on the verandah of her vacation home and contemplating the view. If anything good came out of Katrina, concludes Forte, it was when Beauvoir was restored. "We got to see how the Browns built the house and discover things like the original faux finish on the doors, the faux marble on the mantels, the brilliant colors on the walls, the frescos on the ceilings. They were exciting finds. I tell everybody to look at the photographs of the house right after Katrina. Look at it now. It looks better than it ever has since 1852. It was like going from hell to heaven."

19

Merrehope

With one ghost who followed her portrait across state lines and another who sadly felt the walls closing in, Merrehope, a house in Meridian, makes room for these two diverse entities.

Today, Merrehope resembles a multi-tiered wedding cake slathered in white icing. From humble cottage to castlelike abode to confined cubicles and back again, the many stages of the white house on the hill are astounding. The remarkable ladies of the Meridian Restorations Foundation are hopeful that by having swept away the ravaged cocoons of time, their beautiful butterfly will attract a host of eager new visitors to Merrehope. The name itself reflects its magnificent metamorphosis: *Mer* for Meridian; *re* for restoration; *hope* for hopes and dreams fulfilled. Now that the members have the house back in order, they would like one of their more unruly ghosts to observe the etiquette appropriate for a historic home.

"If you want to know the truth," says hostess Donna White, "when I first came to work here, they kept the whole haunted thing pretty quiet. It was kind of hush-hush; nobody told me anything." The novice hostess had been on site less than three weeks when she realized things weren't what they seemed. "First thing in the morning you make your rounds. I went into the Periwinkle room. I stopped dead in my tracks. There was the perfect imprint of a body on the bed. I ran downstairs and called one of the other ladies, and she asked me, 'What's wrong?' I told her what I saw, and she just mumbled something like 'Well, this stuff happens.'" Donna was shaken; it was her first paranormal experience. She stayed downstairs for a while and avoided the upstairs bedrooms. Her reluctance

The pristine white front galleries of Merrehope glimmer in the sunlight.

prompted the manger to ask, "You are not going to quit are you?" Donna replied, "No, I'll hang in here."

In time, Donna adjusted to the weird quirks and habits of the resident ghosts, including the one who persisted in taking a midmorning nap. "I would open the door to the Periwinkle room and fuss at him. 'I hope you had a nice rest, but I really don't like cleaning up after people, so how about next time you straighten up.'" This specter had unresolved issues that ended in a gruesome exit.

By the 1930s, the run down mansion had been subdivided into apartments. One of the renters was a schoolteacher with two deadly demons—drinking and gambling. The manic-depressive was out of control. "One night," reports Donna, "he lined up some whiskey bottles on the wood mantle, shot them off, and then shot himself." His reckless behavior continues in the afterlife.

"We were getting ready for a Christmas party. There was a really big crash upstairs like someone had knocked over an armoire." Donna suspected that an intruder had gotten into the house. Outraged, she decided to trap the bumbling thief. "I ran around and locked the side door. I grabbed the telephone to call the manager and tell her I was going upstairs to see whoever it was and get them out of here. She's on the phone and she says, 'You're not going up there.' I said, 'Yes, I am.'" Donna marched up the front stairs to find nothing—nothing broken, nothing out of place, nothing fallen over. Realization dawned. Hands on her hips, the unfazed hostess planted her feet in the hall between the bedrooms. She barked out orders. "Don't get upset. There's a party tonight, so just behave. We don't want to spook the guests." She softened briefly and let the teacher's troubled spirit know that if he behaved, he could "come down and join us." He didn't take Donna up on her invitation, but, says the pacified hostess, "It stayed quiet up there for the rest of the night."

Long before the unsettled spirit of the schoolteacher disturbed the peace at Merrehope, the house began life on a much smaller scale. On property deeded to her from her father, Richard McLemore, Juriah Jackson and her husband built a three-room cottage, now the rear, ground-floor rooms of the current mansion. During the Civil War, Confederate general Leonidas Polk set up headquarters here. In February of 1864, Gen. William Tecumseh Sherman, adhering to his scorched earth campaign, set the torch to Meridian because it had a Confederate arsenal. After five days, Sherman declared, "Meridian . . . no longer exists." Juriah's cozy cottage was one of only six homes left unscathed by the time the Union troops moved out.

By 1868, the home returned to private hands. John Gary of Alabama did the first major expansion, adding porches to the front of the house with ruby glass in the main entrance. In 1881, J. C. Lloyd, his wife, and thirteen children began a twenty-three-year residence. In 1908, S. H. Floyd "modernized" the house, installing five bathrooms, electric lights, a stairway, and wainscoting. Floyd also pushed back Juriah's original cottage to make room for a grand dining room. Owners number six, the Gossetts, took possession in 1915. Otto Tibbette reshuffled the floor plan in 1930 and turned the former lovely home into eight apartments. After seven owners and numerous configurations, the stalwart women of the Meridian Restorations Foundation arrived to face bullet-riddled rooms and glass shards from the late teacher's whiskey bottle rampage.

An old photo of Merrehope during the time of the Floyds.

If choices could be made in all things paranormal, the ladies would elect to boot the noisy ghost and keep another more suited to Merrehope. White explains that the staff prefers Eugenia's gentler ways. "I was standing at the kitchen sink fixin' a glass of water and all of a sudden I could feel somebody come up behind me. It was cold, and she was blowing on the back of my neck. I drank my water and then turned and said, 'Hello. Would you like some?' It was Eugenia. She floats around the house. I knew it was Eugenia because people before me had seen her face."

Eugenia was the daughter of the Garys, the second owners. What is particularly strange about this haunting is that Eugenia never lived in the house. She died of consumption as a young teen while her parents were living in Alabama. The only debate among the staff is whether her spirit arrived before or after the portraits.

In the early 1970s, the president of the Meridian Restorations Foundation is positive she encountered the young girl standing in the front hall wearing an 1860s-era dress with a wide hoop skirt. Most paranormal images are of the gauzy-white variety. Not so for Miss Eugenia. The startled foundation president reported that the vision before her favored shades of green, wearing a solid green top over a green plaid skirt. A positive identification was confirmed with the arrival of two oval-framed portraits. "Some of the Gary descendants lived on the Gulf Coast. During Hurricane Camille, their house was destroyed, but they managed to save the portraits of Eugenia and one of her sisters. They sent them to Merrehope for safekeeping."

The portraits hang one over the other in the museum room of the twenty-room mansion. While both are scarred by water and wind damage, Eugenia's sweet face shines through. Aquamarine eyes glow under jet-black hair, parted in the middle. Her dress matches the color of her eyes. At the neckline is a small pink flower pinned to a white lace collar.

The spirit of Eugenia Gary followed her hurricane-ravaged portrait to Merrehope.

Merrehope is often the center of Meridian's social scene. Weddings in the double parlor are a popular choice. One of the upstairs bedrooms is reserved for the bride as a changing room. And, it is also a place where this teenage spirit likes to come in and watch the brides get ready. Donna has felt and heard her presence.

"In 2003, I was cleaning the bride's room. It was freezing cold, and we had the heaters cranked up. I had the door to the bedroom shut to keep the heat in and prevent it from escaping into the hall where there were no heaters. I was inside the bathroom of the suite straightening the towels when all of a sudden the door to the bedroom flew open. I stepped into the bedroom, and I could hear the rustle of her skirts and smell her perfume. Eugenia wears rosewater."

Of all the hostesses, Donna has a unique connection to the teenage ghost. Donna grew up in Meridian. Her father's family lived a few blocks from Merrehope. Through marriage, she is a descendant of the Gary family. Although Eugenia's playful spirit seemed to tease her distant relative, Donna was disappointed that Eugenia never put in a personal appearance. "I never saw her until late last year. It was a dark, dreary day, and I had just put the kitchen lights on. I was putting things away when I decided I needed a break." Donna was alone in the house. "I got up to stretch and walk. When I came through the double parlor into the main hall it was dark, and then all of a sudden, I ran into Eugenia, the outline of her. She was heading away from me towards the back of the house. I called out her name, 'Eugenia?' I drew in my breath and she was gone." Donna pauses and smiles, clearly relishing the memory. "Everybody always used to ask me what I would say if I saw her. I'd usually respond, 'I have no idea.' And then, when Eugenia does show herself, all I could say was her name." Donna would still like to see her face instead of just her relative's backside, but the hostess has patience and hopes that one day the teenage ghost will give her a smile.

Since the incident, Donna has made adjustments to her daily ritual. "When I first worked here, I would come in and announce, 'Okay folks, I'm here to work. This is a big house and there is room enough for all of us. Get used to me. I am not going anywhere.' And at closing time, as I was locking the door, I would say, 'I'll see you all tomorrow. Good night.'" Donna, who now works one week off and one week on, directs her greetings to her kindred spirit. "I arrive and say, 'Good morning, Eugenia.' At the end of the day it's, 'Goodbye, Eugenia. Take care of our home. See you next week.'"

Postscript: Rumors about Merrehope's ghosts pique the interest of a wide-range of visitors. "Normally," says Donna, "we don't volunteer and talk about spirits in the house. If they ask, we will. And then we have some who tell us what is going on, like a psychic who called herself Bloody Mary. She said she saw a ghost in the Periwinkle room." Donna also has to deal with the impatient visitors who are not interested in the history of the house. "They just announce, 'All we want are the ghost stories.'"

One persistent group arranged a rare overnight visit. Donna stayed in the house to supervise. "A few years ago we had a ghost busters group here. They set up video and audio equipment all over the house and put down sleeping bags in the front hall. Around midnight, I said, 'Look, you younger folks can stay up. This old lady is going to bed.'" Donna slept in the apartment at the back of the house, which is used for rental income. "I was sleeping soundly. I woke up because there was the sound of dragging going through the hall near the staircase upstairs and then back towards what used to be the servants' quarters. It was right above my head. I sat straight up. At first, I thought, *'What was that?'* I didn't think it was the paranormal group. I didn't hear anything out of them. What it was, I don't know, but I'll tell you this. I peeked out, and they had their sleeping bags in various groups around the hall and the parlor." Thinking they might be worried about her because of the mysterious dragging sound almost like a body being pulled across the wooden floors, Donna yelled out, "I'm okay!" Their response was surprising. "I heard loud snoring." Donna laughs at the irony. "They are supposed to be tracking the ghosts, and I am the one who hears it." She does add that one of the ghost busters was awake but appeared afraid to get out of his sleeping bag at the foot of the staircase. He told Donna that he decided to wait to see if whatever it was would come downstairs, but it didn't.

The Williams' beloved gingerbread house.

20

The Williams Gingerbread House

A short stroll behind the pristine white façade of Merrehope leads to a sagging, mustard-colored Queen Victorian. Despite its haggard outward appearance, it's a home filled with love and the spirits of one devoted couple. *In 1885, on fashionable Eighth Street in Meridian, Frank W. Williams watched the workers apply the finishing touches to his grand new home. He surveyed the area with a satisfied grin. Meridian was booming. The logging and textile industry were thriving. The city sat at the junction of five railroads with three more planned. He already owned a successful insurance agency, and now he and Mamie would soon be married. The Victorian mansion would be his wedding present to his beautiful bride.*

For the next five idyllic decades, Frank and Mamie were one of the most influential couples to preside over Meridian's social scene. Their only sorrow was their inability to have children of their own. To fill the void, the couple adopted a son, a distant relative. They also invited Daisy, Mamie's sister, to live with them. As Frank's insurance business flourished, the Williams family traveled the world, but they always returned to their beloved home in Meridian. With all of its ornamental fretwork, brackets, corbels, spandrels, carved spindles, and wraparound porch, locals tended to refer to the Williams' home as the "Gingerbread House."

As the Williamses approached their eighties, Frank made modifications to the house. Mamie was confined to a wheelchair. Therefore, an elevator was installed so that she could get from her bedroom on the second floor to the living areas below, especially her favorite music room.

Today, the home is on tour as a house museum. Hostess Donna White enjoys showing off some of its special features, especially the stained glass in the windows, door panels, and transoms. The second-floor bedrooms appear as if Frank, Mamie, and Daisy have never left. Books are stacked on nightstands, framed family photos are spread on top of oak bureaus, and dresses, shawls, and shoes spill out of the open doors of armoires, waiting on their owners to select a gown or jacket to wear to dinner.

There is one item that the hostess wishes she never had to explain. The padlock on the elevator door looms large and foreboding. Donna reveals the terrible sequence of events. "Mrs. Williams opened the door and backed her wheelchair into the elevator. The elevator was still on the first floor. She fell into the shaft. Weeks later she passed away from her injuries."

A devastated Frank Williams retreated to his library, his private domain. Ever the Southern gentleman, he realized he could no longer live in his dream home. Mamie was gone. In her will, she had deeded the home to Daisy. Frank respected her wishes. "He didn't think it proper that he should stay there; it might cause a scandal because Daisy was unmarried."

Today, Frank's heaving sighs are audible in the library. Having lost the love of his life, his specter is a sorrowful one. Mamie's spirit seems unaffected by the events leading to her death. Her ethereal presence is like a whisper, a soft swish as she passes by the bed, sits down in the ladies' parlor, or plays at the piano in the music room.

For reasons Donna cannot explain, children who visit the restored residence have a problem with the room used by Frank and Mamie's son and grandchildren. In the corner of the nursery, a chubby baby doll is propped up in a red wagon. "Kids, when they see it, they get spooked out."

Snowbirds from Wisconsin also were "spooked out" on a visit in 2010. The retirees pulled into the gravel parking lot and stepped out of their silver and gray luxury RV. On the recommendation of a friend, the couple wanted to tour the Williams House. After the tour, they couldn't agree on the level of haunting within the home.

They both loved the idea of two sets of doors at the entrance. The outer doors are for security and protection of the inner doors, and the decorative inner doors have double panels of brilliant colored designs in stained glass. When they asked the tour guide why the panels, as beautiful as they were, did not match, she replied, "If you had as much money as Mr. Williams, you could do whatever you want." The couple approved

An older Frank Williams still in love with Mamie.

of the deep-green shade on the walls of the front parlor along with the rich paneling and parquet floors. She loved the idea of the music room, but he seemed more interested in the library at the end of the hall. The husband, a gaunt, stoop-shouldered man in his late seventies, began a slow perusal of the books and historic documents but then made an abrupt exit. As much as his wife tried to coax her once-eager husband to return to explore the artifacts, he balked. "Carl, come see. Here's the picture of Frank Williams standing inside his first insurance office just like Elliot told us. And look at this chandelier; it's got to be a Tiffany."

Mamie Williams as a young woman.

Carl shook his head and mumbled that the room was "oppressive" and that "the man doesn't want me in here." Concerned about her husband's negative attitude, Florence abandoned the library to join him for the tour of the second floor.

The hostess preceded them up the dark and gloomy staircase. She plugged a work light into a dangling extension cord to light their way. Since Katrina, the electrical system in the home has malfunctioned and repairs are on-going. The bedrooms are off an open hallway running the length of the house. Carl was fine, but this time his wife lagged behind.

While the guide extolled the numerous features of the furnishings on this level, she refrained from sharing the terrible tragedy of Mrs. Williams' fall down the elevator shaft. On exiting one bedroom to cross the hall to another, Florence said, "There is something wrong here." Midway down the hall, close to the padlocked door to the elevator, she grimly announced, "It's really bad. I think I would like to leave."

Outside, Carl had the engine of the RV running and the air-conditioning on full blast to cool off the well-appointed interior for the last leg of their return journey north. Both husband and wife were visibly upset by their experiences inside the Williams House. They requested that their full names not be mentioned. Carl refused further conversation. Florence sheepishly confided that they didn't know what to think. "We don't have ghosts in Wisconsin."

The wheels of the RV stirred up a cloud of white gravel dust, and the retired couple left with a completely new paranormal realm to ponder.

Postscript: Frank Williams died in 1949 at the age of eighty-eight. Daisy Watson, Mamie's sister, lived to 104. Daisy never married. By then, Eighth Street had lost its luster; it was no longer a fashionable thoroughfare. There was concern that the house might be slated for demolition. In 1978, Mrs. Hazel Williams Wright, a descendant of the original owners, donated the house to the Merrehope Restorations Foundation. There was one hitch. It had to be moved. Parts of the home were dismantled. The sleeping porch and chimneys were taken off.

Donna White vividly remembers the trauma of seeing the home in pieces. "I had just moved back from California. I was tooling along Main Street with my son and daughter in the back seat. I thought they were tearing it down. I pulled over and parked and my son asked, 'Mama, what are you doing?' I said, 'I have to go up there and stop them from destroying the Gingerbread House.'"

Donna was relieved to learn that the dismantling process was the first step in preparing the home for its move behind the Merrehope mansion in Meridian's historic district. Unbeknownst to Donna, she would one day be working as a hostess at both Merrehope and her beloved Gingerbread House.

The Williams House tucked behind Merrehope.

Eugenia's playful spirit found her way from the Gulf Coast to Merrehope in Meridian. The loving spirits of Frank and Mamie appeared to have accompanied the Gingerbread House as it made its way across town.

21

Rosedale

No sound rings forth from the campanile at Rosedale; it is a bell tower without bells. The design is pure Italian and most closely resembles Giotto's Bell Tower, the freestanding campanile of Florence Cathedral on the Piazza del Dumo in Italy. In 1856, when Dr. William Topp built his showplace in Columbus, Mississippi, he knew what he wanted and got it. The good doctor's prescription? The illusion of a bell tower as the central focus of his mansion, minus the deafening noise a cacophony of bells would create. What Dr. Topp could not foresee was that his bell tower would provide the perfect nest for a fledgling spirit.

With glowing skin, Leigh Imes wears her glossy brown hair in a shoulder-length flip, and even with her plaid shirttail hanging out over skinny jeans, she has that casual-put-together finesse of a runway model. Together with her husband, Gene, Leigh is the owner and proud restorer of Rosedale. "We bought the house twelve years ago. We had a hard time deciding what to do. Dixie and Carl Butler restored Temple Heights, another historic home in Columbus, and Carl came over here and told us that we really needed to redo the house in the period that it was first built. So we did. For those first seven years, we collected the furniture, and then we moved out for four years so the renovations could be completed. We hired George Fore, an architectural conservator from North Carolina, and Skip Tuminello, from Vicksburg, as the architect for the addition in back." And the hauntings began.

Leigh stands in the spacious upstairs hallway. It is larger than most bedrooms. The main stairwell is at the back end of the hall. At the opposite end is a door to a second landing with a separate staircase for

Rosedale mansion sits in isolated splendor on a rural road in Columbus.

the two-storied bell tower. Leigh pieces together the peculiar unraveling of one haunted evening. "We'd been to J. Broussard's restaurant to eat that night. While the renovations were going on, Skip Tuminello slept in the guest bedroom, closest to the tower door. Skip was asleep when we got back. He came down the next morning and said he heard a lady and a child in the hall outside his room, and they woke him up. He said it was two distinct voices, an older woman and a little girl. They were playing a game. He didn't know what game, but the little girl was giggling and the old woman was talking to her. He opened his door to look. There was nobody there. The voices stopped and he went back to bed. This went on three different times in the middle of the night." Leigh hesitates before going on. "It was so real to Skip that he even accused us of tricking him. He kept asking, 'Are you playing a joke on me? Are you sure you all weren't up there?' And we said, 'Why would we be playing in the hall?' And he just said that he thought we all had to be up to something."

Leigh reviewed any other sources that might be mistaken for voices. "Our daughter Megan was asleep, and there was no older woman staying in the house. We keep the door to the tower open from time to time. I've heard the wind blow and shake and all that, and I've heard creaks, but Skip insisted it was two voices and they were playing. He didn't seem to be terrified by it; it just bothered him enough that he told us, 'I can't stay here anymore.' He would stay with a friend in Columbus while he was working here, and he never spent another night at Rosedale."

Skip's experience validates that of a longtime resident of Columbus. "I have a friend," remembers Leigh, "whose husband as a teenager would ride by Rosedale quite a bit. He would say that as he passed he would always check out the window on the top level of the tower, and when he did, he could see a little girl walking up and down the staircase." Leigh catches herself midthought. "That is strange because Skip Tuminello heard a little girl outside his bedroom door, which is right by the landing to the tower. It's weird; two different people talking about the same little girl ghost, decades apart, and Skip, not even knowing anything about the earlier stories."

Rosedale's tower affords a 360-degree view of the surrounding fields. The house sits a good football field back from the nearest road. There are few trees to obstruct the street-level view of the front of Rosedale. French doors on the lower tower level open on to a Juliet balcony with a wrought-iron railing. The upper tier of the tower has four pairs of arched windows facing the four compass points. The stairs inside the campanile pass directly in front of the glass of the upper and lower tiers.

"The children who lived at the Palmer House would also talk about the little girl ghost in the tower," admits Leigh. The residential dorms of Palmer House are like box seats overlooking the pond off the right wing of Rosedale. Palmer House was founded in 1895 as a place for "children with no where else to turn." By 1902, the eighteen-acre facility housed forty "social orphans." Tales of Rosedale's ghost are a common topic among Palmer House alumni, now numbering one thousand strong. "The kids staying there would say that they could see a light on in the tower windows when the house was vacant, and the little girl would go up and down the stairs."

Leigh decided to give the sight lines a little test run. "I actually went outside at night to see if you could spot a figure in the landing." Leigh concedes that anyone mortal or otherwise, ascending or descending these stairs, would be visible from the street. She is just sad that her timing is off. "My husband has said he wished he could see her, but neither of us have. I guess we are not susceptible; still there must be something to it with so many people telling the same story."

Leigh and Gene Imes are the sixth family to own Rosedale. "The first owners, the Topps, had five children here. In 1904, they sold the house to W. V. Grace. The Graces lived here for a very long time, forty years. This house has always been a home for children." On the back stairwell that connects the original house to the new addition, a wall of photos chronicles happy moments in the life of daughter Megan Imes. Her infectious smile shines through from baby pictures to a more adventurous young girl on horseback jumping fences. A proud mother, Leigh extends her arms as if to embrace all the little ones who ever ran through the mansion. "Children were all over this place all the time; if you talk to anybody that's from Columbus, they'll say, 'Oh, yeah, I used to play at that house.'" Leigh continues the happy tradition. "Life is too short not to enjoy it. My daughter had a slumber party. All the girls put on socks and slid up and down the front hall like it was an ice-skating rink. Children haven't changed at all. If something gets broken, it's bad, but things happen; you move on." Leigh's voice has an inviting, intimate, Jackie Kennedy-whisperlike quality. She is thoughtful. "So I guess it was natural that Skip Tuminello heard children's voices in the house. I wish I could hear the little girl's voice."

A tiny ball of gray-and-white shaggy fur scampers into the front hall. Leigh bends over to pet Harvey, a Havanese puppy. Harvey is a perfect fit for this Italian mansion. Harvey shadows Leigh, but sometimes he struggles to keep up; his stubby paws support an eight-pound body barely nine inches off the floor. This time Harvey is knocked off course by a stealthy calico cat hell bent on crossing the black-and-white, diamond-patterned floor. "We have a Noah's ark here," says Leigh, scooping up Harvey in her arms. "I've heard that animals are more aware of spirits." Harvey gives Leigh a look of pure puppy devotion. "My cats will freeze as they are climbing up the stairs. I don't see anything, and I can't figure out what they are staring at."

Leigh Imes is not troubled by any potential ghosts that came to the home before her; however, she does own up to a mild form of *furniphobia*. In February of 2009, *Fear of Furniture,* an animated documentary, captured the anguish of a man on a new-furniture-buying expedition; he saw the looming purchases as a symbol of submission to a life of drudgery. Leigh has a leery, getting-to-know-you, cooling-off period with recent antique acquisitions at Rosedale, where an unsurpassed collection of American-made antiques grace the halls.

If ghoulies and ghosties can take over rooms and towers, why can't they hitch a ride inside an armoire, burrow in a draw, or wrap their tenacious spirits around the sinewy curve of a cabriole leg? "You know how sometimes someone can buy an old piece of furniture and bring something with them to your house?" Leigh's question is rhetorical. "That always kind of freaked me out at first when we bought this furniture. . . . I always worried where the pieces came from and what might be attached to them." Leigh's mother has similar concerns.

Against a backdrop of gold *fleur-de-lis* on deep-red wallpaper, the Gothic Revival bed in the guest room is breathtaking. The spires on the canopy soar to the fourteen-foot ceiling, and the headboard and footboard are designed with carved vaulted arches reminiscent of cathedral architecture. "My mother will not sleep in this bed. She thinks it's a beautiful bed, but she gets a funny feeling from it." Leigh makes a face. "She says the bed is creepy; it bothers her." Leigh is unsure whether it is a combination of bed and bedroom that causes her mother to sleep elsewhere. "This was the room that Skip Tuminello slept in when he heard the little girl and the old woman playing outside his door, but this is a different bed. The bed Skip slept in is now in my daughter Megan's room. One of the previous owners, Mr. Grace, died in that bedroom."

And while Leigh swears that "nothing strange has every happened in my daughter's bedroom," the complicated origins of Rosedale's two talking ghosts persist when the present owner says, "We think the older woman is Mrs. Grace because we've heard that her ghost haunts here, but I've yet to know who the little girl is."

During the restoration process, Gene and Leigh Imes found numerous old photos to guide them. They would have preferred to salvage all of the ancillary buildings that had been on the grounds, but most were torn down prior to their arrival. Their new pool house sits on the same footprint of the original kitchen. "We found a little bit of the brick walkway and pieces of china scattered about."

The guest bedroom with its Gothic bed.

Although the historic images of Rosedale also offered clues to the location of the slave quarters, Leigh's visceral experience was more personal. "I walked outside in the back, this is kind of weird, it smelled like somebody struck a match, the smell of sulphur, real strong. I had this image of the slaves, and it made me wonder about how they were treated because the slave quarters were back there."

Although Leigh claims she is not as tuned in to the supernatural as other visitors to the house, she can easily run through a checklist of the inexplicable. "I have been in other parts of the house and heard the front door slam shut when it is already closed. One time the alarm was even beeping and no one was there. I got really upset; it was out of place. You see shadows from time to time as you enter a room. It's hard to tell if your eyes are playing tricks on you or not. And this house feels real warm to me sometimes in certain rooms. It's not anything I am afraid of; just maybe it could be someone who's lived here before."

Leigh Imes is clear on one thing. "This is a historic home to me, not a haunted house. If there is something here, it likes us I guess."

Postscript: Rosedale is open to the public only by appointment or during the Columbus Spring Pilgrimage tour of homes. Leigh, Gene, and Megan live at Rosedale full time. The campanile, the bell tower, is currently devoid of furniture. Future plans include furnishing the campanile as a comfortable space to "watch the sunset or drink a glass of wine." Perhaps the anonymous little girl ghost will also enjoy having a comfy chair to curl up in and enjoy the view.

Temple Heights on a bluff in Columbus.

22

Temple Heights

What's happening to us?
—from the movie *The Amityville Horror*

In the 1979 paranormal blockbuster movie *The Amityville Horror,* actor James Brolin is losing his mind. He and his wife have just purchased an old deserted home, and it's possessed. A door blows off its hinges, windows slam shut, ooze drips from nail heads in the walls, swarms of flies invade a room, and malevolent manifestations stalk the house. The movie is based on the actual experiences of newlyweds George and Kathy Lutz.

"When we first went to see *The Amityville Horror,* everybody in the audience was scared. Carl and I just laughed." Dixie and her late husband, Carl Butler, found the movie's paranormal antics paled in comparison to the haunted happenings at Temple Heights, their historic home in Columbus. "I mean, I even have stuff that oozes out of the walls. I just had it repaired again this year. You scrape it out, put some mud on it, smooth it out, and then its back." This former elementary school principal presents the facts in a manner that leaves no room for doubt.

In some aspects, Dixie and Carl Butler's lives mirrored those of George and Kathy Lutz, the couple who purchased the Amityville house. George and Kathy were newlyweds when they first saw High Hopes, the house at 112 Ocean Drive on the south shore of Long Island, New York. Although the Dutch colonial sat vacant and was in need of repair, the Lutzes fell in love with the house's gambrel (barn-shaped) roof and a pair of quarter-circle windows on the end. On the market for a bargain price of $80,000, the Lutz family jumped at the opportunity to snag their dream house for $40,000 below the appraised value.

Dixie Butler's initial reaction to Temple Heights in Columbus was not so favorable, but like High Hopes in Amityville, the price was right, and Dixie's future husband made an offer she couldn't refuse. "Carl had already seen the house. We were both grad students in Nashville. One day he drew the floor plans for me and asked, 'Do you think you'd like to live in it?' And I said, 'Do you mean with you?' And he said yes, and I said yes." After the unusual marriage proposal, Carl warned Dixie, "Now, don't get your hopes up. It is really going to be in bad shape." Dixie is forthright. "I have to tell you, it was so much worse than I possibly could have imagined. It really was. It was really pretty dreary when I first saw it on a cold November day."

In an interview for *Reflections: Homes and History of Columbus, Mississippi,* by Sylvia Higginbotham, Carl Butler describes the circumstances leading to the purchase. "I'd always been interested in historic properties and knew about Temple Heights but was told it was uninhabitable. It was in terrible shape visually; it had not been painted in forty years. . . . After Dixie and I got engaged, we decided we wanted this house and made the commitment to restore it." Owner Kirk Egger cut the young couple an unbelievable deal. "Since we were both in graduate school in Nashville—Dixie at Peabody, I was at Vanderbilt—he let us pay one thousand dollars down."

Dixie's hair has turned a soft gray now, but she remembers the excitement of that first home purchase. "We bought Temple Heights the last day of 1967. We didn't have to pay any more until we were out of school. We got married in 1968 and started living here in 1969."

Both couples, the Butlers and the Lutzes, would soon come to question their decisions. When George and Kathy Lutz purchased High Hopes, the real estate agent disclosed that on November 13, 1974, a father, mother, and their four children—two girls and two boys—were murdered in the house. Many potential buyers were scared off. However, George Lutz was not dissuaded, saying, "Houses don't have memories." But at the urging of a family friend, he invited a priest to bless the house. In subsequent television interviews with talk show host Merv Griffin and ABC's Elizabeth Vargas, George says the blessing had the opposite effect.

Father Delany believed the house had an evil spirit and tried to perform an exorcism. Kathy had nightmares about the murders. Their daughter was convinced she had a ghost, a malevolent spirit, for a playmate. George's work suffered, and the evil vibes in the house repulsed his business partner's wife.

Dixie scoffs at the movie version's exaggerated portrayal of what may have happened to the Lutzes. "I've had people who had *real* experiences. When we first got married, we would bring Mrs. Wakefield, our landlady from Nashville, with us. She stayed in this room [second-floor guest bedroom], and she saw a little wispy thing coming down the steps from the third floor to the second-floor landing. So she closed this door [and] put a chair against it. She said later that that probably wouldn't do any good. And she was a really intelligent lady not prone to over imagination." A shadow of a smile tugs at the corners of Dixie's lips. "And we knew it wasn't either Carl or I that she saw because we aren't *wispy*." When asked to describe the ghostly form, Dixie says that Mrs. Wakefield "couldn't put her finger on whether it was a child or an adult. I have had some people stay in here, they felt a presence, but they couldn't identify it either."

Dixie, on the other hand, is confident she knows who it is. "I think it is Elizabeth. One of the ladies that lived here was named Elizabeth Kennebrew. She lived and died here. When things happen here, we just say that is Miss Elizabeth."

The wispy ghostlike figure was identified by someone who knew Elizabeth well. "We were having a dinner party here," says Dixie. "One of my friends went upstairs to use the bathroom [until recently the only bathroom in the house was on the second floor]. My friend heard somebody outside waiting. After she rejoined us at the table, she said, 'I just had the strangest thing happen. When I was leaving the bathroom, I passed somebody in the hall, and I thought she was waiting for me to get out.'" Dixie says there were no other guests in the house except the ones seated at the table, so they asked the woman who had just come from the bathroom to tell them more about the person she saw. Everyone in the dining room was astonished as an older friend of Dixie's exclaimed, "You're describing Elizabeth Kennebrew. I knew Elizabeth."

At High Hopes in Amityville, the manifestations, as depicted in the horror movie, had no intention of waiting their turn. The Lutzes called in a second priest to cleanse the house. This exorcism also failed. After twenty-eight days, the Lutz family fled Amityville and moved to another state, their dreams and hopes in ruins. At Temple Heights, Carl and Dixie Butler were not so easily dissuaded.

The Butlers handled their ghosts and tackled the restoration with equal aplomb. "Since we knew we couldn't afford to redo everything, we could mop the floor and we could put Johnson's paste wax on it. We found that we could paint a room in a weekend, so we would come down from Nashville and paint over whatever was here, knowing that we would come back and sheetrock when we could afford it, but at least it made the rooms feel livable," explains Dixie.

As for the ghosts and other questionable activities around the house, they addressed them each in turn. "My goodness, we heard noises when there was no one around. Doors opened and closed by themselves. One time there was a big crash when Don Schollander, the Olympic swimming star, and his wife were staying with us." As the local high-school swim coach with an impressive winning record, Carl Butler had persuaded the four-time gold-medal winner of the 1964 Summer Olympics to give a clinic for the swim team. "Don and his wife were by the pool at the house; we were getting ready to have lunch, and we heard the crash. We never could find anything that fell to make such a loud noise."

Random sounds are a common occurrence at Temple Heights. "We will hear music or voices, and you'll think you've left the radio or the television on upstairs, and there won't be anybody. We climb the stairs to the second floor and the lights turn on and off."

There is one piece of the paranormal puzzle that annoys Dixie more than the others. "Carl's parents were staying here. I had gone to bed, and they were downstairs. Out of curiosity, Mr. Butler asked Carl if we knew which rooms the Kennebrew sisters used." Dixie walks over to the *faux bois,* paneled door in the guest bedroom. "We knew this was Laura Kennebrew's room because she wrote her name on it; her signature was etched into the door." Dixie's tone is precise. "Carl brought his parents up to this room to show them where Laura had signed her name, and he couldn't find it. The master bedroom is the room next to this. I was reading, and Carl called, 'Dixie, come show Mother and Daddy where Laura wrote her name. I can't find it.'" Frustration filters in. "I couldn't find it either. After they left, I got a flashlight and I went to every door in the house looking for Laura's name." Dixie briefly tried to convince herself that maybe she and Carl had gotten confused about which door had the name; it had been awhile since they had looked at it. Then years of listening to students try to wiggle out of a situation when they are caught in the act kicked in. "It was right across here." Dixie indicates a spot at eye level on the inside of Laura's bedroom door. "It was in big print. We had shown it to a lot of people before Carl's parents asked about it." Dixie refuses to entertain the possibility that she might have been hallucinating. "No, it was there. And it has never reappeared. There are a lot of things you just can't explain. You just have to accept."

Elizabeth Kennebrew had a different view. She refused to accept the apology from a suitor who stood her up. Dixie carefully unfolds a handwritten letter. The pages are delicate parchment paper. They crinkle as she smoothes them out.

Laura Kennebrew's bedroom where her name disappeared from the door.

Dear Lizette,

I know that you will never speak to me again and I think you have a right not to after what happened last evening. I feel as if I never can look at you in the face again. You may not believe me, but I never had anything to happen that bothered me more, but listen, I will explain. Yesterday, a week ago, I made a date with Miss Haley to accompany her to church, but had forgotten all about it when I asked you if I may walk home with you . . . I want to ask you to forgive me and promise you it will never happen again. Will you?. . . Please let me know for I am bothered to death. Hoping you will have compassion on me.

I am so ever your sincere friend, Joseph Wilbur, September, 1908

Elizabeth spurned her would-be suitor. "She remained an old maid," says Dixie. Elizabeth never married, but her mother's will provided for Elizabeth and her sisters, Laura, Daisy, Ruth, and Jessie. "Mrs. Kennebrew's will said that as long as there was an unmarried daughter,

Dixie Butler reads Joseph's letter to Lizette.

the house couldn't be sold." Elizabeth was able to live out the remainder of her days at Temple Heights.

Now that Elizabeth inhabits another realm, free of the physical restraints of old age, she seems to enjoy floating down from the upper floors to the lower. Dixie Butler is pleased to have her.

Downstairs in the brilliant blue foyer another woman's signature has caused some confusion. "Mrs. Francis Jane Fontaine owned this house from 1867 to 1887. Her daughter, Annie, scratched her name in the pane of glass to the right of the front door. People say she scratched it with her diamond ring." Dixie Butler stares at the flourishes in the lower panel of the glass sidelights on the right side of the door. "You can't really do that unless you take the diamond out of the ring. I don't know how she did that; if I knew I would put my name in here." A broad smile brightens her face. Dixie is ever vigilant about Annie's signature. "This glass has cracked, and I hope it lasts under my watch. I am the only one who washes it." Unlike Elizabeth's signature on the bedroom door, Dixie intends to make sure Annie's signature stays put. "I have a sense of all of the people who have lived here. I am in awe of their stories."

Temple Heights is on the National Register of Historic Places and a featured stop on the annual Columbus Spring Pilgrimage Home, Garden and Church Tour. In 1847, Richard T. Brownrigg, a native of Edenton, North Carolina, arrived in Columbus and soon made his fortune as a cotton planter. Brownrigg built Temple Heights as a singular testament to his achievements.

"We had a party for the house in 1987 to celebrate its 150th birthday." Dixie Butler is beaming. "People came from all over the country. Since that time, we came to know a descendant of one of the Brownrigg slaves, Dr. Morris Henderson of Richmond. He teaches at Virginia Commonwealth University." Dixie is excited to have a fellow scholar come to visit and share "the other side of the story of Temple Heights."

"During Columbus's annual pilgrimage, I have a story in every room of someone who lived in the house. I had someone in the kitchen playing the part of General Brownrigg. Dr. Henderson sat down next to him, and they kind of fed off each other, telling the history of the families who lived here, each with a very different point of view. People were fascinated." For the first time since the middle of the nineteenth century, the voices of slave and owner spoke freely on common ground. "One man came here and then he came back one summer with his family, and he said, 'I want them to see their history.'" For Dixie Butler, knowing that Temple Heights serves as a place where the past is rekindled in the present day makes all her efforts worthwhile, and she's not done. "I would like to have a reunion of the Brownrigg slaves and the Brownriggs at the same time.'"

Postscript: The history of Temple Heights is well documented, and despite all that has happened in the ensuing years, Dixie Butler is not afraid. "It's not a spooky house. It is a friendly house so whatever is here, I am comfortable with."

23

Waverley

Yet, with a stern delight and strange
I saw the spirit-stirring change.
As warr'd the wind with wave and wood
Upon the ruined tower I stood.
—Sir Walter Scott, *Waverley*

A traveling salesman spins a whopper of a tale to Robert and Madonna Snow about a haunted house in the deep weeds of Clay County near West Point, Mississippi; lost on a dirt road, he spied a decrepit mansion in the tangled overgrowth. The Snows, antique dealers from Philadelphia, Mississippi, are intrigued. They hop a ferry across the Tombigbee River and clamber up a knoll. Poking through the treetop is an octagonal cupola crowning an H-shaped, four-storied, eight-thousand-square-foot behemoth. Thirty-eight-year-old Robert and thirty-six-year-old "Donna" are in love.

Three months later, in October of 1962, Robert and Donna sell their antiques shop, farm, and timberland to raise money to purchase Waverley, an 1852 antebellum mansion. They pack up their children—Allen, eleven; Melanie, seven; and little Cindy, five—and move in. An adult Melanie Snow remembers it as more like camping out. "We loaded up our old station wagon and threw caution to the winds. My parents weren't money people; they had all they could do to buy the house; they had no idea how they would be able to restore it." The family pulled up and hacked their way to the rotting porch. The front steps were missing, and the front door had been wedged ajar. Honeysuckle vines snaked up over the house,

Waverley Plantation amid acres of forest land in West Point.

and branches poked through broken windows. A few faded-green shutters dangled askew while the rest lay scattered on the ground.

Conditions inside were even more deplorable. A moldy mat of leaves, branches, and human refuse carpeted the floor. An infestation of possums, squirrels, birds, bats, insects, and one very loud ghost had settled in. "We slept on mattresses in the dining room because we couldn't even get into the bedrooms on the second floor." The family's sleep was interrupted by sonic boomlike crashes from above that felt like the ceiling was caving in.

The heavy-handed, foot-stomping ghost was the least of their problems. "We had no electricity or plumbing; we hauled water up and down the muddy dirt roads, miles back and forth from the nearest neighbors." But there was plenty of reading material.

Graffiti covered every square inch of the walls. There were thousands of names. During the fifty years that Waverley sat vacant, campers, hunters, and fishermen used it as a way stop. Curiosity seekers filtered in and out and scrawled their names on every available space. "Mississippi State

University in Starkville, thirty miles away, sent their pledges over here for decades. If you could spend the night in the spook house, you could be in the club." Melanie laughs, "That's the truth. The worst thing we found scribbled on the walls was *'For a good time, call Lulu in Cowtown, Texas.'* She must have been a bad, bad, girl." Rather than tear out the old plaster to remove all of the signatures and writing on the walls, the Snows worked for more than two years cleaning out each name. "Every crevice, every crack, we worked with boxes of toothbrushes, toothpicks, and wooden kitchen matches to remove the wood daubers. Irishmen worked over two years to install the plaster and it took us two and a half years to clean and repair it."

Although pounded by the elements, the house was structurally sound and survived the onslaught of five decades of uninvited visitors. Other than the wall-to-wall graffiti, there was little vandalism. In the rotunda, a matching pair of self-supporting staircases curves upwards to cantilevered balconies on the second, third, and fourth floors. Of the 718 hand-turned, mahogany spindles, only one was missing. Less than twenty windowpanes were broken, and there was only one BB hole in the house. "No one took the marble mantles; there were eight in the house," reports a blue-eyed, red-headed Melanie. "They left the original French gasoliers in each of the rooms and the large, gold-leaf mirrors."

Miraculously, Waverley also escaped going up in flames. "We have a number of photographs of this entrance hall, and in the rotunda, someone had placed a big metal barrel. They had campfires inside to keep warm. They had drinking parties." Melanie testifies to the horrific dangers. "We found thousands of cigarette butts in the house. The rotunda is open; it goes sixty-five feet straight up. It was designed to carry the heat up and then be let out of the sixteen windows in the cupola. If a fire had gotten out of control here, Waverley would be nothing more than ashes."

The Snow family believes that the ghosts guarded the house. "We have had so many people tells us through the years that they would sneak into Waverley to go ghost hunting or picnicking, and any time somebody was up to no good, or thinking about maybe stealing a wall sconce, there would be loud noises like shotguns and boards popping together, it would scare them and they would run away."

There is one little spirit that seems to be particularly active, and

Melanie knows her well. As a child, Melanie roamed in and out of every inch, every hidden corner, and every obscure cubbyhole of Waverly. She is a gifted storyteller. "Legend has it that the little ghost girl has been here over one hundred years, long before we ever heard of Waverley. No one knows for sure who she is, but we make the bed in the ghost room, the first room at the top of the stairs, and when we go in there, the imprint of her little body is on the bed; the bedspread is wrinkled, just like a little child has crawled up to nap or play. Many people hear her. We've been at Waverley for forty-eight years. I've heard her. My mother heard her; the family has heard her a number of times. She's in the gardens and in the woods and in the house in that ghost room. A sweet angelic voice calls, *Mama, Mama.*' We believe she is the guardian angel that protected the house all the years it was vacant and protects the house today."

Having inspired many love stories, Waverley is an unusual haunted house. "This was the *play* house for the area and everybody courted out here and wrote on the walls and woodwork who knew who. This past weekend, a lady on a tour said that when she and her husband were courting out here, they wrote their names in that room [the main parlor]. My mom always said we knew every love affair for fifty years. When people in the community come back to visit now, they tell us that they were proposed to out here, their children were conceived out here." Melanie jumps to their defense. "They never dreamed of doing anything wrong to the house. They will say, 'I crossed the ferry on the river just to look around and met this darling boy over there looking around, and we had a picnic, and we fell in love, and we've been married for forty-nine years.' It's a love house. A house of romance that's for sure."

Col. George Hampton Young and his wife, Lucy Woodson Watkins Young, designed the house with a romantic theme from its inception. Brackets of lyres frame the front door. Seven of the ten Young children said their vows under the framed archway of the "wedding alcove" in the parlor. "The little babies were also baptized here. This was like a little chapel. The Youngs built it knowing they would hold all of the family's important moments here." The tradition lives on. "Since we've been here, we've had a number of wedding proposals; sometimes they'll drop to their knees in the wedding alcove or under the magnolia tree or in the original lover's lane to the left of the house." The trail Melanie indicates winds past

The bedroom where the little girl ghost likes to nap.

Lyres frame the front entrance of Waverley.

the house into a secluded glen. The lovers are probably blissfully unaware that they are stepping over the grave of Maj. John Pytchlyn. His ghostly gallivants take him on spectral jaunts through Waverley's grounds.

John "Jack" Pytchlyn was an Englishman by birth who lived among the Mississippi Choctaws and served as an interpreter for the United States government after the Revolutionary War. He married a Choctaw woman. He loved riding his horse along the Tombigbee River, near the future landing of Colonel Young's plantation. Pytchlyn died in 1835, and his gravesite was the vacant field where Waverley would one day stand. The funeral was conducted in the Choctaw warrior tradition. His rifle, boots, and saddle were deposited with his coffin. Mrs. Pytchlyn called for his horse to be killed and buried in the grave with his master. Judge Samuel Gholson intervened on behalf of the horse and assured the widow that a horse befitting the major's rank would surely be furnished by "the Great Spirit in the Happy Hunting Grounds." The widow Pytchlyn acquiesced and ordered a brick wall to be erected to protect the grave. She made semiannual visits to check on the gravesite. After reports of the grave being disturbed, the neighbors noticed that the widow's visits had ceased. Local gossip speculated that Mrs. Pytchlyn had removed the body to Indian Territory. No evidence of the brick wall or the grave remains, but at night, the faint sound of pounding hoofs rises to a crescendo, the earth is said to shudder, and a powerful whoosh of wind carries a phantom horse and rider past Waverley.

The Waverley mansion sits back from a narrow country road. The cupola is the only visible sign that something magnificent lies beyond the surrounding forty-acre forest. During the era of the Young family, the cotton plantation operated as a self-sustaining village with 50,000 acres of cleared land. One thousand slaves labored in the fields or as skilled craftsmen. Melanie lists a few of the operations. "There were grist mills, saw mills, molasses mills, a brick kiln, a cotton gin, an ice house, and a huge leather tannery operation. They manufactured for sale straw hats, leather hats, and boots for men, women, and children." While their labors were the backbone of the plantation economy, servitude forced the enslaved men and women to tread in the realm of uncertainty where even basic beliefs were questioned. One anonymous slave gave voice to their predicament: *"It ain't the things you don't know what gets you into trouble; it's the things you know for sure what ain't so."*

Colonel Young kept a desk in the cupola where he could see for miles. Melanie has read many of the first owner's journals. "He named his plantation Waverley after the title of his favorite novel by author and poet Sir Walter Scott."

The Youngs lived on a palatial level, yet there were also moments of tragedy. In 1836, George and Lucy and the first born of their ten children moved into a two-story log cabin where they could watch the construction of their grand mansion rise from dream to reality. Poor Lucy had little time to savor its magnificence. She died in 1852, the year the mansion was completed.

Exploring Waverley is a treasure hunt on an immense scale. A chip of red brick in the front yard might be from the brick wall that once enclosed the grave of Major Pytchlyn, the phantom rider. Across the country road, broken slabs of marble hint at the luxurious lifestyle of the Youngs and the visit of one famous spy. "At one of the artesian wells on the property, Colonel Young built an Italian marble-lined swimming pool with bathhouses for men and women. People have taken most of the marble over the years, but few of them know about one lady who came here to hide out."

Melanie's voice drops to a whisper as if the woman's secret identity must still be protected. "Belle Edmundson was a female Civil War spy. She's been called the lost heroine of the Confederacy. She smuggled money and mail under her petticoats. There was a letter issued for her arrest in Memphis so she came to Waverley as a refugee. She was friends with Lucy [the Young's daughter named after her mother] and stayed for six months. Belle kept her diary here, and she wrote, '*On hot humid afternoons, the ladies went down early to bathe but did not linger long because the gentlemen were anxious.*'"

Colonel Young loved to experiment. A copper-domed brick retort near the house burned rich pinewood to produce pine-rosin gas, which fueled the gasoliers. "Colonel Young had lighting before anyone else." Melanie has read the accounts. "People at that time wrote in their journals about riding out to Waverley by horseback to see the lights, see the gasoliers. It was a novelty." The gasolier in the master bedroom went from novelty to nest when baby squirrels were discovered in the glass globes by the Snow children after they moved in. "We called this room the Possum Condominium because possums liked the chandeliers as much as the squirrels. We'd take a little stick and the possums would wrap their tails around it, and we'd carry possums all over the house." Melanie nods her head in satisfaction. "The ghost girl did a good job protecting everything, because even with all the animals running around here, none of the glass globes were broken."

Waverley Plantation was the social center of the region with weekly dances and masquerade balls in the rotunda. The pink flounce of a taffeta ball gown, golden curls caught up in ribbon and lace, a gentleman's starched white collar, and a red ruby necklace—fleeting images of the family and their many guests have been seen in the mirrors. "This mirror was cracked at a dance held here during the Civil War but not from vandalism." Melanie is in the rotunda. A jagged crack runs the length of a gilded, pier mirror mounted on the wall. "It is documented in one of the old journals that during a big dance here, candles were placed in

The four-story main rotunda with the cracked pier mirror and ghostly images.

front of the mirror to add a warm glow to the party." One candle was too close to the leaded glass. "When it overheated, it popped so loud that in the journal notation it said, *'We thought we were under attack; we secured the house and the women.'*" Melanie laughs. "I bet the petticoats were flying." After a thorough search of the grounds, the men found nothing; they realized the sound came from the crack in the mirror, and the ball resumed. The cracked glass is said to give a distorted image of phantom dancers.

Melanie steps into the parlor and stares into the mirror over the white-marble fireplace mantle. "This mirror holds fifty years of faces; thousands of faces are reflected back if you look hard enough." Young brides with tentative smiles; stern-faced grooms; a baby, mouth open in rage at the cold christening water on its forehead; and a distraught father and husband mourning his beloved Lucy lying in a coffin in the alcove. They are all here: the hunters and fishermen, the college pledges, the lovers, and the vagrants.

Even the spindles on the cantilevered second-floor balconies harbor a tale, one linked to the identity of the little girl ghost. During the Civil War when Memphis and New Orleans were under attack, Waverley housed dozens of refugee girls from those cities. They doubled up in the bedrooms, slept in the guesthouses, and on cots in the parlor. The Young boys— Watt, Valley, Beverly, Thomas, Erskine, James, and William—had joined the Confederacy. Colonel Young stayed behind to protect his plantation and supply the Confederate troops with food, horses, and clothing.

At the neighboring Burt plantation, all the men had gone to war. Dr. Burt's daughter and two granddaughters were left behind. Colonel Young sent his house servants to bring them to Waverley for the duration. Nine-year-old Carrie Hampton contracted diphtheria. Five days later, eighteen-month-old Cynthia Hampton joined her sister in death. Melanie Snow and historian/tour guide James Denning do not know with 100 percent certainty how Cynthia died. However, Melanie and James are inclined to believe that baby Cynthia was the curious toddler who slipped away one day, stuck her head through the spindles of the second-floor railing, and broke her neck. All that can be confirmed is that the event happened and that both of Susan Burt Hampton's little girls died at Waverley. "That's factual," confirms Melanie. "It's in the family records."

The mirror in the front parlor that reflects hundreds of ghostly faces.

Those who have seen Waverley's little girl ghost describe her as being quite small. "We have the birth and death records of the Young children and grandchildren. They all lived to be adults, so we know the spirit haunting the house is not one of them." The Snow family can only surmise that the one who protects the house and is still calling for her mama is likely little Cynthia Hampton.

After the war, all but one of the Young boys returned home safely. The girls married and moved away as did three of the remaining six boys. Colonel Young died in 1888. James and Billy lived on at Waverley. James spent his bachelor days reading the Bible. William, or "Billy," the youngest, sought livelier pursuits.

Captain Billy served for a time as Waverley's postmaster. When the post office near the river landing closed, Billy took the walnut secretary and installed it in Waverley's library. A note from Billy dated December 26, 1898, reads *"No mail today. Messenger got drunk."* This is an ironic commentary from a man with a reputation for overindulgence. The library also features a silver dipper passed from friend to friend during Billy's infamous late-night poker parties. Luke Richardson, the last houseboy employed at Waverley and a descendant of Waverley slaves, returned during the restoration by Robert and Donna Snow. Richardson's account validates history. As a twelve-year-old, he and the staff "stayed up all night serving food and drink to the poker-playing guests."

When Billy died in 1913, distant nieces, nephews, and cousins inherited the estate. "As with the best of families," explains Melanie, "they argued for fifty years about what to do with the house. Waverley sat vacant for half a century."

In his eighteenth-century novel titled *Waverley,* English author Sir Walter Scott could have been describing twentieth-century conditions at Waverley in Mississippi when he wrote, *"The very trees mourned for her, for their leaves dropped around her without a gust of wind; and indeed she looked like one that would never see them green again."*

The Snows see their role at Waverley as caretakers of this National Historic Landmark and National Restoration Award winner. They are grateful to all of the ghosts who ensured that there would be a Waverley for years to come, but they retain a special fondness for their little guardian angel and encourage her to stick around.

Donna Snow's entire face pivots inside this portrait.

Postscript: The Snow family has created a mysterious aura of their own. When Madonna "Donna" Gutherie Snow first stepped into Waverley in 1962, she described it as "a magnificent mess" and then began a lifelong restoration. Like Lucy Young before her, matriarch Donna Snow had only a short time to enjoy Waverley in full bloom. With a face full of emotion, Donna's daughter, Melanie, remembers, "We finished the last room, the parlor, eighteen years ago, just before Mom died; she was able to see all the bricks restored and all the house done."

When Donna Snow died, the Mississippi legislature observed a moment of prayer and passed a resolution citing her work promoting Mississippi through Waverley. The Snow family commissioned a painting to honor Donna. The portrait hangs above the mantle in the dining room. Passing in front of the portrait, Donna follows you. Her head turns. "We watch people walking by; they stop and have the most perplexed look on their faces. As you start at one end of the dining room, mother is facing right. As you continue, she faces left." Madonna Snow, dressed in a black, lace, high-collared ball gown is seated. Her hands gently clasp a dozen long-stemmed yellow roses. Her oval face is in quiet repose. If you stand directly in front of the portrait, her brown eyes look past you to a view of the gardens through the windows. But if you move, so does she. There are no hidden wires or digital special effects. The illusion is magical.

24

Cemeteries

I am not now
That which I have been.
—George Gordon Byron, *Childe Harold's Pilgrimage*

Cemeteries are where mortal bodies are buried. To soften the blow, the dead are spoken of in an array of euphemisms: *The dearly departed. The recently deceased. They have either passed, passed on, been laid to rest, gone to their final reward, met their maker, or moved on to a better place.* The collective dead are buried *six feet under,* or as one novice television reporter recently gushed, "waiting to be *funeralized.*" They have in more colloquial terms *kicked the bucket, croaked, or given up the ghost.*

Mississippi's cemeteries are a haven for haunted tales. The gravesites that fuel the stories range in size and scope. At McRaven House in Vicksburg, they are just depressions in the ground. Caretaker Leonard Fuller watches over them. "Outside this window here, you see a flat area, just past the oak tree. There are twenty-eight gravesites. McRaven House was used as a hospital during the Civil War, and a battle took place in the side yard near the railroad tracks where the Kansas City Southern goes by now. We've done some soundings. By the way they are buried, we know they are old military graves. We don't know who they are, but their ghosts still walk around here. The ghosts of Confederate soldiers have been seen since I was a kid."

In 2000, the current owner of McRaven, Leyland French, placed a simple gray stone plaque into the ground to mark the spot.

KNOWN BUT TO GOD
UNKNOWN CONFEDERATE DEAD
1863
LEST WE FORGET

A family graveyard is hidden in a tangle of fallen limbs and thick vines in West Point, Mississippi. The body of the little girl ghost who haunts Waverley Plantation is buried by the side of her grandfather, Dr. William Burt. Next to the Burts are the mortal remains of the Youngs, their neighbors in life and in death. The Youngs and the Burts both lost sons in battle during the Civil War. Descendants of the Youngs still return. They plant daffodils. They mourn the dead. And they worry.

Across the road at Waverley Plantation, Melanie Snow sighs, "Halloween is a big time here. People come and expect to see ghosts." Vandals covered the walls of Waverley in graffiti when it sat vacant for fifty years. The Burt and Young family plots have suffered an even greater

The Burt family plot across the road from Waverley Plantation.

indignity. The Burt vaults are set in the ground. Hooligans have shifted the heavy slab covers aside and have chipped away at the graves. On the Young side, a metal sign with white block letters is nailed to a filigreed iron fence surrounding the tombstones.

GEORGE HAMPTON
YOUNG
FAMILY CEMETERY
PLEASE RESPECT THE
RESTING PLACE OF OUR DEAD

Although the small cemetery is crowded, Melanie Snow believes there is room for one more grave. A nagging dream haunts her sleep. "Beverly Young was the only one of Colonel Young's sons to be wounded in battle. He died from infection and was buried up north. Forty-something of the Youngs are buried in that cemetery which used to be part of the Waverley Plantation property, all except Beverly. He haunts my dreams. I want to bring him home." Melanie Snow has even made plans. "He would come down this one-mile road in front of Waverley Plantation in a horse drawn carriage, and then he could finally be at peace with his family." Melanie is not sure if her persistent dream, inspired by the spirit of Beverly Young, will ever be a reality, but she is not giving up hope.

Neither did Richard Forte. His quest for another lost Confederate soldier began in 1979. Unlike Melanie Snow, who knows the identity of her missing soldier, the name of Forte's young man is lost to the ages. "I was hunting a battlefield in Mississippi on private property with a metal detector. I had hunted there many times." Richard Forte is the director of Beauvoir, a historian, and Civil War expert. Armed with histories of the battles and topographical maps of the terrain, his expeditions are well planned. "I was behind the main Confederate line in a section of the battlefield that was thickly wooded with a lot of high ridges and deep ravines. I got a reading on my metal detector, and when I dug down, I found this canteen—pewter and tin—a cartridge box with ammunition in it, and then buttons and a buckle; that's what set the metal detector off. Forte cautiously sifted through the dirt, and what he found next changed everything. "I saw bones. The main bones were intact. The smaller bones

The vandalized Young family tombs adjoin their neighbors.

were like dust in the ground. It was a pretty emotional thing for me. I never dreamed I would find something like that. Unbelievable." Forte also picked out some nonmetal items. "There were porcelain buttons, his shirt buttons."

The bones were later examined by a physician who determined that the young man was between sixteen and seventeen years of age. Most important to Forte was to "have a decent burial for him." Forte chose the Confederate veterans' cemetery on the grounds of Beauvoir. On June 6, 1981, the Tomb of the Unknown Confederate Soldier was unveiled. The marble top has the seal of the Confederacy and at the foot is a poem by Father Abram J. Ryan, a poet and priest of the Confederacy.

Ah! Fearless on many a day for us
They stood in front of the fray for us
And held the foeman at bay for us
And tears should fall
Fore'er o'er all
Who fell wearing the gray for us.

"Every time I walk the grounds, which are about a mile all the way around, and I walk by him, I think about him. I really believe that things were meant to be; they just are. It was like he was calling to me. I believe in predestination a lot; it was meant for me to find him."

Yet, despite thirty-five years of diligent searching, there was one gravesite Forte couldn't find. Forte is a direct descendant of Napoleon Bonaparte Pardue who fought with the Mississippi Calvary during the Civil War. Like the unknown Confederate soldier, Forte came to believe that his great-great-grandfather was buried either in an unmarked plot or in a small private cemetery somewhere in the vast southern region of the country. He had virtually given up hope until two months ago when Napoleon Bonaparte Pardue made his presence known.

"Two friends of mine, both members of the Sons of the Confederate Veterans, shared the same great-great-great-grandfather." One friend was showing the other their mutual ancestor's grave, which he had located in a small, private family cemetery. "The cemetery had names like Easterling and James," says Forte, nothing even close to Pardue. Suddenly, one of

The Confederate Veterans Cemetery behind Beauvoir in Biloxi.

The tomb of the unknown Confederate soldier contains the remains discovered by Richard Forte.

Forte's friends felt a mysterious pull that compelled him to explore a wooded area about twenty yards away from the family plot. "Low and behold," proclaims Forte with wonder in his voice, "he found my great-great-grandfather's grave with a marker on it. He died April 6, 1910. We had a memorial service for him April 3, 2010, which was three days short of the one hundredth anniversary of his death. If my friends hadn't been there, if one of them hadn't walked into the woods, I never would have found him."

Burial records are problematic whether they sit on private property or state and federal lands. Names and dates are lost; tombs are vandalized or erode away from the effects of nature and time.

In Columbus, Mississippi, Nancy Carpenter, the project manager for the Columbus/Lowndes County Convention and Visitors Bureau, works feverishly to clear leaves and fallen branches from the pathways in the seventy acres of Friendship Cemetery. Volunteer students move into place for the twentieth anniversary of the dramatic rendering of Tales of the Crypt, the annual cemetery tour. Carpenter, an energetic woman with a wedge of blond hair and arresting blue eyes, warns that this is not a "pop-out-of-the-grave, I'm-going-to-get-you, blood-curdling affair." Tales of the Crypt was created by Carl Butler to help visitors see beyond the tombstones and learn how the deeds of the deceased continue to have impact.

On a bluff overlooking the Tombigbee River, the blossom-laden branches of sun-dappled magnolia and dogwood trees shroud row upon row of small, anonymous headstones. The bloody battle of Shiloh delivered more than two thousand Confederate dead and a smattering of their foe to be buried here. Friendship Cemetery has a small town ambiance and a well-justified reputation as the cemetery where "Flowers Healed a Nation."

On April 25, 1866, a group of mothers and wives met at Twelve Gables, the home of the John Morton family. The women devised a plan to honor the Confederate soldiers newly interred in the cemetery. As the flowers were placed on the graves, one woman's heart broke. "I am a mother; I cannot put flowers on the Confederate graves and leave those of the Union boys barren." Carpenter quotes from this tearful episode. "And in a spontaneous moment all the other mothers joined her in showering flowers on the graves of all the young boys on both sides."

The Teasdale angel grieves for the dead in Friendship Cemetery.

This act of kindness in Friendship Cemetery sparked the American celebration of Memorial Day to honor fallen veterans no matter the battle, the war, or sides taken. Pale figures in uniform, restless spirits all, they are honored for their courage and sacrifice.

> *From the silence of sorrowful hours*
> *The desolate mourners go.*
> *Lovingly laden with flowers*
> *Alike for the friend and foe;*
> *Under the sod and the dew,*
> *Waiting the Judgment Day;*
> *Under the roses, the Blue*
> *Under the lilies, the Gray.*
> —F. M. Finch, "The Blue and the Gray"

Five young girls buried together at the Natchez City Cemetery did not die defending any cause. They simply went to work. On March 14, 1908, Carrie Murray, Ada White, Inez Netterville, Luella Booth, and Lizzie Worthy sat at a long, wooden table and poured chemicals from large beakers to smaller ones in the fourth-floor laboratory of the Natchez Drug Company. Carrie, the oldest, was twenty-two. Mary Elizabeth Worthy, "Lizzie," was one month short of her thirteenth birthday. At eleven o'clock in the morning, Sam Burns of the F. Mack Plumbing Company arrived to check on a recently installed gas heater. He detected a leak in the meter, tightened it up, and left. At 1:30 in the afternoon, Sam was called back. Someone still smelled gas. He rechecked the joints and junctions in the laboratory and found nothing. He headed downstairs to the first floor.

Sam did as he had been trained. He ran a lit candle along the gas line; if his candle flame flared, it would reveal the location of the gas leak. Sam found the leak. The explosion rocked the city and blew a hole twenty feet wide. Like a house of cards, the brick building imploded. The rear wall fell in, the east wall came down, and the upper floors collapsed all the way to the cellar. The flames spread out fueled by drugs, chemicals, oils, and other combustibles.

The body of seventeen-year-old Inez had been blown to the north part of the building near the sidewalk. Carrie was found in the rubble; rescue workers identified the body by her corset cover. Nineteen-year-old Ada's body had to be carried away in pieces. Luella's body was charred almost beyond recognition. She was nineteen. Workers didn't find Lizzie until three days later. They knew it was her because it was the smallest body recovered.

The girls' simple headstones are lined side by side. Over them looms the Natchez cemetery's signature statue, the "Turning Angel." She sits on a pedestal, a book open in her lap. Those who drive by Cemetery Road at night swear the white angel turns her head to look at them. As their cars pass the angel, she turns back to guarding her young charges, resting in their tombs beneath her. The effect is unsettling.

Eerier still is the Angels on the Bluff walking tour conducted in the weeks leading up to Halloween. Actors, portraying some of the cemetery's more notable citizens, take their place beside the tombs. On this night, a grieving father holds a lantern in his hand. "My name is

The mysterious Turning Angel guards the graves of five young girls buried together in Natchez City Cemetery.

Quinn Booth. They searched the rubble for three days before they found the charred remains of my daughter Luella. They buried her here with four others, and later the Natchez Drug Company raised this angel to look over the poor innocents." The tragic father figure laments, "They should have buried me at the same time." Quinn Booth never got over his daughter's death. For eight years, he stumbled about in a cloud of grief and depression. He blamed himself for insisting that his seventeen-year-old daughter get a job, no matter how menial. "It was my fault she was sitting at that table the day Sam Burns held a candle to check for gas leaks." Quinn Booth's grave is to the left and a few yards behind that of the girls. "It was the closest they could get me to my darling Luella."

It is an unseasonably warm October night in Natchez, the air stifling. Those gathered to hear Quinn Booth's tale clasp their arms around their chests to ward off a sudden chill. They make futile attempts to dispel the tingles creeping up and over their bodies. Tears flow as visitors bend to read the names etched into the headstones. A woman in her forties is rooted to a spot in front of young Lizzie's weathered grave. "She's staring at me. I can see her eyes. They are so sad. She still doesn't understand what happened." The woman in the navy-blue pantsuit appears as traumatized by her vision as the young victim in the grave at her feet.

Other markers in this massive cemetery date back to the late 1700s. The graveyard is divided into plots like small neighborhoods, where the long-deceased residents still mix and mingle. In the Washington Ford lot, many believe that the mother of poor little Florence "Irene" Ford still tries to comfort her daughter. Certainly, this inconsolable parent went to extraordinary lengths to allay her daughter's fears.

Ten-year-old Irene died of yellow fever on October 30, 1871. She was terrified of storms and lightning. Ellen Ford had a concrete stairway built behind her daughter's headstone that led down to the level of the casket, where a glass window allowed her to look in. The child's casket also had a glass window on top. When it stormed, heedless of the rain pelting her head and shoulders, the protective mother climbed down the stairs. Ellen Ford was said to have talked, read, prayed, and sang to her daughter, trying to console her even in death. In later years, the grave became a popular draw to curiosity seekers. To keep the inquisitive out, cemetery workers erected a brick wall at the bottom of the stairwell and a hinged metal trap door to cover the opening. Oddly, Ellen Ford is not buried next to her daughter. There is no record of this devoted mother's final resting place. The Natchez City Cemetery is closed at night, but those who have made clandestine forays to little Irene's grave report sightings of the shape of a woman kneeling near the burial site. In *Legends of the Natchez City Cemetery,* author Don Estes describes an "eerie green glow" at the grave. The caretaker picked up a glowing orb from the site and showed it to his wife and daughter. But the orb dissipated when he opened his hands. Estes states that this incident in 1991 is the only corroborated ghost story at the cemetery.

Haunted tales also swirl about two other female graves in this legendary cemetery. One has sunk into the ground so far the inscription may soon be indecipherable. The mysterious headstone bears only a first name and a very strange two-word epitaph.

LOUISE
THE UNFORTUNATE

Louise was a prostitute who worked in Natchez-under-the-Hill, the city's notorious red-light district, which hugged a steep bank of the Mississippi River. In the spring of 1849, she fell ill. Reverend Stratton, the local Presbyterian minister, offered assistance. Although she accepted his offer of food and medicine, the stubborn woman would only reveal her first name. When she died, the reverend raised money for her burial and erected a tombstone. Research conducted in 2005 by Don Estes, the former director of the Natchez City Cemetery, finally produced a surname—Leroy. Feisty Louise has a last name at last, yet no one seems in any hurry to claim her as their own and inscribe Leroy on the stone. If her troubled spirit could change anything, the first task on her list would likely be to erase her rather ignominious "Unfortunate" epitaph.

No one has reported hearing Rosalie Beekman speaking up for herself in the afterlife, but her dying words are the stuff of legends. Seven-year-old Rosalie was the only person killed in Natchez as a result of the Civil War. In September of 1862, the Union gunboat USS *Essex* shelled Natchez for three hours. The citizenry panicked. Rosalie's father, Aaron Beekman, tried to lead his daughters to safety. As they scurried up Silver Street,

A little cherub marks an infant grave in Columbus's Friendship Cemetery.

Rosalie's nine-year-old sister screamed, "Papa, Rosalie fell down." The harried father urged her to get up and run. She is said to have solemnly replied, "I can't Papa. I'm killed."

Carved into the upper curve of her headstone are a cluster of roses. The center rose is a tightly closed bud, a symbol of life that will never open its fragrant petals and bloom. "Rosalie Beekman would have been my great-great-great-aunt. My mother's grandmother was Hattie Beekman." Caroline Guido, owner of Glenburnie in Natchez, lives with the residual effects of senseless tragedy every day. Jennie Merrill, the previous owner of Glenburnie, was shot down trying to escape from her murderer. Rosalie was shot while trying to keep up with her sister and her father. The loss of innocent Rosalie still resonates in Caroline's family. Rosalie's grave is a challenge to find. Visitors scramble through narrow winding paths hoping to connect with the spirited little girl.

Wherever there is a cemetery, it is hallowed, haunted ground. Each tomb that survives is like a chapter in an old, discarded book, its edges frayed, its binder broken, its pages wrinkled and yellowed. However, the story that lies within is more than myth and legend. It is the final place where a once-vibrant person left his imprint in the fertile lands of Mississippi. Their stories are there to be gathered and cherished.

Postscript: The statue on the cover of this book can be found in Friendship Cemetery in Columbus, Mississippi. The epitaph on the baby's grave reads:

Louis Fox Green
Born December 31, 1879
Died November 25, 1880
Budded on Earth
To Bloom in Heaven

Epilogue

And life will be
as it has always been—
cycles within a circle,
whirling
without starts or finishes,
through the timeless places
of forever.
—Jim Metcalf, "Exodus"

If we see them only as shadows, wispy figures, or momentary aberrations, how do we know they are real? Why do we believe?

Personal experiences can transform nonbelievers into believers. Kathy Hall had never given much thought to the ability of the dead to return until she was twenty-one. "I was three-months pregnant with my first child when my husband passed away. I never expected to have such a drastic thing happen to me. It was hard for me to get a grip on reality. After several months of trying to deal with the idea of his death, I sat out in my front yard one night and I just looked up at the sky and I said, 'I can't do this. You've got to help me through this.'" Hall takes a deep breath. "It was like he put his hand on my shoulder. I could feel it. So yeah, I believe they can come back. I believe they do come back."

Before she came to work the front desk at Cedar Grove Inn in Vicksburg, Hall had never heard the stories about its ghosts. Seven years into the job, she has met most of them. "I have seen the little handprints on the wall in the Bonnie Blue room. I have smelled the cigar smoke in the gentlemen's parlor before the guests arrive. I have seen the photographs."

Hall was present on one occasion when the ghosts had their pictures taken. "I took a couple on a tour one morning. The husband took pictures inside and outside of the library suite, room 21. Afterwards, he loaded the pictures in his laptop and showed them to me. One was in the sitting room; you could see the settee and over it the gold frame of the painting with birds in it, except in the photo the birds were gone. There was just a white blur blocking them. I jokingly said, 'Well, Mr. Klein was in here with y'all.' I guess he stepped into the frame just when they snapped the picture."

In a second photo, there is a close-up of the oval plaque on the door to the suite. "There were these fire flames shooting up. Really cool," declares Hall. The front desk manager's explanation of the paranormal evidence is that the flames were from Mr. Klein's cigar as his spirit was about to enter his favorite room. "Each one of us who have been at Cedar Grove Inn for a while, John, Joe, myself, we all respect this house and we respect the ghosts."

Joe Connor, the head bartender, says that occasionally things get a little too real for some staff members. "We had a waitress, Christina, who had been here off and on for a couple of years. During Halloween, she'd get dressed up as Mrs. Elizabeth Klein, the former lady of Cedar Grove. The last time, last October, in the middle of the tour, she got out of her costume and quit. She said the ghosts were messing with her; she could hear them whispering, 'We're back.' She just ran off, that's how spooked she was."

Chef John Kellogg feels the ghosts are usually a bit more subtle. "Joe will be standing at the bar and you'll see him do this." Kellogg takes his hand and flicks at the back of his neck as if trying to shoo something or someone away. "We put Ashley, one of our new girls, behind the bar one night to train, and she said, 'I don't know what it is. Something keeps tugging at my hair or pulling at my shirt collar.'" The executive chef offers reassurance. "It is never anything scary. It happens so often that we don't even pay attention to it anymore. It's nothing major."

Dixie Butler, the owner of Temple Heights in Columbus, is philosophical on the subject of ghosts. "There are a lot of things you just can't explain; our minds are so finite we can't conceive of what it could be."

Kay McNeil lived and worked at Magnolia Hall in Natchez. She regrets that she never reached a more personal level with Mr. Henderson whose spirit roams the house. "I don't know if you have to be in a special mode or a special person for him to want to talk to you. Many times I would sit in the hallway right by the room where he died, or I would play the piano with my back to his bedroom, hoping he would talk to me. I felt him there, but he would never say anything. I still get goose bumps. Maybe I just wasn't the right person, so I guess he is still waiting to get his message across."

Tom Miller, the proprietor of King's Tavern in Natchez thinks it's a seasonal thing. "Since it has turned warm, we usually go through some stale periods where not much happens in the way of haunting. Nobody reports seeing our ghost girl Madeline. We get very little paranormal activity in the summer." Miller shrugs. "I don't know why, maybe the ghosts head up north where it's cool." Miller is not worried. He's confident alluring Madeline will be back come fall.

Historian and cultural anthropologist, Dr. Elizabeth Boggess doesn't believe it has anything to do with the weather or any earthly outside influences. For Boggess, spirits tend to behave in the same manner that they did when they were alive. "My husband died in a plane crash. Right after his death and before he was buried, they were about to bring the body home, and I had gone to my mother's house because I couldn't be left alone. I woke up from a nap, and I knew that my husband was on one side of the bed and his best friend, who was killed with him, was on the other side. I am convinced that a spirit comes back because they may have something else to do." Boggess is a practical woman resigned to the inevitable. "After the funeral, I never had any sense that my husband was there, but his best friend was. He was a born wanderer, and I think he just had a need to keep wandering."

Jeanette Feltus runs Linden solo. When her husband was alive, he assisted with the operation of the popular bed and breakfast on the outskirts of Natchez. "I would fuss at Richard because he would spread paperwork all over the kitchen." Feltus had an office built for her husband's exclusive use over the garage. "He didn't like being so far removed from what was going on here, so he'd dump his stuff back on the kitchen table." She looks over her kitchen with a sly grin. An answering machine, a copier, a fax machine, brochures, and reservation forms are stacked up on every level. "I can hear Richard laughing whenever I am in here because the kitchen is where I run the business now." Feltus embraces all of her family ghosts and informs overnight guests that while Linden is definitely haunted, all of the spirits, including her late husband, are quite friendly.

"Of course," nods a sage Tom Miller, "nobody wants to scare anybody off telling them there are evil spirits. Each of the homes I owned here in Natchez had an entity in it, different kinds. People ask me if I'm scared, if they keep me up at night." Miller sits in the bar he owns along with King's Tavern, the adjacent haunted restaurant. "I'm used to it. I don't think we have evil entities here, but we had an investigative team here once and they recorded this demonic voice." Miller boots up his computer and plays the recording. A deep voice intones, *'I'm here on the porch.'* Miller closes the laptop and polishes off his drink. "Yeah, it does alarm me a little bit."

Patricia Taylor runs into ghosts no matter where she goes. During the annual Spring Pilgrimage in Natchez, she puts up with the antics of Thomas Henderson's spirit at Magnolia Hall. When she's on a break from docent duties, apparitions like to check her out. "There is a courtyard at the Eola Hotel where on a nice day you can sit outside and eat lunch. I was there with a friend, and I could see this gentleman standing in the corner. He didn't move, and I asked my friend if she knew the man because he kept staring at us. She said, 'There is nobody there, Patricia.'" Taylor allows that she tends to be "a bit sensitive" to the paranormal. This time she decided the ghost should acknowledge her. "I walked past him, and I sort of nodded, and he nodded back at me." Taylor would love to know the identity of the courtyard ghost. "The man was there for a reason. There's got to be a picture of him in this town somewhere; he was wearing a frock coat when I realized it."

With Taylor, spectral encounters are like tag teams; one hooks on to another. "I talked to the manager of the Eola, and she found my experience quite interesting. She took my friend and I into one of the rooms she believes is exceptionally haunted. She and her family used the room when they first moved to Natchez. They had to move out because she said all four of them heard strange noises, not normal hotel noises." Taylor felt very ill at ease in the room. She discovered that the hotel has an untold quantity of what she refers to as "residual memories." The staff speaks of literally running into the ghost of Isadore Levy, who built the hotel in 1927, and his daughter, Eola, for whom the hotel was named. Eola died at sixteen, and her spirit often gives guests a little nudge on the staircase. Patricia Taylor would have preferred bumping into Eola rather than what she saw as she tried to ascend the staircase.

"Bodies wrapped in shrouds, in rows, about yeah far off the floor," Taylor raises her arm waist high. "I couldn't walk upstairs because that meant I would have to walk through them. I have tried and tried to find out what went on there. It was not a Confederate hospital; it was built in the early 1920s I think." Taylor did a little research and arrived at a more likely scenario for her vision at the hotel. "Someone told me that there was a hurricane that came through here in the early 1800s and it killed a lot of people. They would have had to store them somewhere, so maybe before this was a hotel, there was an open space that they used as a triage center of some sort."

Judy Grimsley served as head docent at Magnolia Hall in Natchez for many years. She argues on the side of ghosts. "To me, hauntings are just like déjà vu. Those feelings you get like you were there before. You already know what someone is going to say. No one can explain that. Why is it so hard to believe that there are ghosts?"

Kathleen Blankenstein, who has served on the board governing nearby Magnolia Hall, is puzzled. "Why do people want to believe—just because it's fun?" Although she is firmly in the doubter's camp, this longtime resident of

Natchez does try to keep an open mind—until proven otherwise. On an outing to the Natchez City Cemetery, she met with Donald Estes, the cemetery director. "Don was telling me he thought there was a body here at this place where we were getting ready to put a tombstone to this Spanish American soldier. He said he was pretty sure, but he would use his equipment to confirm it." Blankenstein visibly winces. "He believes in dousing. He had these two coat hangers and he held them like this." Blankenstein crosses her arms. "He passed these hangers over the ground and told me if they bent one way it meant something and if they went the other way it meant something else. I was just laughing, but he was quite serious. He said, 'It will not only tell you if there is a body there, it will tell you whether it was male or female.'"

Blankenstein backtracks in her story and gives a brief run down of some family names. "We had a Josephine, a Lily, and a Shirley. My father's given name was Shirley. He was named for a friend who's surname was Shirley. Now most people think of it as a girl's name. My father said he never had a fight over it until Shirley Temple came along."

A doubtful Blankenstein watched as Estes demonstrated his dousing method. "He held the dousing hangers over Josephine's grave without looking down and said, 'It's a female.' He came to Lily, did the same thing and said it was another female," Blankenstein can barely contain a wide grin. "He got to my father's grave and said, 'That's a female.' And I shouted, 'Gottcha!' Don leaned over to read the name and he couldn't understand. He said, 'Let me see. That says Shirley, so that's a female.' I said, 'Don, that's my father, and he's not a female.'" Blankenstein's good-natured laugh erupts. She composes herself and tries for a bit more understanding of people's fascination with all things paranormal. "Maybe there is something to it. It's just not for me."

Nancy Carpenter is on the same page. "I personally don't believe in ghosts, but I love a good story."

Grayce Hicks of Rosewood Manor in Columbus isn't sure how the stories got started at her historic Greek Revival mansion. Over the years, the home has been known by many names—Birdhaven, Wooten Manor, Fairleigh Manor, Maydrew Manor—before settling into Rosewood Manor. The cavernous home was built in 1835 by Richard Skyes as a townhouse to entertain his many acquaintances. "This house has a complete basement, almost an entire other house underneath where the servants' quarters were." During the Skyes era, the servants were slaves. Grayce and her husband, Dewitt Hicks, use the space now for storage, but aspects of its past can't be erased. "Some people are scared to death of our basement. They think it is haunted."

On a beautiful spring day, gardeners are busy sprucing up the grounds. There are more than 4.5 acres of gardens, three thousand boxwoods, a rose garden, and an herb garden in this floral fantasyland. Hicks observes one of the maintenance men skirt the basement door. "They think there are ghosts in our basement because the slaves lived there." Hicks finds the notion nearly incomprehensible. "I have lived here for thirty-three years and haven't met a ghost yet." With her distinct Southern inflection, she states with no hesitation, "I don't feel like I am missing anything because I might be scared if I was. This is a large house and you know, as they say . . . *if walls could talk.*"

Mattie Jo Ratcliffe, the former chairwoman of the Natchez Pilgrimage Club, also has definite opinions. "I know there is an element out there that we don't understand and we don't know about. And in my opinion, a house, a home, a building that's been sitting there since the 1800s that has witnessed laughter and tears and emotions of all kinds . . . why wouldn't it absorb some of those feelings, some of those emotions?" She answers her own question. "I think having ghost stories is good. I do. When my husband and I bought a historic home, it was a tremendous redo. There was a threshold in the back of the hall that originally had been the back gallery. The threshold was a worn-away, wide cypress log. I told my husband that I would just love to know how many feet had crossed that log and who they belonged to. I think when you personalize history, it makes it alive. That's what ghost stories do; you get to meet the people before you."

Appendix

For more information about the sites visited in this book, refer to the following list. The entries are grouped here by geographic region north to south.

HILLS REGION

Rowan Oak
719 Old Taylor Road
Oxford, MS 38655
662-234-3284

Saint Peter's Cemetery
Jefferson Avenue and North
    Sixteenth Street
Oxford, MS 38655

**Oxford Convention and Visitors
    Bureau**
102 Ed Perry Boulevard
Oxford, MS 38655
800-758-9177

**Elvis Presley Birthplace and
    Museum**
306 Elvis Presley Drive
Tupelo, MS 38801
662-841-1245

Lyric-Tupelo Community Theatre
200 North Broad Street
Tupelo, MS 38802
662-844-1935

**Tupelo Convention and Visitors
    Bureau**
399 East Main Street
Tupelo, MS
800-533-0611

DELTA REGION

**Greenville-Washington County
    CVB (The Old Armory)**
216 South Walnut Street
Greenville, MS 38701
800-467-3582

**Greenville Iron Works (Artist John
    Puddin' Moore)**
214 South Walnut Street
Greenville, MS 38701
662-332-8266

Delta Democrat Times (original building)
Corner of Walnut and Main Street
Greenville, MS 38701

Delta Democrat Times (office)
988 North Broadway
Greenville, MS 38701
662-335-1155

Delta Center Stage Community Theatre
E. E. Bass Cultural Arts Center
323 South Main Street
Greenville, MS 38701
662-332-2246

Mt. Holly Plantation
(private)
Susie B. Law House
(private)

Evergreen Cemetery and St. John's Ruins
East Lake Washington Road
Glen Allan, MS 38744

Southern Star/Bait-n-Thangs
1940 Lake Washington Road
Chatham, MS 38731
662-827-2666

PINES REGION

Waverley Mansion
1852 Waverley Mansion Road
West Point, MS 39773
662-494-1399

Rosedale
1523 Ninth Street South
Columbus, MS 39701
800-920-3533

Rosewood Manor
719 Seventh Street North
Columbus, MS 39701
662-328-7313

Temple Heights
515 Ninth Street North
Columbus, MS 39701
800-920-3533

Friendship Cemetery
Fourth Street South
Columbus, MS 39701
662-328-2569

Tennessee Williams Welcome Center
Columbus Spring Pilgrimage: Tales from the Crypt and Ghosts & Legends Tour
300 Main Street
Columbus, MS 39701
800-920-3553

Merrehope
The Frank Williams House
905 Martin Luther King Drive
Meridian, MS 39301
601-483-8439

CAPITAL/RIVER REGION

Anchuca Historic Mansion & Inn
1010 First East Street
Vicksburg, MS 39183
888-686-0111

Cedar Grove Inn & Restaurant
2300 Washington Street
Vicksburg, MS 39180
800-862-1300

McRaven House
1445 Harrison Street
Vicksburg, MS 39180

Vicksburg Convention and Visitors Bureau
Vicksburg Pilgrimage "Tapestry"
3300 Clay Street
601-636-9421

The Old State Capitol Museum
100 South State Street
Jackson, MS 39205
601-576-6920

The Chapel of the Cross
674 Mannsdale Road
Madison, MS 39110
601-856-2953

Glenburnie
551 John R. Junkin Drive
Natchez, MS 39120

Homewood (private home)
30 Laub Road
Natchez, MS 39120

King's Tavern Restaurant
619 Jefferson Street
Natchez, MS 39120
601-446-8845

Linden Bed & Breakfast
1 Linden Place
Natchez, MS 39120
800-254-6336

Longwood
140 Lower Woodville Road
Natchez, MS 39120
601-442-5193

Magnolia Hall
215 South Pearl Street
Natchez, MS 39120
601-442-6672

Stanton Hall
401 High Street
Natchez, MS 39120
601-442-6282

Natchez City Cemetery
2 Cemetery Road
Natchez, MS 39120
601-445-5051

Natchez Visitor Center
640 South Canal Street
Natchez, MS 39120
800-647-6724

Coast Region

Beauvoir
2244 Beach Boulevard
Biloxi, MS 39531
228-388-4400

The Old Place/La Maison Gautier
2800 Oak Street
Gautier, MS 39553
228-497-1222